mystics and sceptics

Celebrating
30 Years of Publishing
in India

Also by Namita Gokhale

Travelling In, Travelling Out: A Book of Unexpected Journeys
(edited anthology)

The Himalayan Arc: Journeys East of South-east
(edited anthology)

Betrayed by Hope: A Play on the Life of Michael Madhusudan Dutt
(with Malashri Lal)

mystics

IN SEARCH

and

OF HIMALAYAN MASTERS

sceptics

edited by

NAMITA GOKHALE

HarperCollins *Publishers* India

First published in hardback in India by HarperCollins *Publishers* 2023
4th Floor, Tower A, Building No. 10, Phase II, DLF Cyber City,
Gurugram, Haryana – 122002
www.harpercollins.co.in

2 4 6 8 10 9 7 5 3

Page 317 is an extension of the copyright page.

P-ISBN: 978-93-5629-572-8
E-ISBN: 978-93-5629-573-5

Typeset in 11/15 Adobe Caslon Pro at
Manipal Technologies Limited, Manipal

Printed and bound at
Thomson Press (India) Ltd

MIX
Paper from responsible sources
FSC® C010615

This book is produced from independently certified FSC® paper
to ensure responsible forest management.

Contents

Introduction — 1
Namita Gokhale

1. The Living Presence — 11
Holly Gayley

2. Milarepa — 17
Andrew Quintman

3. Tibet's Great Yogi Milarepa — 25
W.Y. Evan Wentz

4. Lal Děd — 45
Ranjit Hoskote

5. The Mountain Sojourns of Guru Nanak and Guru Gobind Singh — 53
Navtej Sarna

6. Moving Mountains — 63
Makarand R. Paranjape

7. Magic and Mystery in Tibet — 91
Alexandra David-Néel

8. Reincarnation — 101
H.H. the Fourteenth Dalai Lama in conversation with Rajiv Mehrotra

9. My Interrupted Flight toward the Himalayas — 113
Paramhansa Yogananda

10. Rahul Sankrityayan's Tibet Story — 123
Sujata Prasad

11. Siddha Traditions — 133
Romola Butalia

12. Letting Go — 149
Madhu Tandan

13. Neem Karoli Baba and Siddhi Ma 163
Namita Gokhale

14. Where the Gods Are Mountains 177
René von Nebesky-Wojkowitz

15. The Sage from the Valley of Flowers 191
Swami Rama

16. From Kishori to Swami Rama of the Himalayas 197
Devyani Mungali

17. In Search of the Miraculous 207
Bhushita Vasistha

18. Laal Baba 217
Sidharth, translated by Nirupama Dutt and Jaspreet Mandher

19. The Handsome Monk 225
Tsering Döndrup, translated by Christopher Peacock

20. Into the Heart of the Himalayas 245
Jono Lineen

21. Trance Runners 251
Tshering Tashi

22. Mystic Marathon 257
René von Nebesky-Wojkowitz

23. Divination 263
Bijoya Sawian

24. My Devi, My Shakti 273
Alka Pande

25. Terrains of Transcendence: An Inner Geography 285
Vaibhav Kaul

Acknowledgements 309

Notes on the Contributors 311

Copyright Acknowledgements 317

Index 319

Front Cover Image: Pearl of Searching

The powerful and evocative cover image is from a tempera on canvas artwork by Roerich titled 'Pearl of Searching', painted in 1924.

Nicholas Roerich (Nikolai Konstantinovich Rerikh), a Russian artist, writer, philosopher and visionary, was a deeply spiritual figure who engaged with the world and other spheres at multiple levels. A lawyer by training, he worked tirelessly on the cause of protecting art and architecture during times of war. The Roerich Pact (for the protection of cultural objects) was signed into law by the United States and other nations in 1935.

Maxim Gorky described Roerich as 'One of the great intuitive minds of the age'. Sitting amidst the serene splendour of the Alps, Roerich observes: 'It is true, mountains everywhere are mountains, water everywhere is water, sky everywhere is sky, and men everywhere are men. But nevertheless, if seated before the Alps, you attempt to picture the Himalayas, something inexplicable but convincing will be lacking.'

A citizen of the world, Roerich had made the Himalaya his home. He died in Kullu, Himachal Pradesh, in 1947.

Words and Image: Emanations by Sidharth

The painter Sidharth has contributed an essay to this anthology titled 'Laal Baba', which is appropriately about red ochre, the colour of earth. He has worked on the line drawings that accompany each chapter as a part of his meditative and artistic practice, incorporating elements from his study of Tibetan Buddhism and thangkha paintings as well as his background in Sikhism.

The works are executed on litho paper using dark lead pencil.

In one's sojourns across the Himalaya, it is best to be cautious in chance encounters, for it is impossible to decipher if one is encountering a saint, a siddha, a madman or a charlatan. This was the advice given by an intensely religious man, an elderly tantric and a scholar, when I was young, and I have kept this counsel close to my heart.

'The gods come to us in many disguises,' he told me. 'They may come to you with a boon, or they may leave you with a curse if you do not conduct yourself in the right way.'

Introduction

NAMITA GOKHALE

Of Immovable Things, I am the Himalaya.

—Bhagavadgita

The Himalaya are sacred to Lord Shiva and Goddess Parvati. Growing up in Kumaon, I felt their presence everywhere, in every leaf and cloud, in every temple bell that chimed or clanged across the rarified air, in the mooing cows and leaping langurs and the occasional slithering snakes that were all blessed by the Lord of All Creatures. I saw Shiva in the visage of his consort Parvati, reflected in the rugged Pahari women who went stoically about their everyday chores and were often named after her. I saw Nanda and Sunanda, the beloved tutelary deities of Kumaon, in the strength and sorority of hill women. I imagined a pantheon of divinities observing us from the clouds above, and sometimes interceding in our lives.

I grew up in Nainital in the central Himalaya, where my mother's younger brother, the handsome and unpredictable Mukul Pande, was deeply drawn to the spiritual life. He gave up college and a brilliant future to search for something—he knew not what—in the dense forests and steep mountains of Kumaon, in the swift, treacherous currents of the Alaknanda river, in the ultimate refuge of a sannyasin's 'Jal Samadhi'—that final immersion in the waters of the sacred Ganga river. In retrospect, one might conclude that the intensity of his passion, the relentlessness of his quest, had left him somewhere shaken up, broken; but I believe he also experienced the ecstasy of those who glimpse some divine vision as the mists part and the grace of Shiva descends to open the third eye.

Outside of the missionary Christian schools where I studied in Nainital and New Delhi, I had the chance through, among others, my beloved Mukki mama, to move outside the blinkered worldview of an anglicized middle-class education to spend time from an early age with seers and saints, sadhus and seekers.

Although many of these spiritualists were deluded, dysfunctional, propelled by addictions and habitual substance abuse, they also had a sense of seen and unseen presences, of wisdom beyond words, of divine understanding, intuitive prowess and mystical powers.

This is not in any way a representative or encyclopaedic collection of essays. The narratives you will find herein, the figures you will encounter, have walked towards me from different directions. They are as varied as the flora and fauna of the mountains and their quests are so diverse, their goals so guardedly obscure, their words so deliberately cryptic that is difficult to untangle their riddles.

These holy men and women work assiduously to protect their mysteries, their 'rahasya'. Everything is not to be deciphered at the plane of pragmatic understanding. They communicate with each other across the ages in an enigmatic secret language, which is sometimes referred to as sadhu-vani.

Of the many acts of omission in this book, I have this to say in my defence. These are encounters, emanations, revelations. I would wish to invoke the great lords of the Himalaya to bless this book. There is Guru Padmasambhava, the lotus-born. The Great Master Rinpoche, whose life is too vast to be encompassed in an essay. His presence informs the geography of the Himalaya in the form of shrines, relics and folklore, and he exists for his followers as surely as the day and the night, the sky and the stars.

Among the great masters who have had a deep impact on me personally, the figure of Drukpa Kunley, the Divine Madman, is missing. While I have others of his lineage, from Jetsun Milarepa to my Guru, Neem Karoli Baba, the expanse of Drukpa Kunley's intuitive understanding, his ability to bend a beam of sunlight, as it were, is left to another book and another time.

I have since childhood been a devotee of Golu Devata, the mediaeval king who is worshipped as the God of Justice and is the patron saint of Kumaon. He is not there in these pages, but his presence is imprinted in the paper and ink, and the words and thoughts, that make up this book.

I seek blessings of the other guardians of these mountains—the Nagas, the Kinnaras, the celestial beings, the shamans and seeresses, the demons and dakinis, who embody the spirit of the tallest and youngest mountains in the world. I invoke Airee, the demon archer, who still walks across the mountain trails of the central Himalaya, if we could only see him.

I beseech Avalokitesvara, the Bodhisattva who is the embodiment of compassion, to bless us believers and seekers, sceptics and those who smile and sneer alike, and light a lamp within us.

The sequence of these essays is roughly linear. The pieces vary in length, style and subject. Some of them display the resilient scepticism that is the foundation of true belief. Others make the leap of faith. The conversations with artist Sidharth, himself an evolved practitioner of iconographic representation and religious symbolism, contributed deeply to my understanding.

Some of the main threads that run through this collection of essays are the joint strands of Indian and Tibetan tantric understanding.

We have an essay on Yeshe Tsogyal—pre-eminent among Tibetan women practitioners and the consort of Padmasambhava, the Vajra master from India who went to Tibet in the eighth century and built the first Buddhist monastery there. The essay by Holly Gayley then steps across time to present Khandro Tare Lhamo (1938–2002) as an emanation of Yeshe Tsogyal.

Perhaps the greatest of masters was the Tibetan Buddhist adept Milarepa (1052–1135) who became the foremost disciple of Marpa, the great translator, whose guru was the Indian master Naropa. In one of his famous 'Songs of Milarepa' (translated by Andrew Quintman), he affirms his commitment to meditative practice.

No footprints upon my doorstep
And no sign of blood inside—
If thus I can die in this mountain retreat
The aims of this Yogina will be complete.

The extract from W.Y. Evan Wentz's enduring biography of Milarepa vividly brings the great master and his times to life.

We move then to the poems of the fourteenth-century mystic Lal Děd, one of Kashmir's best-known spiritual and literary figures. The excerpted essay from Ranjit Hoskote's book, *I, Lalla—The Poems of Lal Děd*, takes us through the enigma of her life.

After that we follow Guru Nanak (1469–1539), the founder of Sikhism and first of the ten Sikh gurus, on a spiritual journey to Sumeru Parbat. This was a reference perhaps to Mount Kailash, the abode of Shiva and Parvati, where he encountered eighty-four siddhas and engaged with them on the true path of devotion. Guru Gobind Singh, the tenth and last Sikh Guru (1666–1708) also spent his formative years at Paonta Sahib by the banks of the Yamuna river in the foothills of the Himalaya.

Swami Vivekananda (1863–1902) rejuvenated the very roots of Hindu religion and philosophy during his brief time on earth. Makarand Paranjape explores Vivekananda's wanderings across the Himalaya with his band of disciples, and the emotional and spiritual journeys they set upon during those long and demanding physical treks through Kumaon, Garhwal and Kashmir.

Alexandra David-Néel (1868–1969) lived an incredible life that spanned an extraordinary range of adventures and experiences. Most known for her visit, in the year 1924, to the Forbidden City of Lhasa, Tibet, she was an explorer, spiritualist, anarchist, writer and opera singer. The excerpt in our book, taken from her classic *Magic and Mystery in Tibet* tells us, among other things, of her meeting with the Thirteenth Dalai Lama—a thread we pick up with the transcript of an interview by Rajiv Mehrotra with His Holiness the Fourteenth Dalai Lama.

The revered monk Paramhansa Yogananda (1893–1952) was the author of the worldwide bestseller *Autobiography of a Yogi,* first published in 1947. We present a light-hearted excerpt revolving around a childhood escapade where he tries to run away to the Himalaya with a band of school friends, foreshadowing his later life as a renunciate.

Rahul Sankrityayan (1893–1963) was many things and many people—Buddhist, Marxist, scholar, mystic, seeker, sceptic, activist, peripatetic, polyglot. Sujata Prasad explores his physical, intellectual and spiritual journeys across Tibet and Nepal, and his friendship with the outstanding scholar and poet Gendum Choephel.

There is a timelessness to Romola Butalia's musings as she tells us mystical tales and elemental rituals of the fire tongs, the chimtas, that are at the heart of Siddha practice in 'Siddha Traditions: Dhuni and Chimta'.

My piece on Neem Karoli Baba (1900–1973) and Shri Siddhi Ma (1928–2017) is a tribute to some of the most important figures in my own life passages, including Swami Chidananda Saraswati (1916–2008). Neem Karoli Baba and Siddhi Ma are revered in places as different and distant as Taos in New Mexico, Silicon Valley and rural Kumaon. To have had proximity to a living guru is an experience that is difficult to explain, but is described in several of the pieces in this book.

Madhu Tandan speaks of her guru, Sri Madhav Ashish (1920–1997), born Alexander Phipps in Edinburgh, an aeronautical engineer during World War II, and her stay in his ashram. Her insightful piece, excerpted from her book *Faith and Fire: A Way Within* takes us deep into the heart of the complex relationship between guru and disciple.

René von Nebesky-Wojkowitz (1923–1959) was an intrepid Czech Tibetologist and ethnologist who, in his short life, assiduously gathered a wealth of material on ritual practice. An inspired raconteur, both mystic and sceptic, he could tell a tale, as the reader will discover in this essay from his book *Where the Gods are Mountains*.

Swami Rama (1925–1996) was a spiritual teacher and a yoga guru with tremendous physical powers and the ability to control his body in Yoga Nidra, or guided meditation. His daughter, the educationist Devyani Mungali, reminiscences about her unusual childhood and her memories of her father. This is followed by a delightful piece penned by Swami Rama himself, about an unexpected journey across the famed Valley of Flowers with an eccentric Baba, a Japanese seeker and a blanket with mystical powers!

We come next to Bhushita Vasistha's searing story about her time in an Osho commune on the outskirts of Kathmandu. It is a reminder and testimony to the ego and power play that can distort the spiritual quest, especially for the tender and vulnerable.

Painter and poet Sidharth's meditative account of Laal Baba takes us to another plane and dimension—of earth and stars and snow-capped mountains, of herbs and leaves and healing plants, of stones and rocks and rushing turbulent waters. Sidharth's evocative illustrations, accompanying each chapter, add a deep spiritual context to the book.

The continuity of past and present, as well as the fractures and fault lines of historical change, can be glimpsed in Tsering Döndrup's compelling story, 'The Handsome Monk'. Döndrup, born in 1961, is a major contemporary Tibetan writer of Mongolian nomadic descent. He writes unblinkingly not of the land of lore and legend, but of a Tibet situated firmly in the People's Republic of China, and the inexorable march of the present. He is a brilliant storyteller, and 'The Handsome Monk', a tale both sceptical and mystical, is a work of immense literary merit.

Dr Jono Lineen brings us an unexpected story from the Ganga-Mai temple in Gangotri, the source of the sacred Ganga river.

Bhutanese historian and culturalist Tshering Tashi then takes us to the Trance Runners, who can ride the wind and travel long distances in an incredibly short time through arduous spiritual and physical training. We have juxtaposed his piece with a long passage from Nebesky-Wojkowitz's *Where the Gods are Mountains,* about a distant past when a mystic marathon was held on the Land of Snow every ten years.

In her essay on Khasi traditions, Bijoya Sawian examines the oracular traditions of the Khasi hills, and the arts of divination, prophecy and soothsaying.

Lord Shiva is interpreted in the Tibetan traditions as Bhairava and as Mahakala, the manifestation of Time; he who nourishes and sustains the universe. His wife Parvati, in her form as Sati, offered her body to fire on being insulted by her father, a dedicated ritualistic. Her husband's grief knew no bounds, and he held on to her inert body as he performed the Tandava, the mystic dance of death. The gods watched in alarm as Shiva's divine frenzy began to threaten the equilibrium of the universe. Lord Vishnu flung his disc, the Sudarshan Chakra, to amputate Sati's charred body and bring it to rest on earth, where the pieces consecrated whichever spots they fell upon. These shaktipeeths, which include Vaishno Devi, Shardapeeth, Jwalamukhi, Naina Devi, Kamakhya and so many others, represent the feminine energies of the Himalaya. Alka Pande writes an intensely personal piece about her relationship with the mountains, titled 'My Devi, My Shakti' where she summons the strength of these sacred spots.

The closing chapter, by mountain geographer and Himalayan scholar Vaibhav Kaul, is perhaps the most enigmatic and emblematic of the essays in this anthology. He tells of the fragile environmental balance of the Himalaya and the incipient wrath of the guardian spirit, Palden Lhamo, as well as her bountiful blessings.

There is an inner logic to these stories that may not at first be apparent to the reader. These are encounters and quests, wanderings and lost paths, disappointments and betrayals, but they carry the spirit of the seeker, of the search and the continuing journey, within them. If the reader gets a sense of our mountains, the mysteries that lie hidden in the Himalaya, and the blessings and benedictions they carry, the book's task is done, its mission accomplished.

The story of Yeshe Tsogyal exists in a continuum of existence. Holly Gayley, associate professor at the Department of Religious Studies, University of Colorado Boulder, gives us an introduction to the princess-turned-yogini. A consort of Guru Padmasambhava and a teacher in her own right, Yeshe Tsogyal continues to be a living presence through her emanations across the centuries.

This deep and empathetic essay takes us through the story of Yeshe Tsogyal to the present century with the life of a contemporary saint, a female exemplar who lived through the conflicted history of Chinese annexation, with its impact on Tibetan faith and spiritual practice. Khandro Tare Lhamo (1938-2002) was considered a living embodiment of Yeshe Tsogyal. The multitude of miracles attributed to her, as well as the courage and fortitude with which she faced the censorship and repression of the Chinese regime, established her across the rhythms of cyclic existence as a manifestation of the great saint, with access to the teachings of Padmasambhava and to the spiritual treasures of the sacred geography of Tibet.

Women who tread the mystic path tend to become invisible, even more so in the high reaches of the Himalaya. This essay on the hidden, forgotten presences of female adepts, mystics and divinities moved me and found deep resonance, as it will with readers.

CHAPTER 1

The Living Presence

Yeshe Tsogyal and Khandro Tare Lhamo

HOLLY GAYLEY

Yeshe Tsogyal is the preeminent lady of Tibetan Buddhism. While most—if not all—of what we know about her life is highly mythologized, she is revered by Tibetans as a foremost disciple and consort of Padmasambhava, the eighth-century Tantric master credited with a seminal role in establishing Buddhism in Tibet. Yeshe Tsogyal is also celebrated for transcribing Padmasambhava's teachings and concealing them as treasures across the Tibetan and Himalayan landscape, to be revealed by successive tertöns or 'treasure revealers', during times of strife.

In her well-known namthar or story of 'complete liberation', which was revealed by the seventeenth-century tertön Taksham Nuden Dorje, Yeshe Tsogyal is portrayed as a gutsy woman striving for enlightenment. She faces various trials while practising meditation in mountain solitudes: scorn from villagers, torment by demons, starvation and sexual assault. Through these trials, she is shown transforming adversity into fuel for her practice and gaining realization. Moreover, in her namthar, one finds the striking statement by Padmasambhava that a woman with strong determination has a greater potential for attaining enlightenment than a man. In this way, Yeshe Tsogyal serves as an important example of a woman who traversed the Buddhist path.

However, if we think of Yeshe Tsogyal primarily as an ancestor who demonstrates that enlightenment is possible in female form, we grossly underestimate her significance for Tibetans. Moreover, we run into the problem (as with so many female figures in Buddhist literature) of establishing her historicity.

For Tibetans, Yeshe Tsogyal is not just a figure from the distant past; she remains an active and enduring presence. In the outer frame of her namthar, we see her portrayed as a timeless being—an emanation of Saraswati—who took human form in Tibet for the sake of propagating the dharma. And at the end of her tale, before dissolving into space, Yeshe Tsogyal promises to continue to respond to the prayers of devotees, to appear to religious adepts in visions and to continue to send forth emanations.

But her story does not end there. Over the centuries, Yeshe Tsogyal has remained accessible to ordinary Tibetans through numerous liturgies that supplicate her. In addition, her potent blessings are understood to remain in the places she practised as well as the objects she touched (strands of hair, articles of clothing, ritual implements, etc.), considered to be relics of contact. To spiritual virtuosos, both male and female, Yeshe Tsogyal also appears in visions, posing riddles, offering encouragement or expounding on the contents of a treasure teaching.

What's more, Yeshe Tsogyal's presence continues in the lives of historical women who are regarded to be her emanations. Indeed, exceptional women in the Nyingma school of Tibetan Buddhism are often identified as an emanation of Yeshe Tsogyal and sometimes referred to as 'Yeshe Tsogyal in person'. Her emanations include the few female tertöns known to us, such as Jomo Menmo (thirteenth century) and Sera Khandro (early twentieth century), as well as Mingyur Paldrön, the daughter and successor of the famed seventeenth-century tertön Terdak Lingpa, founder of Mindroling Monastery outside of Lhasa.

From one perspective, we could say that Yeshe Tsogyal serves as an authoritative precedent, creating a cultural space for female religious authority within the otherwise male-dominated Buddhist milieu in Tibet. From another perspective, through the women identified as her emanations, Yeshe Tsogyal continues to be an active presence, intervening in the lives of ordinary Tibetans.

To illustrate this, let me introduce a contemporary female tertön from the region of Golok in eastern Tibet: Khandro Tare Lhamo (1938–2002), an emanation of Yeshe Tsogyal, who served as a beacon of hope for her local community during a devastating chapter of Tibetan history. The period leading up to and including the Cultural Revolution (1966–76) witnessed the destruction of most visible symbols of Tibetan culture: monasteries were closed, texts were burned, sacred objects were looted, monks and nuns were forced to defrock and public religious observances were forbidden. Many lamas fled into exile or died in prison, including Khandro Tare Lhamo's first husband and three brothers, who were incarcerated in the late 1950s.

Perhaps because she was a woman, Khandro Tare Lhamo was spared imprisonment, though I was told that she did endure beatings. On one harrowing occasion, officials placed her bare chest on a hot wood-burning stove. According to the old woman who told me this story, Khandro Tare Lhamo reflected on the far greater sufferings of beings in the hell realms, and as a result she had no burn marks afterwards.

One cannot find such tales in her namthar, *Spiraling Vine of Faith*. Since it was published in China, most of her personal misfortunes and hardships are left out, likely due to the continued sensitivity of the 'Tibet question'. For this reason, the stories told about Khandro Tare Lhamo in her namthar emphasize the miracles she performed for her local community rather than the trials she endured. For example, during a famine in the wake of the Great Leap Forward, there is no mention of the hunger she and others must have faced; we read only of her miraculous ability to multiply a measure of rice to feed those around her. And while working as part of a crew constructing a pen for wild yaks, she is reported to have carried a stone too heavy for a group of men to lift, leaving an imprint of her hand in it.

These stories show how Khandro Tare Lhamo, as an enlightened being who took rebirth for the sake of others, embodied the paradox of being confined to her historical circumstances while seeming to transcend the laws of nature. Though miraculous in tenor—as when she reportedly stopped a rockslide threatening to overwhelm a crowd with a simple gesture of her hand—her activities were nonetheless grassroots in scale, addressing the immediate needs of her local community.

Khandro Tare Lhamo's role in the Buddhist revival in Golok, beginning in the 1980s, was possible in part due to her identification with Yeshe Tsogyal. With the onset of China's policy of 'reform and opening', religious observances were once again allowed, and Tibetans began an arduous process of rebuilding monasteries and recovering and reprinting precious texts. In Golok, treasure revelation played a significant role in this revival as a means to recover ancient teachings from amidst the debris. For the Nyingma, treasures are meant to be revealed during troubled times, when they promise to heal the damage to the teachings and beings, thereby heralding a new era for Buddhism and society to flourish.

As an emanation of Yeshe Tsogyal, Khandro Tare Lhamo was understood to have access to the teachings of Padmasambhava in the form of treasures, sealed in the Tibetan landscape and also in the mind stream of the tertön. Together with her second husband, Khandro Tare Lhamo revealed a twelve-volume corpus of treasure literature, including a volume dedicated to Yeshe Tsogyal and a series of female deities. From the mid-1980s onward, the couple traveled and taught together, propagating these treasures.

As these stories show, for Tibetans, Yeshe Tsogyal is more than an ancestor from the distant past or simply a role model to affirm women's potential for enlightenment. Indeed, she remains an active presence in the lives of Tibetans—both men and women—through rituals dedicated to her and through the historical women who serve as her emanations. The well-known emanations of Yeshe Tsogyal mentioned above are only the tip of the iceberg. As time goes on, more and more stories of female adepts and spiritual teachers in Tibet are coming to light. Indeed, if present circumstances are any indication, for every female Buddhist teacher who made it into the historical record, there were at least a dozen or more on the ground. As the number of studies on exceptional Tibetan women grows, let us hope that we can consider not only issues of gender but also the impact and influence of these women on Buddhist history.

—

Of all the great masters to bless this book across the portals of time, none is closer to me than Milarepa. It is perhaps because of the intensity of his inner struggle, the hungry lure for revenge and the rigour of the repentance imposed upon him by his revered Guru Marpa, who had studied under none other than the Indian sage Naropa.

The first short piece by Andrew Quintman was originally published in the invaluable Treasury of Lives and includes an excerpt from one of the 'songs of realization' recorded by Milarepa's early biographer, Tsangyon Heruka. This is followed by an evocative excerpt from W.Y. Evan Wentz's classic text, Tibet's Great Yogi, Milarepa*—an account of Milarepa's last days, when he willingly ate the poisoned curds offered by the jealous Geshé Tsakpuwa.*

CHAPTER 2

Milarepa

The Greatest of Masters

ANDREW QUINTMAN

Milarepa is one of the most famous individuals in the Tibetan Buddhist tradition, but very little of his life is known with any historical certainty. Even the dates of his birth and death have been notoriously difficult to calculate. Tsangnyon Heruka (1452–1507)—Milarepa's most famous biographer—records that the boy was born in a water-dragon year (1052) and passed away in a wood-hare year (1135), dates also found in biographical works from a century earlier. Numerous other sources, including the important mid-fifteenth-century *Religious History of Lhorong* push back the dates one twelve-year cycle to 1040–1123, a life span widely accepted by modern scholars. He is usually said to have lived until his eighty-fourth year. In any case, it is clear that he lived during the eleventh and early twelfth centuries, at the advent of the latter dissemination of Buddhism in Tibet.

According to Tsangnyon Heruka's account, Milarepa's ancestors were nomads of the Khyungpo clan from the northern region of the 'Central Horn', one of two administrative regions of Tibet's central province. One early ancestor was a Nyingma tantric practitioner named Josey. Khyungpo Josey became famous for his exorcism rites, a practice that earned him both respect and a good deal of wealth. While residing in a place called Chungpachi in the region of Lato Jang, he had an encounter with a particularly fierce spirit and at last caused the demon to cry out in horror, 'mila, mila', an admission of submission and defeat. Josey subsequently adopted this exclamation as a new clan title and his descendants came to be known by the name Mila.

Khyungpo Josey eventually married and had a son. This son in turn had two sons, the elder of whom was known as Mila Doton Sengge. The latter's son was named Mila Dorje Sengge. Dorje Sengge, who was fond of gambling, lost his family's home and wealth in a fateful game of dice. The family was thus forced to seek out a new life elsewhere and eventually resettled in the small village of Kyangatsa in Mangyul Gungtang, close to the modern border of Nepal. The father Doton Sengge served as a local village priest, performing various rituals and religious activities, while the son undertook trading trips in Tibet and to Nepal. In this way they were able to regain a good deal of wealth. Dorje Sengge married a local woman and had a son they named Mila Sherab Gyeltsen; the latter in turn married a woman named Nyangtsa Kargyen. This couple then gave birth to the boy who would become Milarepa.

When the boy turned seven, his father was stricken with a fatal illness and prepared a final testament that entrusted his wife, children, and wealth to the care of Milarepa's paternal uncle and aunt, providing that Milarepa regain his patrimony once he reached adulthood. The uncle and aunt, usually depicted as greedy and cold-hearted, responded by taking the estate for themselves, thus casting Milarepa's family into a life of abject poverty. The boy was sent to study reading and writing with a Nyingma master while his mother and sister were forced to labour as servants for their uncle and aunt.

Nyangtsa Kargyen then sent her son to train in black magic in order to seek revenge upon their relatives. Carrying out his mother's wishes, he trained with Nubchung Yonten Gyatso and thereby murdered thirty-five people attending a wedding feast at his aunt and uncle's house. From Yungton Trogyal he then learned the art of casting hailstorms. Unleashing a powerful storm across his homeland, he destroyed the village's barley crops just as they were about to be reaped, washing away much of the surrounding countryside.

Milarepa eventually came to regret his terrible crimes and in order to expiate their karmic effects, he set out to train with a Buddhist master. He first studied Dzogchen with Rangton Lhaga in Nyangto Rinang. His practice, however, proved ineffective, and Rangton instead directed Milarepa to seek out Marpa Chokyi Lodro (circa 1012–1097), the great translator residing in Lhodrak in southern Tibet.

Milarepa eventually reached Lhodrak where he met a heavyset plowman standing in his field. In reality, this was Marpa who had had a vision that Milarepa would become his foremost disciple. He had thus devised a way to greet his future student in disguise. Marpa was famous for his fierce temper and did not immediately teach Milarepa. Instead, he subjected his new disciple to a stream of verbal and physical abuse, forcing Milarepa to endure a series of ordeals, including a trial of constructing a series of four immense stone towers. Marpa eventually revealed that Milarepa had been prophesied by his own guru, the Indian master Nāropa. He further explained that the trials were actually a means of purifying the sins he had committed earlier in his life. The last of the towers, known as Sekhar Gutok ('Nine-Storied Son's-Tower'), still stands at the center of a monastic complex.

Marpa first imparted the lay and bodhisattva vows, granting Milarepa the name Dorje Gyeltsen. Milarepa then received numerous tantric instructions that Marpa had received in India, especially those of tummo, or yogic heat, the aural instructions of tantric practice, and instructions on Mahāmudrā. Marpa conferred upon Milarepa the secret initiation name Zhepa Dorje and commanded him to spend the rest of his life meditating in solitary mountain retreats.

Milarepa returned to his homeland for a brief period and then retired to a series of retreats nearby. Most famous among these is Drakar Taso where he remained for many years in arduous meditation. With nothing but wild nettles to eat, his body grew weak, and his flesh turned pale green. He later traveled widely across the Himalayan borderlands of southern Tibet and northern Nepal, and dozens of locations associated with his life have become important pilgrimage sites and retreat centers. In his account of the life story, Tsangnyon Heruka drew largely upon earlier sources in order to document dozens [of] such locations, but he reorganized them to create a new map of sacred sites—many of which were designated 'fortresses' of meditation—along Tibet's southern border: six well-known outer fortresses, six unknown inner fortresses and six secret fortresses, together with numerous other caves.

Stories of Milarepa's taming and converting demons in these locations, recorded in Tsangnyon Heruka's companion volume *The Hundred Thousand Songs of Milarepa*, echo accounts of the eight-century Indian master Padmasambhava. Many of Milarepa's most famous retreat locations were said to have been previously inhabited by Padmasambhava himself. Tsangnyon Heruka's reckoning of Milarepa's meditation sites therefore reveals a process of spiritual re-colonization, one that effectively claimed much of the Himalayan border for Milarepa's lineage. Three famous sacred sites of southern and western Tibet—Tsāri, Labchi, and Kailāsa – are said to have been established or prophesied by Milarepa, and all three later became important Kagyu retreat and pilgrimage centers, identified as Himālaya/Himavat, Godāvarī, and Cāritra/Devīkoṭa from the list of twenty-four pīṭhas of the Cakrasaṃvara Tantra, as well as the maṇḍalas of Cakrasaṃvara's body, speech, and mind. Drakar Taso became an important monastic institution and printing house under the direction of Tsangnyon Heruka's disciple Lhatsun Rinchen Namgyel (1473–1557).

Milarepa spent the rest of his adult life practicing meditation in seclusion and teaching groups of disciples mainly through spontaneous songs of realization. One of the first of Milarepa's songs recorded in Tsangnyon Heruka's account takes place after returning to his homeland for the first time and poignantly marks his decision to take up a life of solitary meditation:

I bow down at the feet of most excellent Marpa.
Bless this beggar to turn from clinging to things.

Alas. Alas. Ay me. Ay me. How sad.
People invested in things of life's round—
I reflect and reflect and again and again I despair.
They engage and engage and stir up from their depths so much torment.
They whirl and they whirl and are cast in the depths of life's round.

Those dragged on by karma, afflicted with anguish like this—
What to do? What to do? There's no cure but the dharma.
Lord Akṣobhya in essence, Vajradhara,
Bless this beggar to stay in mountain retreat.

In the town of impermanence and illusion
A restless visitor to these ruins is afflicted with anguish.
In the environs of Gungtang, a wondrous landscape,
Grasslands that fed yaks, sheep, cattle, and goats
Are nowadays taken over by harmful spirits.
These too are examples of impermanence and illusion,
Examples that call me, a yogin, to practice.

Lord Akṣobhya in essence, compassionate one,
Bless this beggar to stay in mountain retreat.

While staying at Drakar Taso, Milarepa later reaffirms his commitment to meditation practice in a stirring song about his aim of dying in solitary retreat:

I address my prayers to the lord lama's body.
Bless this beggar to stay in mountain retreat.

My happiness unknown to loved ones
And misery unknown to foes—
If thus I can die in this mountain retreat
The aims of this yogin will be complete.

No footprints upon my doorstep
And no sign of blood inside—
If thus I can die in this mountain retreat
The aims of this yogin will be complete.

No one to stand round my corpse
And no one to mourn for my death—
If thus I can die in this mountain retreat
The aims of this yogin will be complete.

No one to ask where I've gone to
And no one to say I have come—
If thus I can die in this mountain retreat
The aims of this yogin will be complete.

May the prayer of this beggar to die
In a cave of some lonesome locale
Be cast for the benefit of beings.
When cast, my aims are fulfilled.

Milarepa passed away at the age of eighty-four, after eating poisoned curds given by the jealous Geshé Tsakpuwa. After Milarepa's body was cremated, ḍākinī goddesses are said to have carried away his corporeal relics, leaving his disciples with little more than a piece of his robe, a lump of rock sugar, a knife and flint steel, and the yogin's many songs of inner realization.

Milarepa is credited with gathering numerous disciples; the best known are Rechung Dorje Drakpa and Gampopa Sonam Rinchen. The latter helped to establish a lineage of Kagyu masters and institutions that continue to play an important role in the dissemination of Tibetan Buddhism.

CHAPTER 3

Tibet's Great Yogi Milarepa

W.Y. EVAN WENTZ

At the time when Jetsūn had fulfilled his various duties, there lived, in the interior of Brin, a learned Lama named Tsaphuwa, very rich and influential, who was accustomed to take the highest seat in the assemblies of the people of Brin. This man feigned great reverence for Jetsūn, while at heart he was bursting with envy of him, and desirous of exposing what he took to be Jetsūn's ignorance, by putting difficult questions to Jetsūn in a public gathering of his own supporters. In this wise he asked Jetsūn many and various questions, all the while pretending that it was for the clearing of his own doubts.

Then, in the first month of the autumn of the Wood-Tiger year, there happened to be a grand marriage feast to which Jetsūn was invited, and he was placed on the highest seat at the head of the first row of guests, and the Geshé Tsaphuwa was seated next to him. The Geshé bowed down to Jetsūn, expecting that Jetsūn would bow down to him in return. Jetsūn, however, did not do so; for never having bowed down to, nor returned the obeisance of, any person save his own Guru, he did not depart from his usual custom on this occasion.

Much chagrined, the Geshé thought to himself, 'What! shall so learned a pandit as I am bow down to an ignoramus like him, and he not condescend to return the salutation! I shall certainly do my best to lower him in the esteem of the public.' And, producing a book on philosophy, he addressed Jetsūn thus: 'O Jetsūn, please be so good as to dissipate my perplexities by going through this book and explaining it to me word by word.'

Upon this, Jetsūn answered:

'As for the mere word-by-word explication of these dialectics, thou thyself art sufficiently expert ; but to realize their true import it is necessary to renounce the Eight Worldly Ambitions, lopping off their heads, to subdue the illusion of belief in the personal ego, and, regarding Nirvāna and Sangsāra as inseparable, to conquer the spiritual ego by meditation in mountain solitudes. I have never valued or studied the mere sophistry of word-knowledge, set down in books in conventionalized form of questions and answers to be committed to memory (and fired off at one's opponent); these lead but to mental confusion and not to such practice as bringeth actual realization of Truth. Of such word-knowledge I am ignorant; and if ever I did know it, I have forgotten it long ago. I pray that thou wilt give ear to the song which I am about to sing, to show my reasons for forgetting book-learning.'

And then Jetsūn sang this song:

Obeisance to the honoured Feet of Marpa the Translator!
May I be far removed from arguing creeds and dogmas.

Obeisance to the honoured Feet of Marpa the Translator!
My mind hath never strayed seeking various distractions.
Accustomed long to contemplating Love and Pity,
I have forgot all difference between myself and others.

Accustomed long to meditating on my Guru as enhaloed
O'er my head,
I have forgot all those who rule by power and by prestige.
Accustomed long to meditating on my Guardian Gods as
from myself inseparable,
I have forgot the lowly fleshly form.
Accustomed long to meditating on the Whispered Chosen Truths,
I have forgot all that is said in written and in printed books.

Accustomed, as I've been, to the study of the Common Science,
Knowledge of erring Ignorance I've lost.

Accustomed, as I've been, to contemplating the Three Bodies as inherent
in myself, I have forgot to think of hope and fear.

Accustomed, as I've been, to meditating on this life and the future life
as one,
I have forgot the dread of birth and death.

Accustomed long to studying, all by myself, mine own experiences,
I have forgot the need of seeking the opinions of friends and brethren,

Accustomed long to application of each new experience to
mine own growth spiritual,
I have forgot all creeds and dogmas.

Accustomed long to meditating on the Unborn, the Indestructible, and
the Unabiding,
I have forgot all definitions of this or that particular Goal.

Accustomed long to meditating on all visible phenomena as the Dharma
Kāya
I have forgot all mind-made meditations.

Accustomed long to keep my mind in the Uncreated State
of Freedom,
I have forgot conventional and artificial usages.

Accustomed long to humbleness, of body and of mind,
I have forgot the pride and haughty manner of the mighty.

Accustomed long to regard my fleshly body as my hermitage,
I have forgot the ease and comfort of retreats in monasteries.

Accustomed long to know the meaning of the Wordless,
I have forgot the way to trace the roots of verbs and source of words
and phrases;
May thou, O learned one, trace out these things in standard books.

When Jetsūn had sung this song, the Geshé said, 'All this may be very well according to thy yogi creed, but, following our metaphysicians, such religious discourses lead nowhere [i.e. show no real attainment of understanding]. I bowed down to thee imagining thee to be a highly advanced person!'

Upon his saying this, the people (especially his own supporters) showed displeasure, and, as though with one voice, cried, 'O Geshé Tonpa, however learned thou mayst be, and however many professors like thee the world may hold, the whole lot of you are not equal to the smallest downy hair on Jetsūn's body, nor able to fill the tiny pore containing it. Thou hadst better be satisfied with the seat assigned to thee, at the head of our row, and do what thou canst to add to thy wealth by usury. As for religion, thou art not in the least permeated with its perfume.'

The Geshé was much angered by this, but as the whole party were unanimously against him, he could not show fight, and so he merely sat in sulky silence, thinking to himself, 'This ignoramus, Milarepa, by mere display of eccentric doings and sayings and telling of lies, which tend to overthrow the Buddhist Faith, is able to delude the people into making him numerous alms and gifts, whereas I, though so learned in book-learning, and the wealthiest and most influential person in the place, count for less than a dog despite my religious attainments. Something must be done to put an end to this.'

Acting on this resolve, he induced a concubine of his, by promising her a valuable turquoise, to go and offer Jetsūn some poisoned curds, which she did, while Jetsūn was at Brin-Dragkar. Having fulfilled his duty of setting his favoured disciples upon the Path of Emancipation and Perfection, Jetsūn knew that his term of life was almost ended, even if he did not take the poison. But foreseeing that unless the woman procured the turquoise now she would not procure it afterward [i. e. after the commission of the crime], he said to her, 'For the present, I will not accept the food thou offerest me. Bring it later on and I will then accept it.'

Thinking that perhaps Jetsūn knew her intention, the woman, much embarrassed and distressed, returned to the Geshé, relating to him the whole incident at length, [and] said that Jetsūn, in virtue of clairvoyance, had detected her evil design and refused the poisoned food. But her seducer, trying to embolden her, said, ' If Jetsūn possessed this power he would not have asked thee to take the food to him later on, but would have handed it back, telling thee to take it thyself; this is proof that he doth not possess clairvoyance. Thou mayst now have the turquoise, but be sure that he taketh the poisoned food.' Then he gave her the turquoise; and she said,

'That Jetsūn doth possess clairvoyant power is commonly believed, and his refusal of the food the first time proveth it. I am satisfied that he will refuse the food the second time. I do not want thy turquoise; I am too much afraid to go to him again; and most certainly I will not go.'

The Geshé replied:

'Illiterate folk believe that he possesseth the power, but not being conversant with the Scriptures, they are duped by his trickery. The Scriptures describe a person possessed of clairvoyance as quite different from a person such as he is; I am convinced that he doth not possess it. Now, if thou undertake to offer him the food again, and succeed in getting him to eat it, thereupon—seeing that we two have already lived together, and, as the proverb sayeth, "No difference is there in taking a big or a little bite of garlic, since garlic it is"—we will thenceforth live openly as husband and wife. Then not only will the turquoise be thine, but thou wilt be the mistress of all that I own; and we will share weal and woe together. As we thus have the grudge in common, do thine utmost to bring the attempt to a successful issue.'

Taking the Geshé at his word the woman, tempted to try a second time, again mixed poison and curd together and took the mixture to Jetsūn as a food offering, when he was at Trode-Trashi-Gang. Smilingly, Jetsūn took her offering in his hand, and she thought that the Geshé was perhaps right in asserting that Jetsūn did not possess clairvoyance. Just then, however, Jetsūn spoke and said, 'Thou hast procured the turquoise as thy fee for doing this deed.' Overcome with remorse and fear, the woman began to tremble; and, in quavering sob-choked voice, confessed, 'Yes, Lord, I have procured the turquoise' and, prostrating herself at his feet, she begged him not to partake of the poisoned food, but to give it back to her who was guilty of so heinous an intention [that she might drink it].

Jetsūn answered:

'First of all, I cannot, on any account, give it back to thee to drink; my compassion for thee is too great. Were I to do so, I should be transgressing the vows of a Bodhisattva, and thus incur the heaviest of spiritual penalties. Moreover, my life hath almost run its course; my work is finished; the time hath come for me to go to another world. Thy poisoned food would have no effect upon me whatsoever. Nevertheless, I refused it at first, in order to enable thee to gain the turquoise, which was promised to thee as the fee for thy crime. Now that the turquoise is thine, I will take the poisoned food, to satisfy the desire of the Geshé and to secure thee in possession of the coveted turquoise. As regardeth the many promises for the future which he hath made to thee on condition that this crime be successfully accomplished, thou needest place no reliance on them; for he will disappoint thee.

'There is no truth at all in any of the many things which he hath said against me. The time shall come when both thou and he will deeply repent of all these things. When that time cometh, ye will devote yourselves wholly, if possible, to penance and devotion; but if unable to do so much, at least avoid committing such heinous sins, even though your very life be at stake, and pray to me and my disciples in deep and humble faith. Left unassisted, ye two would be cut off from happiness for countless ages, and suffering would thus be your lot; so, for this once, I will see if I can absolve your evil karma. But I command thee to keep this affair secret for as long as I am alive; the time will come when it will be known to everyone. Although thou mayst not believe other sayings of mine upon hearing them, yet in this affair thou wilt have an opportunity of believing in me [or of being convinced]. Therefore, bear this well in mind, and await its fulfilment.'

Then Jetsūn partook of the poisoned food.

When the woman had reported these things to the Geshé he said, 'Everything that is spoken is not necessarily true. [According to the proverb], "Not everything that is cooked is fit [for food]." Enough for me that he hath taken the poison. Now take heed and keep thy mouth shut.'

Then Jetsūn sent word to the people of Tingri and Nyanam, and to all who had known him and had faith in him, to come to see him, each with a small offering. He sent a like invitation to all who had a wish to meet him, but had never done so. Also to all his disciples the message was proclaimed; and, greatly impressed by its ominous nature, each of them, male and female, initiated and uninitiated, acquainted and unacquainted with one another, assembled in a great assembly at Lapchi-Chubar. Then for many days Jetsūn preached to them concerning the Apparent Truth [i.e. the Law of Karma] and the Real Truth [i.e. the Dharma-Kāya].

During these days, the more spiritually gifted of the hearers beheld the skies filled with gods listening [to the Master]. Many others felt [intuitively] that in the skies and on the earth there was an innumerable congregation of divine as of human beings, all joyously listening to the preaching of the Dharma; and they felt a joyfulness pervading the whole gathering. And, to everyone present, there appeared various phenomenal signs, such as rainbows arching a clear blue sky; [then again] clouds, of different colours, assuming the shapes of [royal] umbrellas and banners and different offerings; and showers of variegated blossoms. There was heard by all the most exquisite music from various musical instruments; and the most fragrant odours, such as none had ever before enjoyed, filled the air. Those of moderate spiritual development who experienced these phenomena of good omen inquired of Jetsūn why there was the feeling of wondrous communion between the celestial auditors filling the skies and the human auditors assembled on the earth, and why the various auspicious phenomenal signs, which every person present saw, had occurred.

Jetsūn replied, 'Among human beings, the number who are spiritually developed, inclusive of both the initiated and the uninitiated, is not great, whereas those piously inclined among the divine being, who are eager to hear the Dharma, the very skies and are offering to me in worship the five celestial objects of enjoyment, and radiating, to all alike, joy and cheerfulness of mind. Thus do ye feel thrilled with gladness, and perceive the joyous and favourable signs.'

Thereupon, they asked him, 'Why, then, should the divine beings be invisible to [most of] us?'

Jetsūn replied:

'Many there are among the gods who have attained the Anāgāmi State, and various other degrees of holiness; and, to be able to see them, it is necessary to be endowed with the perfected vision and the highest zeal in the acquirement of the two kinds of merit, and free from the two obscuring impurities born of Ignorance. If the chiefs among the gods be seen, then, too, will their followers be seen. Whosoever desire to see these divine beings, must devote themselves to acquiring merit sufficient for the expiating of all evil karma. Thereupon, one may see in oneself the highest and holiest of all gods [which is the Pure Mind].'

Then Jetsūn chanted a hymn on the way to see the gods:

Obeisance at the Feet of Gracious Marpa!
Bless Thy Spiritual Descendants, that they may multiply.

To me, Milarepa, the Devotee,
Celestial beings, from Tushita Heavens,
And other Holy Regions, come to hear my sermons.
Thy fill all quarters of the skies,
But only those [among my human followers] enjoying the
five kinds of vision,
Can behold them; the common folk behold them not;
Yet I myself without impediment see each of them.
For the good of all the congregation,
They offer reverence unto me, with heavenly offerings.

The heavens are filled with radiance of rainbows;
Celestial showers of sweet-smelling blossoms fall;
All beings alike hear harmonies melodious, and fragrance
of incense enjoy;
Love divine, and happiness, pervade the whole assembly.
Such are the [fruits of] Grace-Waves of the Kargyütpa Saints.

Taking to yourselves the Gracious Refuge of the Faith,
If ye desire to see the Gods and Angels,
Give ear attentively to this, my hymn:

Because of evil karma accumulated by you in past lives,
The moment ye are of your mother born, ye delight in sinning;

The doing of the good and merit-bringing deeds ye like not;
E'en till ye are grown old, your nature is perverse:
Thus surely must ye garner the results of evil actions.

If ye wonder whether evil karm a can be neutralized or not,
Then know that it is neutralized by desire for goodness.

But they who knowingly do evil deeds,
Exchange a mouthful of food for infamy.
They who knowing not whither they themselves are bound,
Yet presume to pose as guides for others,
Do injury both to themselves and others.

If pain and sorrow ye desire sincerely to avoid,
Avoid, then, doing harm to others.

Repenting and confessing of all previous sins,
At the feet of the Guru and the Deities,
And vowing never more in future to commit a wrong,
Are the shortest path to rapid expiation of all evils done.

The greater part of sinners are sharp-witted;
[Of mind] unstable and unfixed, they delight in various distractions;
And unendowed are they with love of the religious life:
This, in itself, doth signify that they are sin-obscured,
And need repentance and confession o'er and o'er.

Do ye each give yourselves, with zeal,
To expiating sins and winning merit;
If thus ye do, not only shall ye see
The Dharma-loving deities celestial,
But the holiest and highest of all gods.

The Dharma-Kāya of your own mind ye shall also see;
And seeing That, ye shall have seen the All,
The Vision Infinite, the Sangsāra and Nirvāna
Then shall your karmic actions cease.

Upon Jetsūn's chanting this hymn, those of the assembled deities and human beings who were highly developed spiritually, obtained the right view of the Dharma-Kāya [or Nirvanic] State. Those of moderate development obtained experience of the super-sensuous divine state of Ecstatic Bliss and Voidness such as they had never before known, and were helped thereby to enter upon the Path [of the Realization of Nirvana]. And not one of all the others who were there but was desirous of gaining the Great Emancipation.

Then Jetsūn addressed the congregation, saying:

'My disciples, gods, and men, and all who are assembled here today, our coming together is the result of good karma from past lives; and in this life we have established a purer and holier relationship by religious communion. Now that I am grown very aged, no certainty is there of our being able to meet again [in this lifetime]. I exhort you to preserve the religious discourses which I have delivered to you, and not to neglect them, but to carry their teachings into practice, in so far as ye can, in your daily lives. If ye do this, in whatever realm I may arrive at the Perfection of Buddhahood, ye shall be the first body of disciples to receive the Truth that I shall then preach. Therefore rejoice in this.'

When those present from Nyanam heard these words of the Lord Jetsūn, they asked of one another whether the Master meant that he was about to leave this world in order to go and benefit some other world; and said that, if this were his meaning, they should entreat him to ascend to the Paradise Realm from Nyanam, or, if that could not be, at least to bless Nyanam by a final visit. So they went to Jetsūn, and, clasping his feet, entreated him with tear-filled eyes and in fervency of faith and love to grant their prayer. In like manner did the disciples and lay-followers from Tingri entreat Jetsūn to go to Tingri. To these entreaties Jetsūn made reply, 'I am now too far advanced in years to go to Nyanam or Tingri; I will await death at Brin and

Chubar. Therefore, each of ye may give me your parting good wishes and return home; I will meet all of you in the Sacred Paradises.'

Then they prayed that, if Jetsūn were unable to visit their countries, he might, at least, utter a blessing upon each of the places which he had visited, and a special good wish for those people who had seen his face, or heard his voice, and listened to his preaching; and, in short, that not upon them alone [should these blessings be], but upon all sentient creatures throughout the universe.

To this entreaty, Jetsūn said: 'Grateful am I for the faith which ye have manifested in me, and for the necessities of life with which ye have kept me supplied. I have shown my thankfulness in having ever wished you well; and, to do good to you, I have preached the Dharma to you, whereby, through obligation, a mutual bond hath been established between us. And, now, seeing that I am a Yogi who hath realized the Truth, it is my duty to utter for you a good-wish for peace and happiness, both temporal and spiritual, for the present time and for all eternity.'

Then Jetsūn sang the following good wishes in verse:

O Father and Protector of all Creatures, Thou Who hast
Thine Own Good-Wishes realized,
Translator Marpa, I bow down at Thy Feet!

O my disciples, here assembled, hearken unto me.
Kind, indeed, have ye been unto me,
And kind have I been unto you;
May we, thus bound together by ties of mutual helpfulness,
Meet in the Realm of Happiness.

Ye donors of alms, who here are seated,
May ye live long, and be e'er prosperous;

May no perverted thought find entry to your minds;
May all your thoughts e'er pious be and lead to your success religiously.

May peace harmonious bless this land;
May it be ever free from maladies and war;
May there be harvests rich, and increased yield of grain;
May every one delight in righteousness.

May all who have beheld my face and heard my voice,
And all who have my history known, and borne it in their heart,
And all who have but heard my name and story,
Meet me in the Realm of Happiness.

May those who make a study of my life
And emulate it, and dedicate themselves to meditation;
And each who shall transcribe, narrate, or listen to my history,
Or whosoe'er shall read and venerate it,
Or take it as their rule of conduct,
Meet me in the Realm of Happiness.

May every being in future time
Who hath the will to meditate,
In virtue of mine own austerities
Be free from all impediment and error.

To them who for devotion's sake endure hardships,
There cometh boundless merit;
To them who shall lead others to the treading of the Path,
Boundless gratitude is due;
To them who hear the story of my life,
There cometh boundless grace:
By the power of this boundless merit, gratitude, and grace,
May every being, as soon as they shall hear [my history], attain Deliverance,
And [True] Success as soon as they shall contemplate [it].

May the places of my sojourn, and the objects whereon I have rested,
And every little thing which hath been mine,
Bring peace and gladness wheresoe'er they be.

The earth, the water, fire, and air,
And the ethereal spaces wheresoever they pervade—
May I be able to embrace them all.

And may the Devas, Nāgas and the Spirits of Eight Orders,
And all the local genii and the sprites,
Do not the least of harm;
But may they each fulfil these wishes in accordance with the Dharma.

May none of living creatures, none e'en of insects,
Be bound unto sangsaric life; nay, not one of them;
But may I be empowered to save them all.

At these words, the lay-disciples showed great joy, for they now doubted whether Jetsūn meant to pass away; so that those of Nyanam and Tingri were all the more eager to seek his grace and blessings, and to listen to his religious discourses.

As soon as the congregation had dispersed and everyone had gone home, the heavenly rainbows and the other phenomena automatically vanished.

Now the people of Brin earnestly begged Jetsūn to preach to them. Accordingly, Jetsūn went to dwell in a hermitage which had been built on the top of a rock known as 'Poisonous-to-Touch', for the rock was believed to be the serpenthood crowning the malignant Serpent-Spirit of Brin, the hermitage having been built there in order that the Serpent-Spirit should be subjugated [in virtue of hermits dwelling therein]; and there Jetsūn continued his preaching to his lay-disciples of Brin. When he had completed his sermons, he said to them, 'Those who have points to be elucidated, or perplexities to be cleared concerning the special teachings which they have received, should make haste to present them, for I am not sure of living much longer.'

So the assembled disciples gathered together offerings for performing a pūjā and having performed the pūjā listened to the completion of the special teachings [as Jetsūn made the elucidations and cleared the perplexities]. Then Bri-Gom-Repa and Seban-Repa, addressing Jetsūn, asked, ' O Jetsūn, from what thou hast [just] said we have come to fear lest thou intend to pass away into Nirvāna. It cannot be that thy life hath run its course?' Jetsūn replied, 'My life and mine influence in converting others have reached their completion. Therefore must I now meet the consequence of having been born.'

A few days later, Jetsūn showed signs of illness, and Ngan-Dzong-Repa began preparations for making propitiatory offerings in the worship of the Gurus, the Devas and the Dākinīs on behalf of the disciples; and, at the same time, he begged Jetsūn to take medical and other treatment He was about to summon all the laymen and disciples to complete the necessary preparations; but Jetsūn said:

'It is commonly the rule that illness befalling a yogi is to be looked upon as an exhortation to persevere in devotion, and he ought not to have any special prayers offered up for his recovery. He should utilize illness as an aid to progression on the Path, ever ready to meet suffering, and even death. As for me, Milarepa, I have, by the grace of my gracious Guru Marpa completed all the special rites for overcoming illness, according to his particular method; and now I need neither forces nor mediators. I have made mine enemies to be bosom friends; so I need not the making of prayers or expiatory offerings. Nor do I need exorcisms or propitiatory rites to any demons; for I have transmuted all bad omens and evil presentiments into Guardian Deities of the Faith, who will perform all the four kinds of ceremonies. The Maladies born of the Five Poisons, I have changed into the Bliss of the Five Divine Wisdoms; therefore do I need not medicines compounded of the six chief spices. The time hath come when the visible, illusory, physical body, the mind-evolved form of the Divine Body [the Dharma-Kāya], must be merged into the Realms of Spiritual Light; and for this no rites of consecration are necessary. Worldly folk who have heaped up evil karma during their lifetime, and who anticipate reaping, as the result, the pangs of birth, old age, illness and death, in this world, vainly seek to evade or ameliorate the intensity and anguish thereof by means of propitiatory ceremonies and medical treatment. Neither through the power or authority of kings, nor the valour of the hero nor the charming form of the belle, nor the wealth of the rich, nor the fleetness of the coward, nor the oratory of an able pleader, can one ward off, or retard for a moment, the Decree of Time. There are no means or methods, be they peaceful, noble, fascinating, or stern, which can buy off or stop the execution of this unalterable decree.

'If any there be who are truly fearful of those pangs, and sincerely seek to prevent their recurrence, and are really eager to attain a state of eternal bliss, I possess the secret rite for the attainment thereof?'

When Jetsūn had thus spoken, some of the disciples prayed him to impart to them this ritual [or science]; and Jetsūn said:

'So be it. All worldly pursuits have but the one unavoidable and inevitable end, which is sorrow: acquisitions end in dispersion; buildings, in destruction; meetings, in separation; births, in death. Knowing this, one should, from the very first, renounce acquisition and heaping up, and building, and meeting; and, faithful to the commands of an eminent guru, set about realizing the Truth [which hath no birth or death]. That alone is the best ritual [or science]. I have yet my last important testament to impart. This, forget ye not, I will do hereafter.'

Again Shiwa-Wod-Repa and Ngan-Dzong-Repa addressed Jetsūn, saying, 'O Jetsūn, were thou to regain health, thou couldst continue to do good to many more sentient creatures. Therefore, even though thou dost not see fit to grant our prayers in full, yet in order that we may not have regrets hereafter, we again pray that thou wilt be pleased to perform an efficacious Tantric ceremonial of worship for thy recovery; and, at the same time, take some medicine.'

Jetsūn answered:

'Were it not that my time had come, I should have done as ye have requested. But, if one were to condescend to perform a Tantric rite for the prolongation of one's life without having, as the plea, the altruistic intention to serve others, it would be as improper behaviour towards the Divine Deities as it would be towards a king to ask him to perform the menial service of sweeping and scrubbing one's floor; and such act carrieth with it its own penalty. Therefore, I adjure you never to perform sacred Tantric rites with a view to success in worldly pursuits; though selfish folk [who know no better] are not to blame in so doing. I have passed my life in incessant practice of the Highest Tantric Truths, in order to benefit all sentient beings; this will serve for religious rites [for warding off evil] now. Because of such devotion, my mind knoweth not how to move away from the firm Seat of Truth [in Samadht]; this will suffice for the rites for long life. Marpa's remedies have eradicated the very roots of the diseases of the Five Poisons [i.e. lust, hatred, stupidity, egotism, jealousy]; this will serve for medical treatment. As for yourselves, merely to be devotees, or to have adopted the religious career, will not suffice; ye must, in addition, use trials and tribulations as aids on the Path. If one's time have not come, and some evil interruption threaten one's life, there is no harm in having recourse to medical treatment and [faith-cure] rituals for one's recovery, providing such shall assist one on the Path. Recent evils can be warded off by exercising the very might of the correlative and interdependent chain of circumstances which result [from them]; and even those evils themselves can be transmuted into blessings at such times. Thus it was that in former times the Buddha, too, thinking of the good of his lesser developed disciples, held out his hand to have his pulse felt by the physician Jivaka Kumara, and took the medicines prescribed. But when His time had come, even He, the Lord Buddha, passed away into Nirvana. Likewise, now, my time hath come, and I will not have recourse to medical treatment or any sort of ceremonies for my cure.'

Thus would Jetsūn not allow anything to be done for him. Accordingly, the two advanced disciples entreated him to instruct them as follows: 'If Jetsūn is really passing away to some other realm, then, for our good, how should the funeral ceremonies be performed, how should the bones and reliques be honourably preserved, and how should the stupas and tsha-tshas be made? Again, who should be elected as thy successor; and how are the ceremonies on the anniversary [of thy passing away] to be conducted? Then, too, which disciple is to follow this or that branch of religious practice, such as listening [to instruction], cogitating, or meditating [in solitude]. In all these matters we solicit thine own verbal directions.'

To this Jetsūn answered:

'By the kind favour of Marpa, I have fulfilled all the duties of the Sangsdra and attained Deliverance [therefrom]. The three principles of my personality [i.e. body, speech, and mind] having been transmuted into the Body of Truth, there is no certainty that I shall leave a corpse behind me. There is, therefore, no need either of stupas or of clay tsha-tshas. As I own no monastery or temple, I need not appoint any one to succeed me. The bleak, sterile hills and the mountain peaks, and the other solitary retreats or hermitages, all of you may possess and occupy. All the sentient beings of the Six Lokas ye may protect as your children and followers. Instead of erecting stupas cultivate loving fondness towards all parts of the Dharma and set up the Victorious Banner of Devotion; and, in place of tsha-tshas let there be uninterrupted daily repetitions of the fourfold prayer. For periodical ceremonies [in memory of my passing away], offer me earnest prayer from the innermost recesses of your hearts. As regardeth the method of acquiring practical knowledge, if ye find a certain practice increaseth your evil passions and tendeth to selfishness, abandon it, though it may appear virtuous; and if any line of action tend to counteract the Five Evil Passions, and to benefit sentient beings, know that to be true and holy Dharma and continue it, even though it should appear to be sinful [to those bound to worldly conventionalities].

'If, after having heard these counsels, one fails to follow them and, instead, infringe and trample upon them in defiance of the [Divine] Law, howsoever well-informed such a one may be, he will merely be earning a place in the lowest Hell. Life is short, and the time of death is uncertain; so apply yourselves to meditation. Avoid doing evil, and acquire merit, to the best of your ability, even at the cost of life itself. In short, the whole purport may be stated thus: Act so that ye have no cause to be ashamed of yourselves; and hold fast to this rule. If ye do thus, ye can be sure of never disobeying the commands of the Supreme Buddhas, notwithstanding any conflicting rules which may be found set down in writing. Herein is contained all guidance concerning listening and deliberating. Satisfied will this old man's heart be if ye act accordingly; for if my heart be satisfied, then will your duties be fulfilled, both towards the Sangsāra and Nirvāna.'

—

Poet, interdisciplinary scholar and curator Ranjit Hoskote's evocative and moving introduction to the fourteenth-century Kashmiri mystic and poet Lal Děd is written with passion and erudition. His book I, Lalla: The Poems of Lal Děd *carries his powerful and authentic translations of her enigmatic, philosophically precise verses. He himself belongs to the close-knit community of Kashmiri Pandits, now for the most part in exile from their beloved home state.*

Lalla, as she was also known, was an accomplished yogini trained in the demanding discipline of Kashmir's Śaivite tradition.

In this essay, Hoskote brings alive Lalla's troubled path to sainthood and the power and pathos of her poetry.

CHAPTER 4

Lal Děd

Life, Poetry and Historical Context

RANJIT HOSKOTE

I didn't believe in it for a moment
but I gulped down the wine of my own voice.
And then I wrestled with the darkness inside me,
knocked it down, clawed at it, ripped it to shreds.

The poems of the fourteenth-century Kashmiri mystic Lal Děd strike us like brief and blinding bursts of light: epiphanic, provocative, they shuttle between the vulnerability of doubt and the assurance of an insight gained through resilience and reflection. These poems are as likely to demand that the Divine reveal Itself as to complain of Its bewildering and protean ubiquity. They prize clarity of self-knowledge above both the ritualist's mastery of observances and the ascetic's professional athleticism. If they scoff at the scholar who substitutes experience with scripture and the priest who cages his God in a routine of prayers, they also reject the renouncer's austere mortification of the body. Across the expanse of her poetry, the author, whose signature these poems carry, evolves from a wanderer, uncertain of herself and looking for anchorage in a potentially hostile landscape, into a questor who has found belonging beneath a sky that is continuous with her mind.

To the outer world, Lal Děd is arguably Kashmir's best-known spiritual and literary figure; within Kashmir, she has been venerated both by Hindus and Muslims for nearly seven centuries. For most of that period, she has successfully eluded the proprietorial claims of religious monopolists. Since the late 1980s, however, Kashmir's confluential culture has frayed thin under the pressure of a prolonged conflict to which transnational terrorism, state repression and local militancy have all contributed. Religious identities in the region have become harder and more sharp-edged, following a substantial exodus of the Hindu minority during the early 1990s, and a gradual effort to replace Kashmir's unique and syncretically nuanced tradition of Islam with a more Arabo-centric global template. It is true that Lal Děd was constructed differently by each community, but she was *simultaneously* Lalleśvarī or Lalla Yogini to the Hindus and Lal'ārifa to the Muslims; today, unfortunately, these descriptions are increasingly being promoted at the expense of one another. In honour of the plural sensibilities that Kashmir has long nurtured, I will refer to this mystic-poet by her most celebrated and nonsectarian appellation, 'Lal Děd'. In the colloquial, this means 'Grandmother Lal'; more literally, it means 'Lal the Womb', a designation that connects her to the Mother Goddesses whose cults of fecundity and abundance form the deep substratum of Indic religious life. In writing of her in this book, I will also use the name by which she is most popularly and affectionately known across community lines: Lalla.

Paradoxically, given Lalla's pervasive presence in Kashmiri culture, it is difficult to construct a biography for her in the conventional sense. All that we know of her life has been communicated orally, through the medium of legend; the skeletal chronology that we possess is derived from Persian chronicles written in the eighteenth century, nearly four centuries after her death.

We cannot be certain of the date and place of Lalla's birth, or the date and place of her death. Sifting through the evidence of the legends and the chronicles, modern scholars have suggested that she was born in 1301 or between 1317 and 1320, either in Sempore, near Pampore, or in Pandrenthan, near Srinagar. She is believed to have died in 1373, although no one is certain where; the grave ascribed to her in Bijbehara appears to be of much later provenance. The details of her early life have crystallized into an archetypal narrative of the misunderstood young woman with spiritual aspirations. Born to a Brahmin family, she was married at the age of twelve, as was the custom, into a family that lived in Pampore; she was given a new name, Padmāvati, but remained Lalla in her own eyes. Her domestic life was a troubled one. Suspicious of her meditative absorptions and visits to shrines, her husband treated her cruelly; her mother-in-law often starved her. From this period in Lalla's life comes the well-known Kashmiri saying attributed to the future mystic: 'Whether they kill a ram or a sheep, Lalla will get a stone to eat.'

At twenty-six, Lalla renounced home and family and went to the Śaiva saint Sĕd Bôyu, or Siddha Śrīkāntha, asking to be accepted as a disciple. He became her guru and instructed her in the spiritual path. On completing her period of discipleship and being initiated, she went out into the world, in the mould of the classical parivrājikā, as a wandering mendicant. It is assumed that Lalla began to compose her scintillating, provocative and compelling poems at this stage in her life. To renounce the state of marriage, to wander, gathering spiritual experience—this was not an easy choice for a Brahmin woman to make in the Kashmir of the fourteenth century. As a disciple, she had been secure within her guru's protection; her true ordeals began only after she had left her guru's house and set off on her own, with no armour against the full force of social sanction. As she says in Poem 92:

> They lash me with insults, serenade me with curses.
> Their barking means nothing to me.
> Even if they came with soul-flowers to offer,
> I couldn't care less, untouched I move on

Braving the trials and humiliations that came her way, Lalla grew in stature to become a quester and a teacher: this passage to maturity and deepening knowledge is recorded vividly in her vākhs. In Poem 93, she defies her tormentors and the system of conventions they represent:

> Let them hurl a thousand curses at me,
> pain finds no purchase in my heart.
> I belong to Shiva. Can a scatter of ashes
> ruin a mirror? It gleams.

Lalla's poems shimmer with their author's experience of being a yoginī, trained in the demanding spiritual disciplines and devotional practices of Kashmir Śaivite mysticism. Since this school is itself the confluential outcome of an engagement with several philosophical traditions, she was receptive to the images and ideas of those other traditions. It would be most productive to view her as a figure whose ideas straddled the domains of

Kashmir Śaivism, Tantra, Yoga and Yogacara Buddhism, and who appears to have been socially acquainted with the ideas and practices of the Sufis.

Revelation comes to Lalla like a moon flowering in dark water. Her symbols and allegories can be cryptic, and yet the candour of her poems moves us deeply, viscerally. She celebrates perseverance in the quest, contrasting physical agony with spiritual flight and dwelling on the obdurate landscapes chat the questor must negotiate. Lalla's poetry is fortified by a palpable, first-hand experience of illumination; it conveys a freedom from the mortal freight of fear and vacillation. She cherishes these while attacking the parasitic forms of organized religion that have attached themselves to the spiritual quest and choked it: arid scholarship, soulless ritualism, fetishized austerity and animal sacrifice. Her ways of transcending these obstacles can seem subversive, even deeply transgressive—as in Poem 59, where she confronts the priest with the brutal exaction demanded by his idolatry:

> It covers your shame, keeps you from shivering.
> Grass and water are all the food it asks
> Who taught you, priest-man,
> to feed this breathing thing to your thing of stone?

For an itinerant, tangential and seemingly isolated dissident—she founded no school or movement, had no apostles, left no anointed successors and scattered her poems among her listeners—Lalla has exerted a profound and seminal influence on Kashmir's religious life. She was a major presence in the life and practice not only of Rupa Bhavani, but also of a number of later Kashmiri mystics, teachers and devotional poets like Parmanand (1791–1879), Shams Faqir (1843–1904), and Krishna Joo Razdan (1851–1926). Vitally, given that Kashmir is now almost completely a Muslim region, it is instructive to recall that Lalla is regarded as a foundational figure by the Rishi order of Kashmiri Sufism, which was initiated by Nund Rishi or Sheikh Nur-ud-din Wali (1379–1442), seen by many as her spiritual son and heir. Nur-ud-din and his fellow rishīs chose to lead celibate lives, abstained from meat, avoided injuring animals or plants, secluded themselves in caves or forests, and employed an ecumenical vocabulary drawn both from the Kashmir Śaivite and Islamic systems. The rishīs instituted solitary meditative as well as collective devotional practices, and their followers convene around a network of khānaqahs or ziyārats: shrine complexes that incorporate mosques, meditation halls and the tombs of saints. This robust regional tradition of spirituality continues to remain strong in the Valley, despite the hardening of Islamic piety along Wahhabi mandates during the low-intensity warfare between insurgents and the Indian State that has raged unabated in recent decades, accompanied by cycles of civil unrest and the killing of countless innocent people, Muslim and Hindu, caught in the crossfire.

Our road, as we map the religious and philosophical lifeworld in which Lalla's poetry emerged, now brings us to Kashmir Śaivism. The foundations of Śaivite philosophy lie in the *Śaiva-agamas* or tantrās, high among which may be ranked the *Vijñānabhairava* (c. 8th century CE), composed in Sanskrit and developed in northern India between the fourth and eighth centuries. These were cast as dialogues between Shiva and Shakti concerning the structure of the cosmos and of human experience, the pathways to spiritual illumination and modes of effecting release from the cycle of birth and death. The tantrās posit a framework of thirty-six cosmic principles, which culminate in Shiva and Shakti, and beyond this dyad, in the ineffable and unitive essence of the universe, which is referred to as Parama-shiva (or the 'Shiva-principle'). The *Śaiv*ite tradition developed through three major branches: the dualist *Śaiva* Siddhanta system that arose in the Tamil country in the sixth century, its texts composed in Tamil; the non-dualist Kashmir *Śaiv*ism that announced itself in the eighth century, its texts composed in Sanskrit with Apabhraṁsa annotations; and the dualist Vīraśaiva or Lingāyat movement that exploded in Karnataka in the twelfth century, its texts composed in Kannada. Non-dualist Kashmir

Śaivism emerged as a distinctive philosophy after intensive dialogue with the thousand-year tradition of Mahayana Buddhism, especially the sophisticated epistemology and psychology of its Yogacara school (also known as the Vijnanavada), which originated in Gandhara and Kashmir. Kashmir Śaivism also benefited from a confrontation with the newly emergent Vedanta monism of the intellectually energetic Kerala monk and systematizer of modern Hinduism, Sankara.

Guru Nanak, the first of the ten Sikh gurus and the founder of Sikhism, spent over two decades on the road, meeting with saints and sages and common people. Navtej Sarna takes us through his travels across the Himalayan reaches, including Tibet, Nepal and Sikkim. He tells us of Guru Nanak's visit to Mount Sumeru, identified by some scholars with Mount Kailash, where he met with eighty-four siddhas (enlightened souls), including ancient souls such as Goraknath and Machendranath or their spiritual successors, to discuss differing approaches to spirituality and engagement with the world.

Sarna also tells us of the time the tenth Guru, Guru Gobind Singh spent by the banks of the Yamuna river in the foothills of the Himalaya. These journeys take us into the living heart of Sikhism, with its deep compassion and its practice of both contemplation and dedicated action.

CHAPTER 5

The Mountain Sojourns of Guru Nanak and Guru Gobind Singh

NAVTEJ SARNA

Babe tare char chak
Nau khand prithvi sacha dhoa
(The Baba traversed the nine regions
Of the earth, as far as the land stretched)

So wrote Bhai Gurdas about the extensive travels of Guru Nanak. This scholar, who was also Guru Arjan's amanuensis for inscribing the first compilation of the Adi Granth, was not exaggerating. Guru Nanak was indeed a mystic master on the move: for more than two decades he was on the road, traversing long distances on foot, accompanied only by his Muslim follower, the rabab player Mardana. His mission was to convey the ultimate truth to all whom he met and show the way to salvation; his message was of universal love, compassion, the equality of all men and the true nature of worship.

Guru Nanak's travels, which can be segmented into four long journeys—called udasis—gave him an opportunity to debate and discuss matters of the spirit with sages and seers, to expose the corruption that was rampant in the name of religion, and to dispel ignorance, blind superstition and empty ritualism. Scholars have laid out detailed routes, even maps, showing these journeys but concrete evidence of the exact order of his travels is difficult to find. Some details can also be discerned from Guru Nanak's own hymns, from the writings of Bhai Gurdas and from the janamsakhis—the anecdotal biographies written a few years after Guru Nanak's passing from this world. Today, old gurudwaras and shrines, enriched by local legends, mark Guru Nanak's travels to far-flung places.

According to some sources, to symbolize the universality of his message Guru Nanak dressed in a composite garb that could not be identified with any sect. On some journeys, he is said to have worn an ochre garment and a white one (presumably like that of the Hindu sanyasi and the Muslim dervish respectively). Around his waist he wore a white cloth or kafni like a fakir and on his head a qalandar's (Sufi saint) conical cap. On one foot was a slipper and wooden sandal in the other and around his neck was a necklace of bones. On his journey west that took him to Mecca, he dressed like a Haji, wore a shirt that was blue, held a thick staff, with a holy book under his arm and an earthen goblet and prayer mat slung over his shoulder. On the journey north he is believed to have worn leather on his head and feet and bound a rope around his body in view of extreme weather.[1] Bhai Gurdas described it as follows:

> *Babe bhek banaia udasi ki riti chalai*
> *Charhia sodhan dharth lukai*
> (The Baba donned robes, starting the tradition of detachment
> Went out to put humanity on the right path)

Guru Nanak undertook his third udasi sometimes between 1515 and 1518. He travelled widely in the Himalaya and several scholars have traced his steps to present-day Himachal Pradesh, Jammu and Kashmir, Uttar Pradesh, Sikkim, Ladakh and even Nepal and Tibet. Several gurudwaras, backed by local legends, mark out this journey. For example, he is said to have visited the settlement of Manikaran, in the narrow valley of the choppy Parvati River, near Kulu. Today, in the old Gurudwara Sahib at Manikaran, the langar is cooked not on any fire but in the steam that rises from the boiling hot springs at the very edge of the ice-cold river. Local tradition has it that Nanak went over the Chandrakhani Pass and down into the village of Malana, situated in a steep rock bowl, the home of an ancient community that generally does not welcome visitors. Further afield, local traditions in Tibet, Nepal and Sikkim speak of his travels: in Buddhist lore, Guru Nanak is referred to as Nanak Lama or Rimpoche (the reincarnate one) Nanak, and in Nepal as Nanak Rishi. In Sikkim, gurudwaras have existed in places such as Gurudongmar, next to a glacial peak of the same name (though it has now been converted into a Buddhist shrine), and Chungthang, at the confluence of the rivers Lachen and Lachung, which combine to form the Teesta. The legend in Chungthang is that the rice given by Nanak enabled the people of the area to grow paddy for the first time. In Nepal, he is said to have visited Janakpur, the fabled birthplace of Sita, and stayed near the Pashupathinath temple on the banks of the Bhagmati. A gurudwara with the impression of the Guru's feet stands on a hillock in Kathmandu. Similar impressions can be found in Skardu in Baltistan and in Srinagar.

---

1 Details of Guru Nanak's dress have been given by several scholars, based on the Puratan Janamsakhi. These include W.H. McLeod (*Guru Nanak and the Sikh Religion*) and Hari Ram Gupta (*History of the Sikhs*, Vol. 1)

Gurudwara Mattan Sahib commemorates his visit to the Amarnath caves and Gurudwara Pathar Sahib, a few miles out of Leh towards Kargil, marks the place where he vanquished a demon.

The central event of this northern udasi is the visit to Sumeru Parbat, recorded in all the janamsakhis and also by Bhai Gurdas. Some scholars identify Sumeru Parbat to be none other than Mount Kailash, the abode of Shiva and Parvati. There the meeting of Nanak with eighty-four siddhas took place, among them ancient souls such as Goraknath and Machendranath or their spiritual successors, who had meditated long and deep and possessed great power and wisdom. It must be mentioned that yogis, predominantly of the kanphata or the split-eared sect, enjoyed immense influence over the people in Punjab and adjoining areas during that time. Through long ascetic practices, they created awe and fear in the minds and hearts of the people who then attributed supernatural and miraculous powers to them. The siddhas lived in the forests or up on the high mountains, away from the trappings of worldly life; yet they depended on gifts from the common folk for their living, who administered to them in order to receive their blessings or out of fear of their curses. Guru Nanak was fundamentally opposed to such practices. He believed that salvation did not lie in ascetic practices or in a display of miraculous powers but rather in living a righteous life of truth, hard work and honesty. This approach, and his opposition to the siddha practices, is underlined in several places in his writings.

In Bhai Gurdas's version of the meeting in the mountains, the siddhas expressed amazement upon seeing Nanak. They asked him: 'O youthful one! What power brings you to these heights?' And Guru Nanak replied: 'I repeated the name of God and contemplated him with loving devotion.'

The siddhas then asked him how the world below was faring. Guru Nanak made no secret of what he felt. He told them that the Dark Age had come. In the dark night of sin, he was searching for the moon of truth. Falsehood and ignorance had taken over the world. Kings were committing sinful deeds and the hedge was eating the crops. The earth was covered with sin and the bull (of dharma) underneath had let out a cry. The wandering yogis were devoid of knowledge; they knew only how to keep their bodies covered with ash. The wise siddhas had escaped into the remote caves and mountains—who, then, could redeem the world?

On hearing this bold reply, the siddhas thought of converting Nanak to their own order. Such a yogi would bring glory to their sect in the Dark Age. They gave him a begging bowl and told him to fetch water from a nearby pond. He reached there to find the pond full of jewels and rubies and precious stones; the siddhas had thought that he would succumb to temptation. But he returned empty-handed and told them that the pond held no water. Through this long dialogue, he established the distinctiveness of his own path by answering their queries and overcoming their doubts.

Guru Nanak had several meetings with siddhas and yogis. Besides the one described above on Sumeru Parbat, he had a major discourse with them at Achal, near Batala, during the Shivratri fair. Guru Nanak later put down the essence of his discourses with these holy men, in question-answer format, in seventy-three verses set to the Ramkali measure. This composition is contained in the Guru Granth Sahib as 'Siddha Gosht'. The entire dialogue is conducted not antagonistically but in a spirit of humility, intellectual inquiry and mutual respect, free of rancour and steeped in tolerance. This bani of Guru Nanak is usually regarded as one of the most thoughtful, symbolic and mature of his compositions, all the more so as it analyses yogic principles and philosophy for their true meaning. In it, Guru Nanak elucidates the concepts of Word, Truth, the Guru, God's grace, simran (meditating on the Name), the gurmukh (the spiritual man), the manmukh (the egocentric person) and so on.

Quoted below is one question-and-answer unit in which the Guru explains how it is possible to be part of this world and yet be detached by following the path of meditation and spirituality.

> Charpat asks: The ocean of the world is deep and impassable, how to get across it, O Nanak! Give me your thoughts about it.
> Nanak: The one who asks that, himself knows. What can I answer him? Truly speaking, how can I answer you, you who think that he has already reached the yonder shore?
> Like the lotus is unaffected in water,
> A duck swimming against the current is dry,
> Similarly, with the mind on the Divine utterances,
> And repeating His Name, we cross the terrible

Ocean of the world
He who lives detached, enshrining the Lord in
His mind
Without desire in the midst of desire,
Sees and shows the inaccessible and
Incomprehensible
Of him Nanak is a slave.

Guru Gobind Singh makes a reference to the mountains in his autobiographical composition, *Bachittar Natak.* He says that he was meditating on the Supreme Creator in his past lives deep in the mountains when he asked by the True Lord to come to the earth and address the evils of the age:

Ab mai apni katha bakhano. Tap sadhat jih bidh muh aano
Hemkunt parbat hai jahan. Sapat sring sobhit hai tahan
(Now I relate my own story. I was brought here while I was absorbed in deep meditation
Where stands the Hemkunt mountain, marked by seven peaks)

The tenth Guru of the Sikhs also spent about four years at Paonta Sahib on the banks of the Yamuna, in the shadow of the Siwalik Range, the foothills of the Himalaya.

Before he went there, the young Guru had spent his early years at Anandpur Sahib. These were years of preparation—both martial and spiritual. Under the inspiring leadership of the young and handsome leader, Anandpur Sahib turned into the birthplace of a new nation. It began to see martial exercises and sports—horse racing, musket shooting, archery and swordsmanship. A huge war drum, known as the Ranjit Nagara, was built and installed; its booming beat announced a hunt or mealtime in the communal kitchen. At the same time, the guru, with his amazing talents, concentrated on literary and spiritual acquisitions. He learned Persian, Arabic, Sanskrit, Braj and Awadhi, and studied the ancient classics and texts. His poetic genius was to result in a cornucopia of highly accomplished literary work.

The Guru's growing influence among the people was watched with consternation by the Rajput rajas of the surrounding hills. These rajas were used as puppets by the Mughal Emperor Aurangzeb and were also given to internal rivalries. It was not just the splendour of Guru Gobind Singh's court that disturbed them but also the casteless nature of the community that he was nurturing, which they saw as a challenge to their time-honoured feudal systems. They also saw the Guru's education, martial training and patronage of the arts as attempts to equate himself with the Rajput rulers.

The first challenge to the Guru came from Raja Bhim Chand of Bilaspur (or Kahlur), in whose territory Anandpur fell. He demanded that the Guru hand over a richly embroidered canopy and a well-trained elephant. When rebuffed, he had to be persuaded by his fellow rajas not to go to war with the Guru; the truce, however, would prove to be temporary.

Raja Medini Prakash of Sirmur, though, was of a different bent of mind and looked towards the Guru for support, fearing that a marital alliance between two other Rajas—Bhim Chand of Kahlur and Fateh Shah of Garhwal—could threaten his kingdom. He made repeated overtures and extended an invitation to the Guru to visit him. Finally, in 1685, Guru Gobind Singh accepted his invitation and set out with 500 soldiers towards Nahan, the picturesque capital of the Sirmur state in the Siwalik Hills. He was warmly received and spent several days in discourse and in hunting game in the surrounding jungles; he is also known to have single-handedly taken on a man-eating white tiger that had spread dread in the population.

The Guru's presence also attracted Raja Fateh Shah of Garhwal, who came to pay his respects. A peace treaty was worked out between Nahan and Garhwal. Medni Prakash was delighted with the Guru's presence in his territory and believed that his kingdom had found its best days. He pleaded with Guru Gobind Singh not to leave. The Guru himself was charmed with the beauty of the mountains, the valley that spread below Nahan to the boisterous Yamuna river where it flows out of the hills. While riding in the area, he reached a spot where his horse came to a halt and would not move any further. Seeing it as a sign and captivated by the beauty of the surroundings, the Guru decided that he would make his camp at the stop where his horse had planted its foot, or 'pau'. That place would be known as Paonta. A small fortress came up quickly and the settlement began to grow. Today, a serene gurudwara stands there as the centre of a thriving town on the banks of the river.

The years at Paonta Sahib were to be the most creative of the Guru's life. He devoted himself to his favourite outdoor activities with his followers and contemplated deeply on the state of the nation and the challenge of reviving the human spirit. He also produced supremely sublime poetry in praise of the Almighty. A number of poets from all over the country—his poetic court included fifty-two—gathered about him, and their creative activity turned Paonta into a cultural and spiritual centre. Sikh lore has it that one day the poets complained to Guru Gobind Singh that the noisy river disturbed their concentration and it is in accordance with the Guru's command that the Yamuna flows soundlessly past that point to this day.

The huge amount of literature produced at Paonta, along with translations of ancient Sanskrit texts—including the Mahabharata, the Puranas and the Niti Shastra—into Punjabi and Braj were compiled into a massive anthology called *Vidyasagar*. This huge exercise had a purpose: to bring about a renaissance of ancient knowledge and thus facilitate a spiritual awakening by making the people aware of a heritage they could be proud of. For this it was necessary to take these texts from the self-serving possession of the priests and render them comprehensible to the masses through translation. Unfortunately, this valuable compilation itself was lost during the crossing of the Sirsa river in flood after the evacuation of Anandpur some years later; some of the translations survived through copies made outside the *Vidyasagar* collection.

But the tranquil spiritual life at Paonta was soon brought to an end. Bhim Chand Kahluria was still determined to challenge the Guru. While visiting Srinagar in Garhwal for the ostensible reason of the marriage of his son, he forced Raja Fateh Shah to join him, along with the other hill rulers, in a conspiracy to attack the Guru. A huge army set out towards Paonta. The Guru's army faced them on the battlefield of Bhangani, six miles from Paonta, on 22 September 1688.

Guru Gobind Singh suffered an early setback when five hundred Pathans who had been commended to his army by a Muslim divine and follower,

Pir Buddhu Shah of Sadhaura, broke their loyalty and went over to the hill rajas. But Buddhu Shah himself joined the Guru with his four sons and seven hundred followers. The Guru's followers, though not professional soldiers, fought with tremendous spirit and resolute determination. The hill rajas and the battle-hardened Pathans were amazed at the spirit that had been instilled into ordinary farmers, workers and shopkeepers, many of whom had never picked up a weapon before. A description of the battle, including the names of the brave warriors, is given in *Bachittar Natak* in the Guru's own words. On the death of Sango Shah, his commander-in-chief and first cousin, the Guru himself took the field and confronted the brave hill chief and ace marksman Hari Chand Handuria. He allowed Hari Chand to fire three arrows at him, the third of which pierced the Guru's belt but did not hurt him. He then killed Handuria with a single gold-tipped arrow. With Hari Chand's death, the army of the hill rajas fell into disarray. The victory at Bhangani belonged to the Guru and his followers and was a decisive demonstration that they could not be trifled with.

After the battle of Bhangani, Guru Gobind Singh did not tarry long at Paonta Sahib but returned to Anandpur Sahib where further battles, both of the sword and the spirit, awaited him.

Makarand Paranjape's engrossing essay recounts Swami Vivekananda's sojourns in the Himalayan regions in the 1890s. Vivekananda travelled on foot from Nainital to Almora, Rudraprayag, Srinagar (Garhwal), Mussoorie, then back to the plains via Rishikesh, Haridwar and Dehradun.

He meditated under a banyan tree in (what was probably) Kakarighat, a spot made sacred by the meditations of other saints mentioned in this anthology, including Sombari Baba and Haidakhan Baba, and which is now an ashram consecrated by Neem Karoli Baba. He returned to the Himalaya in 1898 in the company of Sister Nivedita (Margaret Noble).

They visited Kashmir that same summer, wandering through hills and vales and ancient shrines. Paranjape tells of the tumultuous inner journey of the Swami's devoted disciple Nivedita, as well as his own spiritual passage to worship the Goddess Kali and the mother as manifest in the shrine of Kshir Bhavani.

The chapter ends with the profound and humbling truth of the Vedanta: 'From sand rise these mountains; into sand they go.'

CHAPTER 6

Moving Mountains

Swami Vivekananda's Himalayan Connection

MAKARAND R. PARANJAPE

Introduction

Swami Vivekananda (1863–1902) was one of the most powerful and influential makers of modern India.[2] Although there is scarcely an aspect of his dazzling but brief life of less than forty years that has not been studied, his Himalayan connection demand further exploration. Not only because his relationship with the Himalayas was complex, multi-layered and enduring, but because some of his major life-changing spiritual experiences occurred in the mountainous heights of Uttarakhand and Kashmir.[3] This chapter is an attempt to capture those crucial and momentous events during Swamiji's Himalayan sojourns, which reverberate in the national consciousness to this date.

I
Devatatma

In *Reminiscences of Swami Vivekananda*, K.S. Ramaswami Sastri recalls the nine days Vivekananda stayed at their home in Trivandrum (now Thiruvananthapuram) in December 1892. Swamiji was accompanied by a

---

2 See my study, *Swami Vivekananda: Hinduism and India's Road to Modernity* (New Delhi: HarperCollins, 2020), where I demonstrate this at length. The only detailed examination of Vivekananda's Himalayan connection is *Himalaya Mein Vivekanand* (New Delhi: National Book Trust, 2016) by India's former Union education minister, Ramesh Pokhriyal 'Nishank'.

3 Although Vivekananda's major experiences occurred in Uttarakhand and Kashmir, he also loved the eastern Himalayas, the hill station closest to Calcutta being Darjeeling. He would retreat to the mountains, as his letters in March–April 1897 and April 1898 show, to rest and recuperate from the heat and toil of the cities. For instance, on 23 April 1897, he was writing to Swami Brahmananda that he had just returned from Sandakphu, the highest peak in the Singalila Ridge, near the Indo-Nepal border, Darjeeling district, West Bengal: 'My health was excellent on my return from Sandukphu (11,924 ft.) and other places' (https://www.ramakrishnavivekananda.info/vivekananda/volume_8/epistles_fourth_series/126_rakhal.htm). Future citations from www.ramakrishnavivekananda.info will provided in parenthesis after the reference.

Muslim attendant and, at first, himself taken for a 'Mohammedan'. Sastri was then fourteen years old.[4]

Sastri recalls how one morning, when he was studying from his textbook, Kalidasa's *Kumarasambhava*, Vivekananda asked, 'Can you repeat the great poet's description of the Himalaya?' Sastri recited the verses, so well-known, that open this mahakavya (great poem):

> अस्त्युत्तरस्यां दिशि देवतात्मा हिमालयो नाम नगाधिराजः ।
> पूर्वापरौ तोयनिधी विगाह्य स्थितः पृथिव्या इव मानदण्डः ।। १–१
>
> astyuttarasyāṁ diśi devatātmā himālayo nāma nagādhirājaḥ |
> pūrvāparau toyanidhī vigāhya sthitaḥ pṛthivyā iva mānadaṇḍaḥ || 1-1

The couplet may be roughly translated thus: 'In the northern direction, forming the heartland of Gods, stands the overlord of snowy mountains, Himalayas, like a measuring rod of earth thrust betwixt the eastern and western waters.' [1-1][5]

Pleased, Vivekananda remarked, 'Do you know that I am coming after a long stay amidst the sublimity of the Himalayan scenes and sights?' So saying, he asked the boy to repeat the opening verse and this time also explain its meaning. When Shastri did so, Vivekananda said, 'That is good, but not enough.' Then, repeating the couplet in 'his marvellous, musical, measured tones', he explained:

> The important words in this verse are devatatma (ensouled by Divinity) and manadanda (measuring rod). The poet implies and suggests that the Himalayas is not a mere wall accidentally constructed by nature. It is ensouled by Divinity and is the protector of India and her civilization not only from the chill icy blasts blowing from the arctic region but also

4 His father K. Sundarama Iyer's reminiscences were published in an article, 'My first Navaratri with Swami Vivekananda', available at https://www.ramakrishnavivekananda.info/reminiscences/057_ksi.htm.

5 Sourced from the English notes and commentary of Raghunath Damodar Karmarkar and S.D. Gajendragadkar's edition of *Kumarasambhava* (Bombay: Vishwanath & Co.) 1923.

> from the deadly and destructive incursions of invaders. The Himalaya further protects India by sending the great rivers Sindhu, Ganga, and Brahmaputra perennially fed by melted ice irrespective of the monsoon rains. Manadanda implies that the poet affirms that the Indian civilization is the best of all human civilizations and forms the standard by which all the other human civilizations, past, present, and future, must be tested. Such was the poet's lofty conception of patriotism.

This extraordinary explanation not only underscores Vivekananda's erudition and deep study of classical Indian literature, but more remarkably, his love of the Himalayas.[6] Shastri reminisces, 'I felt thrilled by Swamiji's words. I treasure them even to this day, and they shine in my heart even now with an undimmed and undiminished splendour.'

The travels in the Himalayas that Swamiji mentioned to Sastri occurred earlier that year, in 1890. After Sri Ramakrishna's death on 16 August 1886, Vivekananda had stayed mostly at the Baranagore Math (monastery) for two years, consolidating the order of young sanyasins (renunciates) that he had founded. His itinerant days began in 1888, taking him all across the country, as a wandering monk. That year, he had reached as far as Rishikesh in today's Uttarakhand, but had to return because he contracted malaria. But in 1890, Vivekananda again travelled extensively in the Himalayas, going on foot from Nainital to Almora, Rudraprayag, Srinagar (Garhwal), Tehri, Mussoorie, then back to the plains via Rishikesh, Haridwar and Dehradun.

So well-known was his love for the mountains that his standard biography by his 'Eastern and Western Disciples' devotes a whole chapter to his 'Wanderings in the Himalayas'. Eager 'to see the snow-capped Himalayas', he did not wish to tarry in the sacred city of Varanasi,

6 This incident is mentioned in 'Himalayas—Not Ordinary Mountains, But The Divine Protectors of India' by Pulkit Mathur: 'When we read Swami Vivekananda's in-depth explanation of the verse, which goes much beyond the literal translation, the true spirit in which Kalidasa wrote the stanza, along with the Divine significance of the Himalayas as protectors of India's Vedantic knowledge, shines forth.' (https://www.spiritualbee.com/posts/himalayas-divine-protectors-of-india/).

predicting to his host Pramadadas Mitra, 'When I shall return here next time I shall burst upon society like a bombshell, and it will follow me like a dog!'[7]

From Nainital, Vivekananda, accompanied by his brother monk Akhandananda, planned to walk all the way to Badrinath. But they could not proceed beyond Karnaprayag. The region was famine-struck, with the onward roads closed by the government. Both Vivekananda and Akhandananda fell ill, racked by high fever and chills. Nevertheless, their party spent many memorable days in Chati, Alakananda, Tehri, Srinagar (Garhwal), Ganeshprayag, Rishikesh and Haridwar, before doctors advised them to return to the plains, to convalesce in Dehradun.

There were two notable incidents in this period. Towards the beginning of their Himalayan sojourn, they stopped near a watermill by a stream, not too far from Nainital. Under an ancient peepal tree, Vivekananda sat totally absorbed in meditation. When he came to, he declared to Akhandananda, 'Well, Gangadhar,[8] here under this banyan tree one of the greatest problems of my life has been solved.' This was one of his great realizations, jotted down in a fragment in his notebook in Bangla, translated later as:

> In the beginning was the Word, etc.:
>
> The microcosm and the macrocosm are built on the same plan. Just as the individual soul is encased in the living body, so is the Universal Soul in the Living Prakriti (Nature)—the objective universe. Shivā (Kali)[9] is embracing Shiva; this is not a fancy. This covering of the one (Soul) by the other (Nature) is analogous to the relation between an idea and

---

7 'Wanderings in the Himalayas', https://www.ramakrishnavivekananda.info/swamieastwest/2_files/1-14.html Quotations and information in the next few paragraphs detailing Vivekananda's Himalayan sojourn in 1890 are from this source.

8 Gangadhar Ghatak (Gangopadhyay) was Swami Akhandananda's pre-monastic name. In those days, Swamiji too went by other names, including Vividishananda; Vivekananda became his stable moniker later.

9 Original gloss in the biography: 'The reference is to the Tantrika conception of Kali embracing Shiva. Kali is the Mother of the universe, and Shiva, Her Divine Spouse.' Shivā (long vowel) is feminine, hence refers to Shakti or Kali.

> the word expressing it: they are one and the same, and it is only by a mental abstraction that one can distinguish them. Thought is impossible without words. Therefore, in the beginning was the Word etc.
>
> This dual aspect of the Universal Soul is eternal. So what we perceive or feel is this combination of the Eternally Formed and the Eternally Formless.

Later, he would deliver his famous lecture on the same theme, 'The Cosmos: The Macrocosm', in New York in 1896.

Though these wanderings in the hills suited him temperamentally, he was forced, as it were, to descend once more to the plains to engage with the suffering masses, where he recalled the renunciation and emancipation of the 'stern ascetics' of Haridwar and Rishikesh:

> I saw many great men in Hrishikesh. One case that I remember was that of a man who seemed to be mad. He was coming nude down the street, with boys pursuing and throwing stones at him. The whole man was bubbling over with laughter, while blood was streaming down his face and neck. I took him and bathed his wound, putting ashes (made by burning a piece of cotton cloth) on it to stop the bleeding. And all the time, with peals of laughter, he told me of the fun the boys and he had been having, throwing the stones. 'So the Father plays,' he said. (*Master*, 243–244)

In the same spirit, later in life, he declared in his letter of 9 July 1897 to Mary Hale, one of his spiritual sisters:

> May I be born again and again and suffer thousands of miseries so that I may worship the only God that exists, the only God I believe in, the sum total of all souls: and, above all, my God the wicked, my God the miserable, my God the poor of all races, of all species, is the special object of my worship.[10]

---

10 Letter to Miss Mary Hale, 9 July 1897, https://www.ramakrishnavivekananda.info/vivekananda/volume_5/epistles_first_series/078_sister.htm; also cited in

II
Mayavati

Vivekananda left for Western shores in 1893. His triumphal return to his homeland culminated in Calcutta, his birth city, where he founded the Ramakrishna Mission on 1 May 1897.

Almost immediately after, he travelled back to the Himalayas to rest and recuperate in Almora. There, he was received and welcomed with a moving Hindi oration offered by the prominent citizens of the region. Comparing him to Sankaracharya, the 'welcome address' praised his work in spreading the authentic message of Hindu dharma in North America and Europe and expressed the hope that he would establish an ashram in the Himalayas.

He responded with equal enthusiasm and praise for his hosts:

> This is the land of dreams of our forefathers, in which was born Pârvati, the Mother of India. This is the holy land where every ardent soul in India wants to come at the end of its life, and to close the last chapter of its mortal career. On the tops of the mountains of this blessed land, in the depths of its caves, on the banks of its rushing torrents, have been thought out the most wonderful thoughts … This is the land which, since my very childhood, I have been dreaming of passing my life in, and … yet it is the hope of my life to end my days somewhere in this Father of Mountains where Rishis lived, where philosophy was born … the Himalayas always teach us that one theme which is reverberating in the very atmosphere of the place, the one theme the murmur of which I hear even now in the rushing whirlpools of its rivers—renunciation! सर्वं वस्तु भयान्वितं भुवि नृणां वैराग्यमेवाभयं—'Everything in this life is fraught with fear. It is renunciation alone that makes one fearless.' Yes, this is the land of renunciation.
>
> Friends, you have been very kind to allude to an idea of mine, which is to start a centre in the Himalayas, and perhaps I have sufficiently explained why it should be so, why, above all others, this is the spot which I want to select as one of the great centres to teach this universal

K. R. Ramaswami Sastry's reminiscences.

> religion. These mountains are associated with the best memories of our race; if these Himalayas are taken away from the history of religious India, there will be very little left behind. Here, therefore, must be one of those centres, not merely of activity, but more of calmness, of meditation, and of peace; and I hope some day to realize it.[11]

We get a glimpse of his daily routine and activities in the mountains from his letters written during this period. Writing to his doctor in 1897 from Almora, he says:

> Here I feel that I have no disease whatsoever ... I feel very, very strong now. You ought to see me, Doctor, when I sit meditating in front of the beautiful snow-peaks and repeat from the Upanishads: न तस्य रोगो न जरा न मृत्युः प्राप्तस्य योगाग्निमयं शरीरं—'He has neither disease, nor decay, nor death; for, verily, he has obtained a body full of the fire of Yoga'.[12]

Vivekananda stayed on in Kumaon for two and a half months, returning to the plains on 8 August 1897.

Within two years, his English disciples—Capt. James Henry Sevier and his wife, Charlotte Elizabeth Sevier—along with Swami Swarupananda, whom he had ordained into sanyasa, made his dream of establishing a Himalayan centre come true. Sevier had served as a non-commissioned officer in the British Indian army before returning to England. He and his wife had met Vivekananda in London in 1895. In the following year, 1896, they accompanied him on his continental journey. In July of that year, while recuperating in the Swiss Alps, Vivekananda had expressed his wish that he wanted to set up a spiritual retreat in the Himalayas.

The Seviers travelled back to India with him on the same ship. They rented a house near Almora, where Vivekananda came to stay. Later, in

11 Address of Welcome at Almora and Reply, http://ramakrishnavivekananda.info/vivekananda/volume_3/lectures_from_colombo_to_almora/address_of_welcome_at_almora_and_reply.htm

12 Vivekananda's letter to Swami Brahmananda, 23 April 1898, https://www.ramakrishnavivekananda.info/vivekananda/volume_8/epistles_fourth_series/126_rakhal.htm

1898, they found a secluded tea estate at a height of 1,940 metres, recessed in thicket of deodars, pine and oak, affording spectacular views of the snowy mountains. Nine kilometres from Lohaghat in Champawat district, Uttarakhand, it is known as Mayavati. That is where they, along with Swami Swarupananda, founded the Advaita Ashrama on 19 March 1899.[13]

Vivekananda, who was on his second trip abroad and could not be present at the opening of the ashram, sent a powerful message on the 'Oneness of all beings' as a foundational truth, with its 'particularization' being the aim of sadhana or spiritual practice: '… knowing Him—and therefore the Universe—as our Self, alone extinguishes all fear, brings an end to misery and leads to Infinite Freedom.'

For him, Advaita was the only system that gives 'man complete possession of himself, takes off all dependence and its associated superstitions, thus making us brave to suffer, brave to do, and in the long run attain to Absolute Freedom'. He once declared, 'Dependence is misery. Independence is happiness.' The purpose of the Himalayan ashram was to provide a place where these truths could be realized:

> To give this One Truth a freer and fuller scope in elevating the lives of individuals and leavening the mass of mankind, we start this Advaita Ashrama on the Himalayan heights, the land of its first expiration.
>
> Here it is hoped to keep Advaita free from all superstitions and weakening contaminations. Here will be taught and practised nothing but the Doctrine of Unity, pure and simple; and though in entire

13 The ashram, with its own printing press, library, museum and charitable hospital, was the first to publish Swamiji's complete works. The museum also preserves some objects of Vivekananda's personal use. See Vineet Upadhyay, 'Remembering Vivekananda's affinity with Himalayas', *The Times of India,* 11 January 2016 (https://timesofindia.indiatimes.com/city/dehradun/Remembering-Vivekanandas-affinity-with-Himalayas/articleshow/50537468.cms). Also Jaskiran Chopra, 'His deep spiritual connection with the Himalayas is memorable', *The Pioneer,* 5 July 2018 (https://www.dailypioneer.com/2018/state-editions/his-deep-spiritual-connection-with-the-himalayas-is-memorable.html.)

> sympathy with all other systems, this Ashrama is dedicated to Advaita and Advaita alone.[14]

So keen was he on his Himalayan retreat that on 27 December 1899 he wrote to one of his disciples, Sister Christine:[15]

> I will buy a little place in the Himalayas—a whole hill—about say, six thousand feet high with a grand view of the eternal snows. There must be springs and a tiny lake. Cedars—the Himalayan cedar forests—and flowers, flowers everywhere. I will have a little cottage; in the middle, my vegetable gardens, which I will work myself—and—and—and—my books—and see the face of man only once in a great while.[16]

The following year, still in the US, it is likely that he was referring to Mayavati in his lecture 'Is Vedanta the Future Religion?':

> But on the heights of the Himalayas I have a place where I am determined nothing shall enter except pure truth ... There are an Englishman and an Englishwoman [sic] in charge of the place. The purpose is to train seekers of truth and to bring up children without fear and without superstition. They shall not hear about Christs and Buddhas and Shivas and Vishnus—none of these. They shall learn, from the start, to stand upon their own feet. They shall learn from their childhood that God

---

14 Letter to Swami Swarupananda, March 1899, https://www.ramakrishnavivekananda.info/vivekananda/volume_5/writings_prose_and_poems/the_advaita_ashram_himalayas.htm

15 *A Portrait of Sister Christine by Pravrajika Vrajaprana* (Calcutta: Ramakrishna Mission Institute of Culture, 1996), p. 5. Sister Christine came to India in 1902 to work as a schoolteacher and social worker. After Nivedita's death, she took charge of Nivedita Girls' School, Calcutta.

16 Letter to Sister Christine (Christina), 27 December 1899, http://ramakrishnavivekananda.info/vivekananda/volume_9/letters_fifth_series/161_christina.htm

> is the spirit and should be worshipped in spirit and in truth. Everyone must be looked upon as spirit.[17]

Consequently, Vivekananda, when he visited the ashram in 1901, criticized attempts to institute dualistic worship, as well as images of Sri Ramakrishna. Yet, those used to such modes of worship continued these practices, with the shrine to Sri Ramakrishna present till March 1902. When it was removed, some were unhappy to be deprived of it. It was only when Sarada Ma, Ramakrishna's consort, also known as the Holy Mother, intervened in favour of an unalloyed Advaita, that the matter was resolved.[18]

Capt. Sevier died in October 1900; Charlotte, whom he used to call 'mother', continued to stay at Mayavati for many years before returning to England. She passed away in 1930 at the age of eighty-three.[19]

III
Nivedita

Almora

The most important, at any rate the best recorded, of Swami Vivekananda's Himalayan experiences, occurred in the year 1898 in the company of his greatest female disciple, Margaret Noble (1867–1911), better known as Sister Nivedita.

---

17 Is Vedanta the Future Religion?, https://www.ramakrishnavivekananda.info/vivekananda/volume_8/lectures_and_discourses/is_vedanta_the_future.htm

18 Swami Vimalananda wrote to the Holy Mother about the inner conflict tearing his mind. She made her view amply evident in her letter of September 1902: 'The one who is our guru [Sri Ramakrishna] is an Advaitin. I can emphatically say that you are surely all Adavaitavadins.' See Suchismita Sengupta Pandey, 'Swami Vivekananda's Footprint on Uttarakhand Himalayas,' *The Pioneer*, 13 April 2018 (https://www.pioneeredge.in/5427-2/).

19 Her remarkable story of dedication, idealism, sacrifice and spiritual progress is told in Amrita M. Salm, *Mother of Mayavati: The Story of Charlotte Sevier and Advaita Ashrama* (Advaita Ashrama) 2013.

Margaret, or Margot as she was called, met Vivekananda in 1895 on a 'cold Sunday afternoon in November...in a Westend drawing room' (*Master* 5). When it comes to their Himalayan travels, more detailed, informal and insightful than *The Master as I Saw Him*, is her posthumous account, *Notes of Some Wanderings with the Swami Vivekananda*, an 'authorized' edition of which was published by Swami Saradananda.

Vivekananda and his Western disciples' extraordinary Himalayan journey lasted for a full five months, from May to October 1898. The entire expedition was hosted by philanthropist Sara Chapman Thorp Bull, whom Vivekananda called his 'American Mother,' rechristened as Dhira Mata (the steady mother).[20] The other notable member of the group was Josephine MacLeod, another American devotee and friend.[21] In addition, the wife of the American Consul, Mrs Patterson, and four monks, Swamis Turiyananda (Harinath Chattopadhyay), Niranjanananda (Nityniranjan Ghosh), Sadananda (Sharatchandra Gupta), and Swarupananda accompanied them.

From Calcutta, the group proceeded to Almora, where the Seviers had already set up house in rented accommodation. That is where Vivekananda and his brother monks stayed, while the ladies were put up first in 'a

20 Sara Bull (née Thorp) met Vivekananda in 1894. After her husband's death in 1880, she turned increasingly to philosophy and spirituality. It was she who introduced Vivekananda to William James, the famous Harvard professor and brother of Henry James. She left her entire estate worth about $500,000 to the Vedanta Society. See Pravrajika Prabuddhaprana, *Saint Sara: The Life of Sara Chapman Bull, the American Mother of Swami Vivekananda* (Calcutta: Sri Sarada Math, 2002); and Prothero, Stephen, 'Hinduphobia and Hinduphilia in U.S. Culture' (http://www.bu.edu/religion/files/pdf/Hinduphobia_and_Hinduphilia.pdf.)

21 She met Swamiji in New York on 29 January 1895, which she came to consider her 'spiritual birthday.' As she recalled that life-changing moment, 'It is the Truth that I saw in Swamiji that has set me free; it was to set me free that Swamiji came,' [cited in Chaturvedi Badrinath, *Swami Vivekananda, the Living Vedanta* (New Delhi: Penguin Books, 2006), p. 277.] Remaining unmarried, but not taking vows of renunciation, she became a strong supporter of the Ramakrishna Vivekananda movement. Vivekananda called her 'Joe', 'Tantine', 'Jo Jo' and 'Jaya', which is how she is referred to in *Wanderings*. *Udbodhan* was started with her initial donation of $800.00.

quaintly placed Dak bungalow, on the mountain side in the midst of trees' (Wanderings, 22),[22] then in a rented cottage (Reymond 107). Every morning, Vivekananda would visit them, both to instruct and entertain, preparing them, especially Nivedita, for her Indian mission. On her part, Nivedita, since her arrival, was eager to be assigned some work. She had even complained to Josephine, 'What am I doing for so long? Why doesn't the Swami speak to me about work?' (Reymond, 77). But Vivekananda seemed none too eager to put her, so to speak, in harness.

The guru-shishya relationship is as intimate and sacred as it can be complex and difficult. Nivedita's strong spirit chafed and revolted under what appeared a strange and hurtful indifference on her Master's part. Speaking of her anguish in third person, she talks of the 'strange new element, painful but salutary to remember' (Wanderings, 23)[23] that had crept into her heart. Her biographer, Reymond, is more explicit:

> Nivedita felt herself suddenly seized with an indescribable feeling of grief, and plunged into such solitude that, for a moment, her spirit wavered ... For four days she was sunk in a sorrow that she could not understand. And then she recognized its cause: her guru had withdrawn from her. (108)

The struggle of the personal against the impersonal was extremely hard for Nivedita to handle. As Reymond puts it, 'Deprived of her work, prevented from loving, she did not know how to express herself. She felt herself abandoned.' (109)

It seemed that the more she tried to mend things, to please her Master, the more he ignored her. The fact is that through the entire year, Vivekananda hardly spent an hour alone with her. 'In all that year of 1898 I can remember only one occasion when the Swami invited me to walk alone with him for half an hour, and then our conversation for it was towards the end of the summer' (*Master* 131). She craved for and

22 'Wanderings in the Himalayas', https://www.ramakrishnavivekananda.info/swamieastwest/2_files/1-14.html

23 Ibid.

felt deprived of personal attention. She tried to learn how to meditate from Swarupananda, who had recently been initiated into sanyasa. But her mind was disturbed and confused: 'My relation to our Master at this time can only be described as one of clash and conflict' (*Master* 136). She saw, theoretically, the need for detachment and the dangers of making her guru her idée fixe. Indeed, all the European women had lived practically isolated in Belur, in a cottage away from the monks and other Indians, since they had arrived. Vivekananda had to worry about this unconventional mixing not just of Indians and Westerners, which was practically unheard of, but also of a monk with a single American woman accompanying him.

Nivedita took the Swami's distancing very badly: 'But I had been little prepared for that constant rebuke and attack upon all my most cherished prepossessions' (Ibid.). The dream of 'a friendly and beloved leader' (Ibid.) was shattered. Instead, she found herself having to reconcile to 'one who would be at least indifferent, and possibly, silently hostile,' (*Master* 137). She did not, however, consider leaving Vivekananda or retracting her offer of serving him. But, 'as the days went by', she came to realize that 'there would be no personal sweetness' (Ibid.) in their relationship.

As Reymond puts it,

> Profoundly as she loved and trusted him, she reacted now with obstinacy. She was annoyed because Swami Vivekananda seemed unaware of everything she did for him, because he paid no attention to anything she said to him, because he snubbed her ... She felt an increasing bitterness welling up within her. She was surprised by this, but she could not master it; and her reproaches only aggravated the tension between her guru and herself.
>
> (Reymond 109)

She retreated into herself, bruised and bewildered. Part of the problem was Nivedita's fierce patriotism and national sentiment, as well as her European upbringing and values. Vivekananda seemed to trample upon both of them. It is significant that later, in her work in India, Nivedita Indianized herself so much that she supported the revolutionaries who strove to overthrow the British Empire. She had to return to England to save herself from the wrath of the colonial authorities.

The Almora episode reached its climax when Nivedita was at her breaking point. Josephine was moved to intervene on her behalf. Vivekananda listened, retreated then returned in the evening to admit that the situation needed to be rectified. He admitted, 'with the simplicity of a child, "You were right. There must be a change. I am going away into the forests to be alone, and when I come back I shall bring peace"' (*Master* 137).

So saying, he blessed his kneeling disciple: 'It was assuredly a moment of wonderful sweetness of reconciliation' (*Master* 138). Yet, as she put it, 'such a moment may heal a wound. It cannot restore an illusion that has been broken into fragments' (Ibid.). That evening, during her meditation, Nivedita, for the first time, had a glimpse of the beatitude she so longed for, 'gazing deep into an Infinite Good' (Ibid.). Later she wrote, 'I understood for the first time that the greatest teachers may destroy in us a personal relation only in order to bestow the Impersonal Vision in its place' (*Master* 139).

Amarnath

The party next moved to Kashmir, so beloved to Vivekananda. Arriving in Srinagar on 20 June 1898, the group soon made itself comfortable, moving into houseboats on the Dal Lake. Vivekananda took his party to the Sankaracharya temple, exclaiming: 'Look! What genius the Hindu shows in placing his temples! He always chooses a grand scenic effect! See! The Takt commands the whole of Kashmir. The rock of Hari Parvat rises red out of blue water, like a lion couchant, crowned. And the temple of Martanda has the valley at its feet!'[24]

The party also visited the root shrine of Kashmir, Kshir Bhavani, where Swamiji would later see a vision of the Divine Mother. They also went to see other famous temples, including the ancient Pandrenthan shrine, 'sunken

24 In Kashmir: Amarnath And Kshirbhavani, https://www.ramakrishnavivekananda.info/swamieastwest/2_files/1-32.html.

in a scum-covered pond within a wood by the side of the Jhelum', besides the great temples of Avantipur and Bijbehara (or Vijeshwara) (Ibid.). The Pandrenthan temple had 'a fine image of Buddha, standing with his hands uplifted, in one of the trefoil arches of the eastern door' (Ibid.). Nivedita recalls that the Swami thought the Buddha 'was the greatest man that had ever lived. He never drew a breath for himself ... he never claimed worship. ... Buddha is not a man, but a state. I have found the door. Enter, all of you!' (Ibid.). Of Martand, Nivedita writes: 'It had been a wonderful old building evidently more abbey than temple,' with trefoil arches, originally 'three small rectangular temples, built with heavy blocks of stone, round sacred springs' (*Wanderings* 135). There were many profound discussions about Egyptian, Zoroastrian, Christian, Islamic, and other religious and faith traditions, Vivekananda in each instance presenting the broadest and deepest ideals of each tradition, leavened with his unique insights.

In all, enjoying the sights and listening to Vivekananda's teachings on various aspects of Indian culture and spirituality was their daily routine. On one occasion at Islamabad, Kashmir, Vivekananda picked up two pebbles, saying, 'Whenever death approaches me, all weakness vanishes. I have neither fear, nor doubt, nor thought of the external. I simply busy myself making ready to die.'(Ibid.)

Striking them against each other, he continued, 'I am as hard as that—for I have touched the feet of God!' (Ibid.)

As if anticipating their trip, the previous year, the Swami had written a passionately beautiful letter to Margot from Srinagar, the capital of the princely state: 'I shall not try to describe Kashmir to you. Suffice it to say, I never felt sorry to leave any country except this Paradise on earth.'[25]

Vivekananda's lessons in leadership to his chosen disciples continued: 'Some people do the best work when led. Not everyone is born to lead. The best leader, however, is one who "leads like the baby". The baby, though apparently depending on everyone, is the king of the household' (ibid). Vivekananda was well-aware that without personal magnetism and

---

25 Letter to Sister Nivedita, 1 October 1897, https://www.ramakrishnavivekananda.info/vivekananda/volume_8/epistles_fourth_series/110_margo.htm.

charisma no leader could inspire others to do his bidding. Yet, there was a great danger in the adoration and adulation that such leadership induced:

The great difficulty is this: I see persons giving me almost the whole of their love. But I must not give anyone the whole of mine in return, for that day the work would be ruined. Yet there are some who will look for such a return, not having the breadth of the impersonal view. It is absolutely necessary to the work that I should have the enthusiastic love of as many as possible, while I myself remain entirely impersonal. (Ibid.)

Every guru faces the jealousy and competition between members of his flock. Vivekananda was well-aware of that. He repeats:

> A leader must be impersonal. I am sure you understand this. I do not mean that one should be a brute, making use of the devotion of others for his own ends, and laughing in his sleeve meanwhile. What I mean is what I am, intensely personal in my love, but having the power to pluck out my own heart with my own hand, if it becomes necessary, 'for the good of many, for the welfare of many,' as Buddha said. Madness of love, and yet in it no bondage. Matter changed into spirit by the force of love. Nay, that is the gist of our Vedanta.[26]

Such clear warning, unfortunately, neither saved Nivedita from the suffering in store for her when she came to India, nor prevented critics of Vivekananda from accusing him of misleading her.

By 25 July, the party left for Achhabal, enjoying the Mughal Gardens. That is where the plan was made for Nivedita to accompany Vivekananda to the sacred grotto of Amarnath, with its seasonal giant ice Shivalinga. The duo reached Amarnath on 2 August, travelling via Islamabad, Pahalgam, Chandanwari, Seshnaag, and Panchtarani. The journey itself was as arduous as it was picturesque, the pilgrim host of two or three thousand marching

26 During the Kashmir visit, Vivekananda observed, 'I am persuaded, that a leader is not made in one life. He has to be born for it. For the difficulty is not in organisation, and making plans; the test, the real test, of a leader, lies in holding widely different people together, along the line of their common sympathies. And this can only be done unconsciously, never by trying' (*Master* 150-151).

in a neat and orderly fashion, carrying, as it were, 'a bazaar with them,' with hundreds of monks, with their ochre tents 'some no larger than a good-sized umbrella' (*Master* 154). Vivekananda had to convince them that it was all right for a European renunciate to accompany him as also that 'the warmth of his love and sympathy for Mohammedanism' was not misplaced in the interest of human unity though 'the soil of the Punjab ... was drenched with the blood of those who had died for the faith' (*Master* 155).

At Pahalgam, they observed Ekadashi, the auspicious eleventh day of the luni-solar Hindu calendar:

> It was a beautiful little ravine floored, for the most part with sandy islands in the pebble-worn bed of a mountain stream. The slopes about it were dark with pine trees, and over the mountain at its head was seen, at sunset, the moon, not yet full. It was the scenery of Switzerland or Norway, at their gentlest and loveliest. (*Master* 157)

Passing 'through scenes of indescribable beauty' (Ibid.), they finally approached 'the boulder-strewn gorge, in which the Cave of Amarnath was situated' (*Master* 158). Vivekananda 'had observed every rite of the pilgrimage ... told his beads, kept fasts, and bathed in the ice-cold waters of five streams in succession' (*Master* 158-159). What awaited them was spectacular, 'in the Cave itself, in a niche never reached by sunlight, shone the great ice-lingam ... like the waiting Presence of God' (*Master* 158). On entering the cave, to Vivekananda it seemed 'as if he saw Siva made visible before him' (*Master* 159). Not wishing to be overcome by emotion, 'he knelt and prostrated two or three times, unnoticed' (Ibid.).

For Vivekananda, the Amarnath darshan was a peak spiritual experience. As Nivedita records, it was an 'overwhelming vision that had seemed to draw him almost into its vertex' (*Wanderings* 151). Bare-bodied after a bath in icy cold waters, he not only prostrated before the spectacular ice pillar, but clasped its base. It was as if 'in the presence of the Lord Himself' Vivekananda had been granted the boon 'not to die till he himself should give consent' (Ibid.). Speaking of it later in November to his disciple, Sharat Chandra Chakravarty, he said, 'Since visiting Amarnath, I feel as if Shiva is sitting on my head for twenty-four hours and would not come down.' Swami Brahmananda remarked, 'Since returning from Kashmir, Swamiji does not speak to anybody, he sits in one place rapt in thought; you go to him and by conversation try to draw his mind a little towards worldly objects.'[27]

But what about Nivedita? What exactly happened to her inside the Amarnath cave is a matter of some curiosity and controversy. Did Nivedita expect a final consecration of her life in the presence of the Lord himself? Was she to be anointed as Vivekananda's spiritual partner, his Shakti and successor? When that did not quite happen, did she feel disappointed, even abandoned? Did she feel terribly let down that Vivekananda had his own spiritual experience without giving her something equally memorable? These questions do not have easy answers. Vivekananda said to her, 'You do not now understand. But you have made the pilgrimage, and it will go on working' (Ibid.). The official Ramakrishna-Vivekananda literature downplays or even omits Nivedita's experiences inside the cave. On the other hand, her letters, which Reymond also relies on, tell a somewhat different tale.

It is to Reymond that we must turn to catch a glimpse of her state of mind. According to her, while 'Vivekananda experienced one of the supreme moments of his life … Nivedita was sunk and lost in agony' (127). Vivekananda's ecstasy, of which we have already caught a glimpse, is portrayed even more vividly by Reymond:

> He entered the dark grotto with nerves on edge, breath gone, his half-naked body trembling violently. Overcome with emotion, he prostrated himself three times on the ground, and made the one offering he had brought to Shiva: the life of Nivedita. In ecstasy he experienced divine grace, in the Unknowable he found revelation. Dizzy, half-paralyzed, almost fainting, he staggered away. (127)

27 Conversations and Dialogues from the Diary of a Disciple, https://www.ramakrishnavivekananda.info/vivekananda/volume_7/conversations_and_dialogues/from_the_diary_of_a_disciple/scc_iv.htm.

But Nivedita felt lost, alone, and disconcerted:

> Beside him, Nivedita had remained inert, bewildered, anguished. Where was this god to whom she had come to pay homage? The cold and her own suffering of spirit enveloped her like a stifling shroud. She looked for her guru, but he had disappeared. Lost, abandoned, she was choked by a cry of revolt. The Swami's mystical experience became something she could not bear. Why, why had he not shared it with her? She had seen him immersed in beatitude, his hands over his eyes as if he were blinded by too much light, stumbling in the throes of a divine passion, stammering, "Shiva, Shiva." But what was to become of her? She stayed in the grotto until the cold drove her outside. She did not know where to turn. When she found her guru again, she reproached him bitterly, and he looked at her sadly. (127)

This is how Reba Som, Nivedita's more recent biographer, records this important event:[28]

> Nothing could have prepared Nivedita for the sight of the voluminous cave large enough to hold a cathedral, with a huge iced Shivalingam enthroned as it were on its own base. Vivekananda entered the shrine, naked except for his loin cloth, body smeared in ashes, prostrating himself in adoration and almost swooning with emotion. .... Nivedita was the stupefied observer of this scene. Caught in this moment of intense spiritual wonder she felt certain that Swami had also dedicated her to Shiva. But conflicting emotions gripped her. (39)

How do we know what Nivedita went through when she hardly mentions her inner conflict in *Master,* and neither do Vivekananda's biographies by his Eastern and Western disciples or Swami Nikhilananda make much of it? As Som puts it,

---

28 Reba Som, *Margot: Sister Nivedita of Vivekananda* (New Delhi: Penguin Random House, 2017).

> Mentioning none of these in her book *The Master as I Saw Him*, she laid bare her soul in her letter to Mrs Eric Hammond on her return. Swearing her to secrecy and confidentiality, Nivedita confessed how left out she had felt at that moment of spiritual intensity and although 'deeply and intensely glad' of the revelation that her guru had experienced, she felt 'terrible pain to come face to face with something which is all inwardness to someone you worship, and for yourself to be able to get little further than externals. Swami could have made it live—but he was lost.' (Ibid.)

Perhaps, the more appropriate analogy might be with Sri Ramakrishna and the Holy Mother or, some twenty years later, Sri Aurobindo and Mira Alfassa. While both Sri Ramakrishna and Sri Aurobindo anointed the Holy Mother and Mira Alfassa as their spiritual partners and successors respectively, Vivekananda did not do so with Nivedita. As Som puts it,

> In vain did she plead with him to climb down from the position of Master and realise that 'we were nothing more to each other than an ordinary man and woman'. Holding on to his uncompromising reserve, Vivekananda tried valiantly to reason with her, but as she confessed later, she was inconsolable and 'angry with him and would not listen to him when he was going to talk'. (Ibid.)

According to Narasingha P. Sil,[29] Vivekananda's rejection hurt Nivedita deeply. Was his 'uncompromising reserve' an outcome of his fear of deviating, ever so mildly, from his vow of chastity? Or was it a consequence of Nivedita's not yet being ripe for the expected, if not promised, initiation?

---

29 Narasingha P. Sil, 'Prophet disarmed: Vivekananda and Nivedita', Working Paper (Monash University, Centre of South Asian Studies, no. 2, 1997) (https://www.academia.edu/27518931/Prophet_Disarmed_Vivekananda_and_Nivedita). Sil's revisionist criticism of the Ramakrishna-Vivekananda tradition, albeit meticulously researched, tends to be somewhat sensationalist, controversial, and deprecating. Though he, Sankari Basu, and Rajagopal Chattopadhyaya form the 'terrible trio' of those who wish to reconsider and reevaluate the tradition, they are not entirely hostile or inimical to it.

Sil places the responsibility for the lost opportunity on the disciple, rather than the guru:

> In retrospect she realized with bitterness how wrong she had been and lost a chance that would never come again. What she had perhaps sought was an initiation by Vivekananda at that auspicious moment into the divine knowledge and transcendental experience that he seemed to have received. (Ibid.)

Was Vivekananda entirely insensitive and cruel, as Narasingha P. Sil makes him out to be, an outcome of 'his inability to achieve the paramahaṁsa's total indifference to women and hence his personal anxiety about his vulnerability' (Ibid.)? Or was he well aware of how hurt Nivedita was and tried to make it up to her?

As Nivedita wrote to Nell Hammond afterwards, 'The next morning, as we came home, he said, "Margot, I am not Ramakrishna Paramahamsa"'(Ibid.) This extraordinary admission was accompanied by 'The most perfect, because the most unconscious, humility you ever saw': 'He would have liked to reply, "Peace, peace; the felicity lies only in the gift of oneself"/ But Nivedita, shut in by her despair, was incapable of listening to him (Reymond 127-128).

Both master and disciple returned to Pahalgam where Mrs Bull and Josephine were waiting for them. The greatly anticipated Amarnath darshan had unfortunately turned out to be divisive rather than unitive. Though the age gap between them was not even four years, Nivedita began to fashion herself as Vivekananda's daughter. As Sil puts it, 'Nivedita, in turn, realised with time that Vivekananda who had attracted her initially as "King" had to be viewed instead as the "Master" who guided her and, finally, in the last stage as the "Father" for whom her devotion was complete as a daughter' (15).

Despite the readjustment, her love for him did not diminish. Even as she relished the privilege of travelling back with him to England, she was writing to Josephine in 1899, 'While he is alive and here, I will not stir out of reach of him—I could not bear it—I worship—idolize—love him—I dare not risk his wanting me and not being there' (Sil 58-59). The 'love that she felt for her King,' as Sil puts it, was 'irresistible' (59). As she wrote to Josephine during her sea voyage with Vivekananda, 'Blessed be God for making it possible to love like this' (Sil 60). In the same letter, she confessed, 'that awful time at Almora, when I thought he had put me out of his life contemptuously . . . I have grown infinitely more personal in my love' (Sil 60). The six weeks together on the ship, albeit accompanied by Swami Turyananda, was the longest time Nivedita would spend with Vivekananda. They had set sail on 30 June 1899 on the *S.S. Golkonda,* via Aden, Port Said, and Naples, arriving at Tilsbury Dock, London, on 31 July 1899. She considered it 'as the greatest occasion of my life ... I missed no opportunity of the Swami's society that presented itself ... thus I received one long continuous impression of his mind and personality, for which I can never be sufficiently thankful' (*Master* 220-221).

Those who imagine or claim that the Amarnath journey caused a rupture between Nivedita and Vivekananda or irrevocably changed the former's personality are evidently mistaken. In fact, the Amarnath experience culminated 'on the great day of Rakhibandhan', with both Vivekananda's and Nivedita's wrists 'tied with the red and yellow threads of that sacrament' (*Master* 159-160).

Kshir Bhavai

The master and disciple returned to Srinagar on 8 August 1898 after their unforgettable Amarnath yatra. The experience had been momentous, but the Swami's exertions had exhausted and weakened him.

As Nivedita put it:

> To him, the heavens had opened. He had touched the feet of Shiva. He had had to hold himself tight, he said afterwards, lest he "should swoon away." But so great was his physical exhaustion that a doctor said afterwards that his heart ought to have stopped beating, but had undergone a permanent enlargement instead. (*Wanderings* 149-150)

Vivekananda's mood had changed since his return. He was much more aloof and preoccupied. His focus shifted from Shiva to Kali. Singing the songs of his guru Sri Ramakrisha's favourite poet, Ramprasad, his favourite expression was 'Well, well! Mother knows best!' especially when 'some cherished intention had to be abandoned' (*Master* 163). Vivekananda 'complained bitterly of the malady of thought, which would consume a man, leaving him no time for sleep or rest' and strove to instil the 'ideal of rising beyond the pairs of opposites, beyond pain and pleasure, good and evil alike' (Ibid.).

It was during this fever of imagination and thought that Vivekananda composed what became possibly his most celebrated poem: 'writing in a fever of inspiration, he had fallen on the floor, when he had finished … exhausted with his own intensity' (Ibid.).

Kali the Mother

The stars are blotted out,
The clouds are covering clouds,
It is darkness vibrant, sonant.
In the roaring, whirling wind
Are the souls of a million lunatics
Just loose from the prison-house,
Wrenching trees by the roots,
Sweeping all from the path.
The sea has joined the fray,
And swirls up mountain-waves,
To reach the pitchy sky.
The flash of lurid light
Reveals on every side
A thousand, thousand shades
Of Death begrimed and black—
Scattering plagues and sorrows,
Dancing mad with joy,
Come, Mother, come!

For Terror is Thy name,
Death is in Thy breath,
And every shaking step
Destroys a world for e'er.
Thou 'Time', the All-Destroyer!
Come, O Mother, come!
Who dares misery love,
And hug the form of Death,
Dance in Destruction's dance,
To him the Mother comes.[30]

Vivekananda suddenly left for Kshir Bhavani alone on 30 September. He stayed there for a week, worshipping Kashmir's foundational goddess, Maharajni, with its coloured spring. The temple had been destroyed and razed to the ground by Muslim invaders. While worshipping her, Vivekananda thought: 'Mother Bhavani has been manifesting Her Presence here for untold years. The Mohammedans came and destroyed her temple, yet the people of the place did nothing to protect Her. Alas, if I were then living I could never have borne it silently.'[31]

When he was thinking thus, his mind overwhelmed with anguish and anger, it seemed as if he heard the Mother's voice reply: 'It was according to My desire that the Mohammedans destroyed this temple. It is My desire that I should live in a dilapidated temple, otherwise, can I not immediately erect a seven-storeyed temple of gold here if I like? What can you do? Shall I protect you or shall you protect me!' (Ibid.)

As Swamiji reported to Sharat Chandra Chakravarty, 'Since hearing that divine voice, I cherish no more plans. The idea of building maths etc. I have given up; as Mother wills, so it will be' (Ibid.). Chakravarty decides to test his master by saying, 'Sir, you used to say that Divine Voices are the

30 'Kali the Mother', https://en.wikisource.org/wiki/The_Complete_Works_of_Swami_Vivekananda/Volume_4/Writings:_Poems/Kali_the_Mother

31 Conversations and Dialogues from the Diary of a Disciple, https://www.ramakrishnavivekananda.info/vivekananda/volume_7/conversations_and_dialogues/from_the_diary_of_a_disciple/scc_iv.htm

echo of our inward thoughts and feelings' (Ibid.). Vivekananda disabused him of any doubts regarding the experience, 'Whether it be internal or external, if you actually hear with your ears such a disembodied voice, as I have done, can you deny it and call it false? Divine Voices are actually heard, just as you and I are talking' (Ibid.).[32]

Returning to Srinagar in 1898, Vivekananda gave his guests the marigolds that had been offered to the Mother as prasad. Sitting down, he said, 'No more "Hari Om!" It is all "Mother," now! ... All my patriotism is gone. Everything is gone. Now it's only "Mother, Mother!"' (*Master* 167).

Nivedita narrates the Kshir Bhavani realization in a manner quite similar to Chakravarty, 'I have been very wrong ... Mother said to me 'What, even if unbelievers should enter My temples, and defile My images! What is that to you? Do you protect ME? Or do I protect you?' (*Master* 168). From a staunch Advaitin, Vivekananda transformed into someone much more like his own Master—Sri Ramakrishna, a guileless and fully surrendered devotee of the Mother. Perhaps he had also realized, just a few years before his death, that Brahman and Kali were one and the same, two aspects of the ultimate reality and supreme consciousness. So in the 'Mother mood' was Vivekananda absorbed that he worshipped 'Urna, the little four-year-old daughter of his Mohammedan boatman'.[33]

A few days after, on 11 October, the party descended once again, via Baramulla, to the plains of northern India for their last leg of sightseeing, which included Lahore, Delhi and Agra, before returning to Calcutta.

Conclusion

Vivekananda's Himalayan experiences are some of the most intense, uplifting and transformative in his life. Yet he never lost sight of the profound truth of Vedanta: 'From sand rise these mountains; unto sand

32 Vivekananda, who had been so troubled by the destruction of the temple, did not live to see its rebuilding by Maharaja Pratap Singh in 1912. Today, the restored and heavily guarded temple is visited by thousands of pilgrims.

33 In Kashmir, Amarnath and Kshirbhavani, https://www.ramakrishnavivekananda.info/swamieastwest/2_files/1-32.html

they go'.[34] Here, we see him in close contact with his Western disciples, teaching and training them in a personal, intimate manner, combining the roles of tour guide, philosopher, historian, teacher and Guru. Of his projects, although the one in Kashmir did not fructify, the Mayavati Ashram became a huge and lasting success. Some of his greatest poems are also composed here, notably, 'Kali the Mother'. The Himalayas also inspire and nurture significant episodes in his limitless adventures through the realms of consciousness, from an early realization of the relationship between the microcosm and the macrocosm to an experience of immortality in Amarnath to the definitive shift from knowledge and action to devotion and surrender after Kshir Bhavani. When it comes to Nivedita's trials under his stern spiritual tutelage, some might believe that it is best to censor or suppress the personal or human side of a great guru's life. On the contrary, I have always felt the opposite. The more human, the more divine.

Vivekananda was a man who could move mountains. When, as is inevitable, the mountains did not come to him, he went to the mountains himself. He had understood, internalized and actuated the great secret of India's ancient sages: 'It is the Supreme Lord "gets involved in the minute cell, and evolves at the other end and becomes God again. He it is that comes down and becomes the lowest atom, and slowly unfolding His nature, rejoins Himself. This is the mystery of the universe"' (Ibid.). The Himalayas, India's devbhoomi, still home to our shining and immortal gods and sages, kindled in Vivekananda a spiritual yearning, one that still resonates with us after over a hundred years.

34 The Cosmos: The Macrocosm, https://www.ramakrishnavivekananda.info/vivekananda/volume_2/jnana-yoga/the_macrocosm.htm

—

'To one who knows how to look and feel, every moment of this free wandering life is an enchantment.'

The extraordinary life and adventures of Alexandra David-Néel are made of the stuff of dreams and magic. The intrepid Belgian-French explorer, born in 1869, was a traveller and an anarchist, a spiritualist and Buddhist, a scholar, an opera singer, and a powerful and prolific writer. In 1924, at the age of fifty-five, she was the the first European woman to travel across the Himalaya, in the inhospitable winter, and make her way to the Forbidden City of Lhasa.

This excerpt is from her mesmerizing account of her travels, Magic and Mystery in Tibet. *She recounts her unlikely encounters and adventures with sages, saints,shamans, mystic masters and unknown magicians. Here, she tells us of her meeting with the Thirteenth Dalai Lama while he was in exile in Kalimpong, as well as with an enigmatic najorpa—a wanderer in search of wisdom.*

CHAPTER 7

Magic and Mystery in Tibet

ALEXANDRA DAVID-NÉEL

'Well, then, it is understood. I leave Dawasandup with you as interpreter. He will accompany you to Gangtok.'

Is it a man who is speaking to me? This short yellow-skinned being clad in a robe of orange brocade, a diamond star sparkling on his hat; is he not, rather, a genie come down from the neighbouring mountains?

They say he is an 'incarnated Lama' and heir-prince of a Himalayan throne, but I doubt his reality. Probably he will vanish like a mirage, with his caparisoned little steed and his party of followers, dressed in all the colours of the rainbow. He is a part of the enchantment in which I have lived these last fifteen days. This new episode is of the stuff that dreams are made of. In a few minutes, I shall wake up in a real bed, in some country not haunted by genie nor by 'incarnated Lamas' wrapped in shimmering silk. A country where men wear ugly dark coats and the horses do not carry silver inlaid saddles on golden-yellow cloths.

The sound of a kettledrum makes me start, two haut-boys intone a melancholy minor tune. The youthful genie straddles his diminutive courser, knights and squires jump into their saddles.

'I shall expect you,' the lama-prince says, smiling graciously at me.

I hear myself, as if I were listening to some other person, promising him that I will start the next day for his capital, and the little troop, headed by the musicians, disappears.

As the last murmurs of the plaintive melody die away in the distance, the enchantment that has held me spellbound dissipates.

I have not been dreaming, all this is real. I am at Kalimpong, in the Himalayas, and the interpreter given me when I arrived stands at my side.

I have already related[35] the circumstances which had brought me to the Himalayas. Political reasons had, at that time, led the [Thirteenth] Dalai Lama to seek refuge in British territory. It had seemed to me a unique opportunity, while he was stopping at the Indian frontier, of obtaining

35 In a previous book, *My Journey to Lhasa.*

an interview and getting information from him about the special type of Buddhism that prevails in Tibet.

Very few strangers have ever approached the monk-king, hidden in his sacred city, in the Land of Snows. Even in exile, he saw no one. Up to the time of my visit, he had obstinately refused an audience to any woman except Tibetans and I believe, even to this day, that I am the only exception to this rule.

As I left Darjeeling, in the early rosy dawn of a cool spring morning, I little guessed the far-reaching consequences of my request.

I thought of a short excursion, of an interesting but brief interview; while, actually, I became involved in wanderings that kept me in Asia for full fourteen years.

At the beginning of that long series of journeys, the Dalai Lama figures, in my diaries, as an obliging host who, seeing a stranger without the walls, invites him to see over his domain.

This the Dalai Lama did in a few words: 'Learn the Tibetan language,' he told me.

If one could believe his subjects who call him the 'Omniscient',[36] when giving me this advice, [he] foresaw its consequences, and consciously directed me, not only towards Lhasa, his forbidden capital, but towards the mystic masters and unknown magicians, yet more closely hidden in his wonderland.

At Kalimpong, the lama-king lived in a large house belonging to the minister of the Rajah of Bhutan. To give the place a more majestic appearance, two rows of tall bamboo poles had been planted in the form of an avenue. Flags flew from every pole, with the inscription *Aum mani padme hum!*, or the 'horse of the air', surrounded by magic formulas.

The suite of the exiled sovereign was numerous and included more than a hundred servants. They were for the most part engaged in interminable gossip, and quiet reigned round the habitation. But on fête days, or when visitors of rank were to be received, a crowd of busy officials and domestics poured out from all sides, peering at one from every window, crossing

36 *Thamstched mkyenpa.*

and recrossing the large plot of ground in front of the house, hurrying, screaming, agitated, and all so remarkably alike in their dirty, greasy robes that a stranger could easily make awkward mistakes about their rank.

The splendour, decorum and etiquette of the Potala were absent in that land of exile. Those who saw this roadside camp, where the Head of the Tibetan theocracy waited for his subjects to reconquer his throne, could not imagine what the Court at Lhasa was like.

The British expedition penetrating into the forbidden territory and parading his capital, in spite of the sorcery of the most famous magicians, had probably led the Dalai Lama to understand that foreign barbarians were masters in a material sense, by right of force. The inventions that he noticed during his trip through India must also have convinced him of their ability to enslave and mould the material elements of nature. But his conviction that the white race is mentally inferior remained unshaken. And, in this, he only shared the opinion of all Asiatics—from Ceylon to the northern confines of Mongolia.

A Western woman acquainted with Buddhist doctrines seemed to him an inconceivable phenomenon.

If I had vanished into space while talking to him, he would have been less astonished. My reality surprised him most; but, when finally convinced, he politely inquired after my 'Master', assuming that I could only have learned of Buddha from an Asiatic. It was not easy to convince him that the Tibetan text of one of the most esteemed Buddhist books[37] had been translated into French before I was born. 'Ah well,' he murmured at last, 'if a few strangers have really learned our language and read our sacred books, they must have missed the meaning of them.'

This was my chance. I hastened to seize it.

'It is precisely because I suspect that certain religious doctrines of Tibet have been misunderstood that I have come to you to be enlightened,' I said.

37 *The Gyacher Rolpa*, translated by Ed . Foucaux, Professor at the College de France.

My reply pleased the Dalai Lama. He readily answered any questions I put to him, and a little later gave me a long written explanation of the various subjects we had discussed.

The prince of Sikkim and his escort having disappeared, it only remained for me to keep my promise and make ready to start for Gangtok. But there was something to be seen before moving on.

The evening before, I had witnessed the benediction of the pilgrims by the Dalai Lama, a widely different scene from the Pontifical benediction at Rome. For the Pope in a single gesture blesses the multitude, while the Tibetans are far more exacting and each expect an individual blessing.

Among Lamaists again, the manner of the blessing varies with the social rank of the blessed. The Lama places both hands on the heads of those he most respects. In other cases only one hand, two fingers or even only one finger. Lastly comes the blessing given by slightly touching the head with coloured ribbons, attached to a short stick.

In every case, however, there is contact, direct or indirect, between the lama and the devotee. This contact, according to Lamaists, is indispensable because the benediction, whether of people or of things, is not meant to call down upon them the benediction of God, but to infuse into them some beneficial power that emanates from the lama.

The large number of people who came to Kalimpong to be touched by the Dalai Lama gave me some idea of his widespread prestige.

The procession took several hours to pass before him, and I noticed that not only Lamaists but many people from Nepal and from Bengal, belonging to Hindu sects, had joined the crowd.

I saw some, who had come only to look on, suddenly seized by an occult fervour, hurrying to join the pious flock.

As I was watching this scene, my eyes fell on a man seated on the ground, a little to one side. His matted hair was wound around his head like a turban, in the style common to Hindu ascetics. Yet, his features were not those of an Indian and he was wearing dirty and much-torn lamaist monastic garments.

This tramp had placed a small bag beside him and seemed to observe the crowd with a cynical expression.

I pointed him out to Dawasandup, asking him if he had any idea who this Himalayan Diogenes might be. 'It must be a travelling najorpa[38],' he answered; and, seeing my curiosity, my obliging interpreter went to the man and entered into conversation with him.

He returned to me with a serious face and said: 'This lama is a peripatetic ascetic from Bhutan. He lives here and there in caves, empty houses or under the trees. He has been stopping for several days in a small monastery near here.'

My thoughts returned to the vagabond when the prince and his escort had disappeared. I had no definite plan for the afternoon, why should I not go to the gompa (monastery) where he was staying, and persuade him to talk? Was he really mocking, as he seemed to be, at the Dalai Lama and the faithful? And if so, why? There might be interesting reasons.

I communicated my desire to Dawasandup, who agreed to accompany me.

We went on horseback and soon reached the gompa, which was only a large-sized country-house.

In the lha khang (the room containing the holy images) we found the najorpa seated upon a cushion in front of a low table, finishing his meal. Cushions were brought and we were offered tea.

It was difficult to begin a conversation with the ascetic, as his mouth appeared to be full of rice; he had only answered our polite greetings by a kind of grunt.

I was trying to find a phrase to break the ice, when the strange fellow began to laugh and muttered a few words. Dawasandup seemed embarrassed.

'What does he say?' I asked.

'Excuse me,' answered the interpreter, 'these najorpas sometimes speak roughly. I do not know if I should translate.'

'Please do,' I replied. 'I am here to take notes especially of anything at all curious and original.'

---

38 Naljorpa (written *rnal hbyorpa*), literally: 'He who has attained perfect serenity' but usually interpreted: an ascetic possessing magic powers.

'Well, then—excuse me—he said, "What is this idiot here for?"'

Such rudeness did not greatly astonish me as, in India also certain yogins make a habit of insulting anyone who approaches them.

'Tell him I have come to ask why he mocked at the crowd seeking the benediction of the Dalai Lama.'

'Puffed up with a sense of their own importance and the importance of what they are doing. Insects fluttering in the dung,' muttered the najorpa between his teeth.

This was vague, but the kind of language one expects from such men.

'And you,' I replied. 'Are you free from all defilement?'

He laughed noisily. 'He who tries to get out only sinks in deeper. I roll in it like a pig. I digest it and turn it into golden dust, into a brook of pure water. To fashion stars out of dog dung, that is the Great Work!'

Evidently my friend was enjoying himself. This was his way of posing as a superman.

'Are these pilgrims not right, to profit by the presence of the Dalai Lama and obtain his blessing? They are simple folk incapable of aspiring to the knowledge of the higher doctrines—'

But the najorpa interrupted me.

'For a blessing to be efficacious, he who gives it must possess the power that he professes to communicate.

'Would the Precious Protector (the Dalai Lama) need soldiers to fight the Chinese or other enemies if he possessed such a power? Could he not drive anyone he liked out of the country and surround Tibet with an invisible barrier that none could pass?

'The Guru who is born in a lotus[39] had such a power, and his blessing still reaches those who worship him, even though he lives in the distant land of the Rakshasas.

'I am only a humble disciple, and yet—'

It appeared to me that the 'humble disciple' was maybe a little mad and certainly very conceited, for his 'and yet' had been accompanied by a glance that suggested many things.

---

39 Padmasambhava, who preached in Tibet in the eighth century.

My interpreter meanwhile was visibly uneasy. He profoundly respected the Dalai Lama and disliked to hear him criticized. On the other hand, the man who could 'create stars out of dog dung' inspired him with a superstitious fear.

I proposed to leave, but as I understood that the lama was going away the next morning, I handed Dawasandup a few rupees for the traveller to help him on his way.

This present displeased the najorpa. He refused it, saying he had already received more provisions than he could carry.

Dawasandup thought it right to insist. He took a few steps forward, intending to place the money on a table near the lama. Then I saw him stagger, fall backward and strike his back against the wall as if he had been violently pushed. He uttered a cry and clutched at his stomach. The najorpa got up and, sneering, left the room.

'I feel as if I had received a terrible blow,' said Dawasandup. 'The lama is irritated. How shall we appease him?'

'Let us go,' I answered. 'The lama has probably nothing to do with it. You, perhaps, have heart trouble and had better consult a doctor.'

Pale and troubled, the interpreter answered nothing. Indeed there was nothing to be said. We returned, but I was not able to reassure him.

The next day Dawasandup and I left for Gangtok. The mule path that we followed dives right into the Himalayas, the sacred land which ancient Indian traditions people with famous sages, stern magicians, ascetics and deities.

The summer resorts established by foreigners on the border of these impressive highlands have not yet modified their aspect. A few miles away from the hotels where the Western world enjoys dancing and jazz bands, the primeval forest reigns.

Shrouded in the moving fogs, a fantastic army of trees, draped in livid green moss, seems to keep watch along the narrow tracks, warning or threatening the traveller with enigmatic gestures. From the low valleys buried under the exuberant jungle to the mountain summits covered with eternal snow, the whole country is bathed in occult influences.

In such scenery it is fitting that sorcery should hold sway. The so-called Buddhist population is practically Shamanist and a large number of mediums Bonpos, Pawos, Bunting and Yabas of both sexes, even in the smallest hamlets, transmit the messages of gods, demons and the dead.

I slept on the way at Pakyong, and the next day I reached Gangtok.

The Fourteenth Dalai Lama is possibly the most beloved of spiritual leaders anywhere in the world. His laughter and wisdom suffuse those who meet him with a strange, unfamiliar joy. He has witnessed important transitions in history and led his people through a continuing crisis.

We present His Holiness in conversation with Rajiv Mehrotra, writer, documentary film-maker and a personal student of the Dalai Lama, who is also Trustee/Secretary of The Foundation for Universal Responsibility, established with the Nobel Peace Prize. They speak of reincarnation, the theory and implications of karma, and of happiness, suffering and liberation. A tremendous degree of understanding and transcendent insight is compressed in this chapter.

CHAPTER 8

Reincarnation

H.H. THE FOURTEENTH DALAI LAMA IN CONVERSATION WITH RAJIV MEHROTRA

RM: *You are regarded by millions as the reincarnation of Avalokiteshvara, the Buddha of Compassion. Are you consciously aware that you are a reincarnation of Avalokiteshvara?*

HH: Of Avalokiteshvara? No, no, no! That, I think, is a little bit of an exaggeration. I always describe myself as a Buddhist monk. Of course, I believe that with the previous—the First Dalai Lama, the Second and I think up to the Seventh Dalai Lama—there are clear indications. They are, what you say, reincarnations of Avalokiteshvara—especially the First and the Second. For myself, I do not believe I am of the original Dalai Lama. But I do feel that I have a special relationship with the Fifth and the Thirteenth Dalai Lamas.

There are different types of reincarnation. In some cases, it's the same person or same being. In other cases, it's not the same being, but someone else who has in his or her place. In some, the reincarnation has come as a relative.

If you ask me whether I am the reincarnation of Dalai Lama, my answer is yes, but not necessarily in the sense that I came in the tenth Dalai Lama's place to fulfil his work.

RM: *Your Holiness, with your pursuit of the scientific method, logical analysis and rationality, how do you reconcile with being a reincarnation?*

HH: There are various interpretations of reincarnation. For myself, I think it means deliberately taking birth in order to succeed in what was started in a previous life or to complete the work of someone else's previous life. In that sense, I feel I am an incarnation.

Moreover, as a Buddhist, or as a Buddhist who continues to study Buddhist logic and Buddhist philosophy, if it is scientifically proved that certain things do not exist, then theoretically speaking, it has to be accepted. For example, if reincarnation is thoroughly investigated in a scientific way and it is proved 100 per cent that it doesn't exist, theoretically speaking, Buddhists would have to accept that.

But you must see the difference between merely not *finding* proof and having tangible proof that something *doesn't* exist. From the Buddhist point of view, also, if something cannot be found through philosophy, it doesn't mean it doesn't exist. We believe it does exist, but finding it depends on many factors.

RM: *Do you feel you are the reincarnation of the Thirteenth Dalai Lama, and is there 'incomplete' work for you to complete?*

HH: I must answer that with both a yes and a no. In my dream state, I met the Thirteenth Dalai Lama three times. I don't believe that I am necessarily the same being. I feel, however, that I have a very strong karmic link with him. The Thirteenth Dalai Lama made progress in both the temporal and spiritual fields. However, we also believe that he had a more long-term plan for his work that would overlap beyond his lifetime. He died in his late fifties, and the work that he had begun was neither fulfilled nor completed.

RM: *Do you know that for sure?*

HH: Not very sure. But it is what I feel.

RM: *The physical body decays upon death, so is it the mind or the consciousness that is reincarnated?*

HH: First, you must ask yourself the basic question: 'What is "self" or "I"?' Certainly, this body is not the central being, and the mind alone is also not a central being. For me, Tenzin Gyatso is the human being. However, from the Buddhist point of view, in the Mahayana system, they say the central being, Tenzin Gyatso, is designated here as the human being and is the combination of this body and mind. This body comes from parents and is subject to various causes and conditions.

The being is chosen because of a combination of the body and the mind, and also the subtle level of the body and the grosser level of the mind. The process for rebirth is the continuation of the mind or the continuation of the being. Reincarnation is a deliberate birth at a certain time, in a certain area. It could be the same person and the same being, or a different person who has come to fulfil his previous unfinished work.

Ultimately, some Buddhist scriptures ay that the space particle is the original cause of this body, and that particle was also the cause for the whole previous universe. But consciousness or mind is changing every moment. Therefore, it can be shown that causes and conditions will affect anything that undergoes change. As such, the mind is also a product of causes and conditions. That is the basis of the rebirth theory.

RM: *Currently, do you have any memories of your past life?*

HH: Sometimes it is difficult to remember what happened this morning! However, when I was small—say, two to three years old—my mother and some close friends noticed that I expressed some memories of my past life. That is possible! But if you are asking me for a definite memory, I must say it remains somewhat unclear.

RM: *If Buddhism is open to scientific questioning, why does the belief in reincarnation still survive? There is no supporting science or reason for this.*

HH: Science, as we know it, involves investigation of something that can be measured or calculated. The concept of mind or the concept of self itself cannot be measured. Up to now, the scientific field from the Buddhist viewpoint has been limited, I think. Mind and consciousness are outside the present scientific field. Because there have been many sophisticated experiments on the brain about the experience of dying people, these perhaps may lead to a wider field. But at the same time, we must appreciate what science has not found or says is non-existent.

RM: *Your Holiness, would that not be the case with incarnate lamas who to some degree have recollections of past lives?*

HH: This is not necessarily only a Buddhist concept. In fact, there are two girls in two families near Palampur and in Ambala [in north India]. About two years ago, I sent some people to investigate because at that time the girls, who were four or five, talked very clearly about their past lives, and each claimed that the other girl's parents were her own. As a result, these two girls now have four parents each—parents in this life and parents from a past life. Their recollections were so convincing that each set of parents accepted the other girl as their own child.

I studied a similar case where a little boy claimed that he had a wife and children, and his parents beat him, saying he was a liar. Eventually, by chance, a visitor from the village where he claimed to have a family mentioned that there were people by the same names that he was talking about. So, they took the child to the other village, where he identified a lady as his wife from among three or four women and talked about his children!

RM: *Do you think about your reincarnation in your next life?*

HH: Of course! The words of Shantideva were, 'As long as space remains, as long as suffering of sentient beings remains, I will remain in order to serve, in order to work for them.' That verse gives me the inner strength, hope and a defined purpose of my being.

I am definitely ready as long as my reincarnation is of some benefit, some usefulness. I'm quite sure I will take rebirth. In what place, in what form or with what name, I don't know. But the reincarnation of the Dalai Lama is a different matter. The time may come when the institution of the Dalai Lama may no longer be beneficial and there would be no reason for it to continue. On this, I remain open.

As far as my rebirth is concerned, until Buddhahood is reached, I firmly believe my rebirth is always there. Even after Buddhahood, I will continue somewhere in different manifestations. That is the Buddhist belief, the Buddhist thinking. I really feel that a teaching of this kind sustains one's optimism, will and determination.

RM: *The need for birth control is justified by the finite resources of our planet, which cannot sustain an infinitely growing population. Some people believe we are thus denying large numbers of sentient beings birth in human form. What do you think?*

HH: This can be summed up in a comment by Gandhiji: there is enough for everybody's need, but not for everybody's greed. This balances out the karmic concept of reincarnation. The world has enough to feed everybody if the divisions were better and people did not tend to accumulate more than they should. These two theories balance out to some degree if one could in that sense distribute the well-being of others. There is so much food being destroyed, dumped into the ocean, while millions of people are going hungry. This, I think, is in part both moral and karmic weakness.

I think the confusion is about what is reborn. Is it the entity, the identity? Does it become part of a larger consciousness, part of which manifests itself again? I think that is the area of confusion. It also includes the notion that a number of souls are waiting to be reborn. That suggests the notion that there are that many different entities or identities waiting to be reborn. If we understand the 'I' correctly, our responses change.

RM: *But I do not know who that 'I' is. If I am born again, I do not remember what I was before! Unless I am conscious that it is me, what difference does it make?*

HH: Whose continuity of consciousness is it? To whom does it belong? The answer to the question is that it belongs to the being himself. Whether one can find that self—'I'—or not is a different question altogether. If one were to say my previous life is my own being, one has to recollect it. Then it is not unrecognized. We can recognize certain experiences; others, even of this life, we cannot. On this basis, we cannot say that was not me.

In other words, there are people who very clearly remember past lives. But ordinary people cannot remember past lives because the level of consciousness during the time of death, the interval state between the previous life and the next life, is most subtle. When that happens, the gross level of mind on which these memories are based cannot function well. A person who has some experience of utilizing deeper consciousnesses has a better chance of having clearer memories of past lives.

RM: *Please explain what happens to the mind at the time of death, or what is it that moves from one incarnation to the next and carries forward the karmic imprints?*

HH: That depends on the previous lives—the mental capacity through samadhi or mental training. Some memories, some sustainable experiences, and other mental qualities of the past life remain intact in the next. But the body changes, as does the grosser level of mind, so that in the next life there are not so many traces present. But then again, there is always some kind of small influence or imprint from the previous life.

RM: *At the time of death, there are to practices and trainings in the Tibetan tradition that teach you how to manage and how to direct the subtle mind. So once the gross body and the gross mind have fallen away, what is it that directs the mind to a suitable incarnation in the next life?*

HH: It depends very much on the quality or the experience carried forward by the subtle mind. Those experiences that have a closer relation with the subtle mind have a greater possibility of being transmitted to the next life. This continuation or transmigration of the subtle mind, in fact, is a kind of natural process; and likewise the 'self' is being designated on the subtle mind, and the transference of that 'self' to the next life is also a kind of natural process. As explained earlier, whether that mind carries with it a positive imprint or negative imprint depends very much on the kind of life lived in the previous life, or karma.

Consciousness requires a substantial cause, an earlier moment of consciousness. This basic reason proves the existence of rebirth. If we look further for the continuity of consciousness of this life, like the time of conception, then this continuity can be traced to the previous life. In that case, there is no reason why the continuity of consciousness should cease at the last moment of this life, at the time of death.

For this reason, we have to be concerned about our future lives. Whether we will have good or unfortunate future lives depends on our actions in this life. While we are busy in this life, we should not neglect to think about future lives.

Then there is another aspect. Everybody wants happiness, and nobody wants suffering. If material progress could provide the complete happiness we are seeking, there should be people in this world who are totally satisfied and who should not have even the slightest experience of suffering. However, as long as we have this physical body, the potential for suffering will always exist; this is the nature of samsara. Birth into this body is the basis of misfortune. If we have the possibility to cease rebirth, this is something worthwhile to achieve. This we call moksha or liberation.

RM: *Would you say that you would be ready to disbelieve in reincarnation if the proof were there?*

HH: Oh yes. I think, strictly speaking, from Buddhist viewpoint, if scientific experiment or investigation convincingly shows with 100 per cent certainty that there is no continuation of mind, then of course, we have to accept it. Normally, when we investigate something, we consider the reasons for establishing that point and whether we accept any opposing factors. The rebirth theory involves two things: one, even today there are people who have a clear memory about their past life; and the other, if there is no continuity of life, how does the whole world or universe exist?

There must be some causes. The concept of the Creator raised many contradictions; therefore, at least for Buddhists, it seems more comfortable to accept the theory of rebirth—that the beginning of life is due to their actions, so the whole universe comes and goes, comes and goes. But there always remains an element of mystery.

RM: *So according to the theory of karma, because of the number of mosquitoes I have killed in this life, I will have to be reborn a mosquito . . .*

HH: As far as that is concerned, unless I do some special method of purification, well . . . otherwise, I remember very clearly that I have sinned. I have killed mosquitoes on one occasion in Lhasa, in Tibet; then on another occasion in south India, I killed a few mosquitoes. Those actions are quite enough to take rebirth as a mosquito.

RM: *Does every karma find the physical or external conditions in this world to balance or complete it?*

HH: If, for example, someone has accumulated the karma to take rebirth as a human being on this planet, but because of some external circumstances this planet has been destroyed or has yet to be evolved and such, in these circumstances either his karmic action will have to wait for its maturation or he will take rebirth on another planet that has identical form. To take rebirth into a specific form does require external conditions for the existence of that specific form. Two things are necessary: in order to take rebirth as a human being, karma alone is not enough; one also needs parents.

RM: *Is it necessary to believe in future and past lives?*

HH: If we do not adhere to the theory of rebirth or do not accept past lives, we have to set some point of beginning for beings.

I usually say that whether you are a believer or non-believer, you should be a kind-hearted person. That can be developed without acceptance of past or future lives or without the acceptance of Buddhist or karmic theory. This is religion in itself.

I strongly feel that even anti-religious people—like Communists, for example—can be very good-hearted, as I have personally experienced. People with good hearts do exist without any Buddhist theory of rebirth—those who sacrifice their own lives for the benefit of the masses either through their inborn qualities or in another way.

Love and kindness are a universal religion. Today we are discussing Buddhism, so I am talking about these things from the Buddhist point of view. If someone without these practices simply tries to he a good person, that is certainly possible and he will succeed. If, however, a person does not accept the existence of a completely enlightened state, then the question of bodhicitta not arise either, because it is a state of mind that aspires to Buddhahood. That is some kind of process in the Buddhist point of view.

RM: *There is one question that many people ask. If Buddhists don't believe in an atman—the self or soul—what is it that reincarnates?*

HH: Buddhists emphasize anatman, and much is dependent on the connotation or understanding of the meaning of the term anatman, or selflessness. Sometimes confusion arises due to the usage of the word in different contexts. So, when we talk about anatman, we do not mean the total non-existence of the nominal or conventional self; we very much accept the existence of such a conventional self. What we actually mean is the non-existence of the self that is thought to be totally independent and has nothing whatsoever to do with the self of the physical aggregates; it is totally separate from the self of the physical aggregates, which is the kind of self that is being denied.

When we talk of past and future lives with conviction, there must be some energy or something that comes from past lives and enters this physical body and goes from this life to the next one, leaving this physical body behind. And that something must be separate from the physical body.

According to some Buddhist schools, it is believed that between the mind and body—since the physical body is only for this life, it must be the mind that goes from one life to another. But the mind is also heavily entangled with various senses and organs, which are again very physical and confined to just one life. Therefore, it must be a very subtle mind. That must be the self. This is one Buddhist school of thought—chitta. Even in chitta there are different levels. So, ultimately, a subtler chitta is the self.

Yet another Buddhist school of thought argues that even the subtle mind, no matter *how* subtle, cannot be considered as 'my' mind. Therefore, that mind itself is self. If the mind becomes the self, both the ownership and what is owned by that owner become one.

RM: *If death is the ultimate state of consciousness, then what about ghosts? Have you ever come across any?*

HH: I do remember that, as a child, I was very scared of ghosts.

In Buddhism, we have six types of rebirths. This division is made on the basis of the degree of suffering or pleasure. When the division is made on the basis of having gross or subtle levels of form, feeling, or mind, we divide sentient beings into three realms. This is further divided into three: six types of devas [supernatural beings] belonging to the desire realm, sixteen types belonging to the form realm and four types belonging to the formless realm. So we have here three realms: desire realm, form realm and formless realm.

Ghosts can belong to any of these three realms or states. Some are positive and some negative; just like human beings, some are very cruel and some are very kind—it is like that.

This excerpt from Paramhansa Yogananda's famed Autobiography of a Yogi *is a lighthearted yet deep account of his schoolboy days. It describes an early attempt by a band of friends to run away to the Himalayas and seek refuge in the spiritual life.*

The autobiography, first published in 1947, has sold millions of copies and inspired readers across the world. Paramhansa Yogananda (1893–1952) belonged to an illustrious lineage of adepts. His guru, Swami Sri Yukteswar, was initiated by Sri Lahiri Mahasaya, who had been blessed by none other than the mysterious, immortal, ever-present figure of Babaji. The karmic bonds of Masters and their disciples are difficult to understand or explain. In these passages, we glimpse the inner call of the renunciate, recalled with humour and insight.

CHAPTER 9

My Interrupted Flight toward the Himalayas

PARAMHANSA YOGANANDA

So near the Himalayas and yet, in our captivity, so far, I told Amar I felt doubly impelled to seek freedom.

'Let us slip away when opportunity offers. We can go on foot to holy Rishikesh.' I smiled encouragingly.

But my companion had turned pessimist as soon as the stalwart prop of our money had been taken from us.

'If we started a trek over such dangerous jungle land, we should finish, not in the city of saints, but in the stomachs of tigers!'

Ananta and Amar's brother arrived after three days. Amar greeted his relative with affectionate relief. I was unreconciled; Ananta got no more from me than a severe upbraiding.

'I understand how you feel.' My brother spoke soothingly. 'All I ask of you is to accompany me to Benares to meet a certain saint, and go on to Calcutta to visit your grieving father for a few days. Then you can resume your search here for a master.'

Amar entered the conversation at this point to disclaim any intention of returning to Hardwar with me. He was enjoying the familial warmth. But I knew I would never abandon the quest for my guru.

Our party entrained for Benares. There I had a singular and instant response to my prayers.

A clever scheme had been prearranged by Ananta. Before seeing me at Hardwar, he had stopped in Benares to ask a certain scriptural authority to interview me later. Both the pundit and his son had promised to undertake my dissuasion from the path of a sannyasi.[40]

Ananta took me to their home. The son, a young man of ebullient manner, greeted me in the courtyard. He engaged me in a lengthy philosophic discourse. Professing to have a clairvoyant knowledge of my future, he discountenanced my idea of being a monk.

'You will meet continual misfortune, and be unable to find God, if you insist on deserting your ordinary responsibilities! You cannot work out your past karma[41] without worldly experiences.'

---

40 Literally, 'renunciate'. From Sanskrit verb roots, 'to cast aside'.

41 Effects of past actions, in this or a former life; from Sanskrit kri, 'to do'.

Krishna's immortal words rose to my lips in reply: 'Even he with the worst of karma who ceaselessly meditates on Me quickly loses the effects of his past bad actions. Becoming a high-souled being, he soon attains perennial peace. Arjuna, know this for certain: the devotee who puts his trust in Me never perishes!'[42]

But the forceful prognostications of the young man had slightly shaken my confidence. With all the fervor of my heart I prayed silently to God:

'Please solve my bewilderment and answer me, right here and now, if Thou dost desire me to lead the life of a renunciate or a worldly man!'

I noticed a sadhu of noble countenance standing just outside the compound of the pundit's house. Evidently he had overheard the spirited conversation between the self-styled clairvoyant and myself, for the stranger called me to his side. I felt a tremendous power flowing from his calm eyes.

'Son, don't listen to that ignoramus. In response to your prayer, the Lord tells me to assure you that your sole path in this life is that of the renunciate.'

With astonishment as well as gratitude, I smiled happily at this decisive message.

'Come away from that man!' The 'ignoramus' was calling me from the courtyard. My saintly guide raised his hand in blessing and slowly departed.

'That sadhu is just as crazy as you are.' It was the hoary headed pundit who made this charming observation. He and his son were gazing at me lugubriously. 'I heard that he too has left his home in a vague search for God.'

I turned away. To Ananta I remarked that I would not engage in further discussion with our hosts. My brother agreed to an immediate departure; we soon entrained for Calcutta.

'Mr Detective, how did you discover I had fled with two companions?' I vented my lively curiosity to Ananta during our homeward journey. He smiled mischievously.

'At your school, I found that Amar had left his classroom and had not returned. I went to his home the next morning and unearthed a marked

---

42 *Bhagavad Gita*, IX, 30-31. Krishna was the greatest prophet of India; Arjuna was his foremost disciple.

timetable. Amar's father was just leaving by carriage and was talking to the coachman.

"'My son will not ride with me to his school this morning. He has disappeared!" the father moaned.

"'I heard from a brother coachman that your son and two others, dressed in European suits, boarded the train at Howrah Station," the man stated. "They made a present of their leather shoes to the cab driver."

'Thus I had three clues—the timetable, the trio of boys, and the English clothing.'

I was listening to Ananta's disclosures with mingled mirth and vexation. Our generosity to the coachman had been slightly misplaced!

'Of course I rushed to send telegrams to station officials in all the cities which Amar had underlined in the timetable. He had checked Bareilly, so I wired your friend Dwarka there. After inquiries in our Calcutta neighborhood, I learned that cousin Jatinda had been absent one night but had arrived home the following morning in European garb. I sought him out and invited him to dinner. He accepted, quite disarmed by my friendly manner. On the way I led him unsuspectingly to a police station. He was surrounded by several officers whom I had previously selected for their ferocious appearance. Under their formidable gaze, Jatinda agreed to account for his mysterious conduct.

"'I started for the Himalayas in a buoyant spiritual mood," he explained. "Inspiration filled me at the prospect of meeting the masters. But as soon as Mukunda said, "During our ecstasies in the Himalayan caves, tigers will be spellbound and sit around us like tame pussies," my spirits froze; beads of perspiration formed on my brow. "What then?" I thought. "If the vicious nature of the tigers be not changed through the power of our spiritual trance, shall they treat us with the kindness of house cats?" In my mind's eye, I already saw myself the compulsory inmate of some tiger's stomach—entering there not at once with the whole body, but by installments of its several parts!"'

My anger at Jatinda's vanishment was evaporated in laughter. The hilarious sequel on the train was worth all the anguish he had caused me. I must confess to a slight feeling of satisfaction: Jatinda too had not escaped an encounter with the police!

'Ananta,[43] you are a born sleuthhound!' My glance of amusement was not without some exasperation. 'And I shall tell Jatinda I am glad he was prompted by no mood of treachery, as it appeared, but only by the prudent instinct of self-preservation!'

At home in Calcutta, Father touchingly requested me to curb my roving feet until, at least, the completion of my high-school studies. In my absence, he had lovingly hatched a plot by arranging for a saintly pundit, Swami Kebalananda,[44] to come regularly to the house.

'The sage will be your Sanskrit tutor,' my parent announced confidently.

Father hoped to satisfy my religious yearnings by instructions from a learned philosopher. But the tables were subtly turned: my new teacher, far from offering intellectual aridities, fanned the embers of my God-aspiration. Unknown to Father, Swami Kebalananda was an exalted disciple of Lahiri Mahasaya. The peerless guru had possessed thousands of disciples, silently drawn to him by the irresistibility of his divine magnetism. I learned later that Lahiri Mahasaya had often characterized Kebalananda as rishi or illumined sage.

Luxuriant curls framed my tutor's handsome face. His dark eyes were guileless, with the transparency of a child's. All the movements of his slight body were marked by a restful deliberation. Ever gentle and loving, he was firmly established in the infinite consciousness. Many of our happy hours together were spent in deep Kriya meditation.

Kebalananda was a noted authority on the ancient shastras or sacred books: his erudition had earned him the title of 'Shastri Mahasaya', by which he was usually addressed. But my progress in Sanskrit scholarship was unnoteworthy. I sought every opportunity to forsake prosaic grammar

---

43 I always addressed him as Ananta-da. 'Da' is a respectful suffix which the eldest brother in an Indian family receives from junior brothers and sisters.

44 At the time of our meeting, Kebalananda had not yet joined the Swami Order and was generally called 'Shastri Mahasaya'. To avoid confusion with the name of Lahiri Mahasaya and of Master Mahasaya, I am referring to my Sanskrit tutor only by his later monastic name of Swami Kebalananda. Born in the Khulna district of Bengal in 1863, Kebalananda gave up his body in Benares at the age of sixty-eight. His family name was Ashutosh Chatterji.

and to talk of yoga and Lahiri Mahasaya. My tutor obliged me one day by telling me something of his own life with the master.

'Rarely fortunate, I was able to remain near Lahiri Mahasaya for ten years. His Benares home was my nightly goal of pilgrimage. The guru was always present in a small front parlour on the first floor. As he sat in lotus posture on a backless wooden seat, his disciples garlanded him in a semicircle. His eyes sparkled and danced with the joy of the Divine. They were ever half closed, peering through the inner telescopic orb into a sphere of eternal bliss. He seldom spoke at length. Occasionally his gaze would focus on a student in need of help; healing words poured then like an avalanche of light.

'An indescribable peace blossomed within me at the master's glance. I was permeated with his fragrance, as though from a lotus of infinity. To be with him, even without exchanging a word for days, was experience which changed my entire being. If any invisible barrier rose in the path of my concentration, I would meditate at the guru's feet. There the most tenuous states came easily within my grasp. Such perceptions eluded me in the presence of lesser teachers. The master was a living temple of God whose secret doors were open to all disciples through devotion.

'Lahiri Mahasaya was no bookish interpreter of the scriptures. Effortlessly he dipped into the "divine library". Foam of words and spray of thoughts gushed from the fountain of his omniscience. He had the wondrous clavis which unlocked the profound philosophical science embedded ages ago in the Vedas.[45] If asked to explain the different planes of consciousness mentioned in the ancient texts, he would smilingly assent.

---

45 The ancient four Vedas comprise over 100 extant canonical books. Emerson paid the following tribute in his *Journal* to Vedic thought: 'It is sublime as heat and night and a breathless ocean. It contains every religious sentiment, all the grand ethics which visit in turn each noble poetic mind ... It is of no use to put away the book; if I trust myself in the woods or in a boat upon the pond, Nature makes a Brahmin of me presently: eternal necessity, eternal compensation, unfathomable power, unbroken silence ... This is her creed. Peace, she saith to me, and purity and absolute abandonment—these panaceas expiate all sin and bring you to the beatitude of the Eight Gods.'

'"I will undergo those states, and presently tell you what I perceive." He was thus diametrically unlike the teachers who commit scripture to memory and then give forth unrealized abstractions.

'"Please expound the holy stanzas as the meaning occurs to you." The taciturn guru often gave this instruction to a near-by disciple. "I will guide your thoughts, that the right interpretation be uttered." In this way, many of Lahiri Mahasaya's perceptions came to be recorded, with voluminous commentaries by various students.

'The master never counselled slavish belief. "Words are only shells," he said. "Win conviction of God's presence through your own joyous contact in meditation."

'No matter what the disciple's problem, the guru advised Kriya Yoga for its solution.

'"The yogic key will not lose its efficiency when I am no longer present in the body to guide you. This technique cannot be bound, filed, and forgotten, in the manner of theoretical inspirations. Continue ceaselessly on your path to liberation through Kriya, whose power lies in practice."

'I myself consider Kriya the most effective device of salvation through self-effort ever to be evolved in man's search for the Infinite.' Kebalananda concluded with this earnest testimony. 'Through its use, the omnipotent God, hidden in all men, became visibly incarnated in the flesh of Lahiri Mahasaya and a number of his disciples.'

A Christ-like miracle by Lahiri Mahasaya took place in Kebalananda's presence. My saintly tutor recounted the story one day, his eyes remote from the Sanskrit texts before us.

'A blind disciple, Ramu, aroused my active pity. Should he have no light in his eyes, when he faithfully served our master, in whom the Divine was fully blazing? One morning I sought to speak to Ramu, but he sat for patient hours fanning the guru with a handmade palm-leaf punkha. When the devotee finally left the room, I followed him.

'"Ramu, how long have you been blind?"

'"From my birth, sir! Never have my eyes been blessed with a glimpse of the sun."

'"Our omnipotent guru can help you. Please make a supplication."

'The following day Ramu diffidently approached Lahiri Mahasaya. The disciple felt almost ashamed to ask that physical wealth be added to his spiritual superabundance.

'"Master, the Illuminator of the cosmos is in you. I pray you to bring His light into my eyes, that I perceive the sun's lesser glow."

'"Ramu, someone has connived to put me in a difficult position. I have no healing power."

'"Sir, the Infinite One within you can certainly heal."

'"That is indeed different, Ramu. God's limit is nowhere! He who ignites the stars and the cells of flesh with mysterious life-effulgence can surely bring luster of vision into your eyes."

'The master touched Ramu's forehead at the point between the eyebrows.[46]

'"Keep your mind concentrated there, and frequently chant the name of the Prophet Rama[47] for seven days. The splendour of the sun shall have a special dawn for you."

'Lo! in one week it was so. For the first time, Ramu beheld the fair face of nature. The Omniscient One had unerringly directed his disciple to repeat the name of Rama, adored by him above all other saints. Ramu's faith was the devotionally ploughed soil in which the guru's powerful seed of permanent healing sprouted.' Kebalananda was silent for a moment, then paid a further tribute to his guru.

'It was evident in all miracles performed by Lahiri Mahasaya that he never allowed the ego-principle[48] to consider itself a causative force. By perfection of resistless surrender, the master enabled the Prime Healing Power to flow freely through him.

'The numerous bodies which were spectacularly healed through Lahiri Mahasaya eventually had to feed the flames of cremation. But the silent

46 The seat of the 'single' or spiritual eye. At death the consciousness of man is usually drawn to this holy spot, accounting for the upraised eyes found in the dead.

47 The central sacred figure of the Sanskrit epic, the Ramayana.

48 Ahankara, egoism; literally, 'I do'. The root cause of dualism or illusion of maya, whereby the subject (ego) appears as object; the creatures imagine themselves to be creators.

spiritual awakenings he effected, the Christ-like disciples he fashioned, are his imperishable miracles.'

I never became a Sanskrit scholar; Kebalananda taught me a diviner syntax.

The extraordinary travels, quests and inner journeys of the enigmatic scholar Rahul Sankrityayan are presented to us in this essay by author, curator, columnist and former civil servant Sujata Prasad. Sankrityayan was a writer and polyglot who wrote in his mother tongue, Hindi. Born in 1893, he spent more than forty-five years in relentless travel. He died in Darjeeling in 1963, leaving behind a legacy that is difficult to comprehend or encompass. Honoured as Mahapandit (Great Scholar) Rahul Sankrityayan, he is said to have known almost thirty languages and could read, write and converse in more than a dozen of them, including English, French, German, Russian, Tamil, Tibetan, Sanskrit, Pali, Urdu, Persian, Arabic and Hindi.

Sujata Prasad's evocative essay documents his four trips to Tibet, bringing to life his all-pervading devotion to knowledge and his commitment to its preservation and transmission.

CHAPTER 10

Rahul Sankrityayan's Tibet Story

SUJATA PRASAD

From studying Brahmanical canons and classical Vedantic learning to Arya Samaj, Buddhism and Marxism, Indian scholar Rahul Sankrityayan (1893–1963) was the quintessential sceptic and seeker. He turned 'onism'[49]—the angst and frustration of being stuck in one body that inhabits only one place at a time—on its head by constantly moving from place to place and from one area of knowledge to another, haunted by the road not taken, by places not mapped, by ideas that remained unexplored. He rationalized his obsessive urge to travel in a treatise for footloose wanderers titled *Ghumakkad Shastra*, (loosely translated as *Wanderer's Scriptures*).

In his memoir, Sankrityayan traces the genesis of his constant need to move to an Urdu couplet that caught his imagination in primary school:

> *Sair kar duniya ki gafil, zindagani phir kahan*
> *Zindagi gar kuchh rahi to naujavani phir kahan*
> (Wander the world, oh thoughtless one, how long will life last?
> Even if life remains, how long will youth last?)

Sankrityayan journeyed through Europe, Japan, China, Korea, Manchuria, Iran, Nepal, Sri Lanka, Afghanistan and Russia, crossing Siberia on the Trans-Siberian railway, and of course the Himalaya.

However, none of these voyages rivalled the combined experience of his four trips to Tibet, the forbidden land, closed to outsiders in the 1920s. It is a story of exceptional strength, resilience and determination. In his travelogues, he confesses that it was difficult to think of another journey as demanding and singular as these.

The trips were not random. Sankrityayan was at that point living the Gandhian dream, immersed in the impassioned tumult of the freedom movement. During this time he was imprisoned in 1922 and then again in 1924. While he was incarcerated, he read a smuggled copy of Leon Trotsky's

---

49 John Koenig's *Dictionary of Obscure Sorrows*.

Bolshevism and World Peace, composed verses in Brajbhasha, worked on the Sanskrit translation of the Quran, learnt trigonometry and wrote his first novel, *Baisvin Sadi*. His tryst with Buddhism also began during his jail term. He taught himself Pali and managed to read the entire Pali text of *Majjhim Nikaya*, the Buddha's middle-length discourses.

Sankrityayan's interest in Buddhism deepened as he travelled to Ladakh in 1926. He met Ras-Pa, a lama at the Hemis monastery, and spent time studying Buddhist texts at the Rizong monastery. He also attempted to travel to western Tibet, taking a route traversed by nomads that was considered dangerous and vulnerable to crime, with only a young Tibetan dog as his companion. The dog died midway, leaving him completely distraught. His memoir takes on a ruminative, poetic tone in the eight Sanskrit shlokas he wrote as an elegy to his companion.

Spurred by the desire to study the Pali Tripitakas under the guidance of renowned scholars, Sankrityayan joined Vidyalankar Parivena, a renowned Buddhist monastic school in Sri Lanka in 1927, where he finally found what he had been searching for:

> When I came upon the Buddha's exhortation: 'do not believe by deference to some book or tradition or to your elders; always decide upon belief by your own examination, and then stand firm', my heart suddenly exclaimed: here is the man whose faith in truth remain implacable, who understood independent intellect within humankind. And when, in the *Majjhim Nikaya*, I read 'the precepts of Dhamma that I have given to you are like a ferry boat…', I realized that what I had been searching for in all my wanderings had now been found.

Sankrityayan translated the *Digha Nikaya* and *Majjhim Nikaya* into Hindi, deepened his engagement with epigraphy and archaeology, and taught himself German and French to follow the work of eminent European Indologists and scholars such as Sylvan Levi, Aurel Stein, Rudolf Otto and Sergei Oldenburg. He dropped his original name, Ram Udar Das, and embraced the Buddhist name of Rahul Sankrityayan. He was conferred the title of Tripitakacharya, a rare honour, but his search was far from over. In a poignant essay on her father, Jaya Sankrityayan observed that the commentaries on original Sanskrit works that were lost when the universities of Odantapurui, Vikramshila and Nalanda were ravaged, piqued his interest. He was also aware that European expeditions to Central Asia and Tibet at the turn of the century had led to the rediscovery of some of the precious text.

The travelogue of European scholar Alexandra David-Néel, who sneaked into Tibet in the 1920s, inspired him, as did Ekai Kawaguchi's seminal 1909 book, *Three Years in Tibet*. The discovery of texts taken away and airbrushed from public consciousness, Sankrityayan felt, was vital for understanding the Indian-Buddhist heritage. He also longed to visit the ruins of the oldest mahavihara in Samye, Tibet, to pay homage to the relics of the renowned Nalanda scholar Santarakshita who, together with masters such as Dignaga and Dharmakirti, formed the Buddhist triumvirate. It was Santarakshita who had ordained the first seven Tibetan monks and strengthened the roots of Buddhism across the Himalaya.

The journey to Tibet, an idea that had been brewing in his mind for years finally took shape in 1929. As someone who was a recognized face of democratic dissent, Sankrityayan knew that he was a marked man and would have to travel incognito. It was not easy for him to enter Nepal, leave alone Tibet. He juggled the subtleties and oddities of assuming different religious personas, entering the Kathmandu valley disguised as a sadhu during the Shivratri celebrations in spring. Once there, he remained largely underground in the attic of a house near the Mahabaudha stupa, clothed in a threadbare chhupa (Tibetan gown). Sankrityayan's travel diaries, *Tibbat mein Sava Vars* and *Yatra ke Panne*, with their essayistic detours, describe his ordeal. Even though he wore a Tibetan dress and remained unshaven and bedraggled, he was petrified of being recognized as a plainsman.

He used Henderson's Tibetan manual to familiarize himself with the language and weighed his options carefully. The best bet seemed to be to use his rather tenuous contact with Dukpa Lama to get to Tibet as a member of his large entourage of monks. When this did not work, he took the help of Dharmaman Sahu, a wealthy Newar trader who had a home and office in Lhasa, and his friend Dasharatan Sahu, to put in place a credible and workable travel itinerary.

Sankrityayan tried to hoodwink the Nepal border police by pretending to be a mystic from Kinnaur. His initial journey was fraught with danger. He had to move cautiously, masquerading as a beggar before potential marauders and predators. A fortuitous meeting with Lobsang Sherab, a taciturn lama he had befriended in Bodh Gaya, radically altered the situation. The lama helped him get an authentic permit to cross into Tibet. They travelled together for three months, navigating the ragged terrain, crossing the icy water of the Kosi river, often taking rest in flea-infested stables, sustaining themselves on a frugal diet of sattu and tea. They reached the important milestones of Narthang, Tashi Lhumpo Gumba and Shigarche, crossing the Jarala Pass and reaching extremely remote areas such as Nagache largely on foot. Their journey ended on 19 July when they spotted the wondrous golden roof of the Dzong fortress of Potala.

One of Sankrityayan's immediate tasks was to reveal his presence to the Thirteenth Dalai Lama and seek his permission to study in the ancient gumbas of Sera and Drepung, where thousands of monks lived in dormitories made for Buddhist devotees from across the world. He spent months in Lhasa, trekking to nearby monasteries, often through frigid darkness. The city spread itself open to him. He absorbed the magic that nested in the quotidian details of its social fabric and enjoyed the fine aesthetic sense embedded deep in the country's DNA. His presence no longer sparked a flurry of speculation. Through his connections, he was able to source prodigious amounts of rare texts and Thangka paintings. Most of these texts were hand-lettered Tibetan manuscripts or printed woodblocks. A few were written with gold and silver powder. In addition to the spiritual canon, there were texts on philosophy, history, art, astronomy, medicine and other subjects.. He also travelled to Samye, a two-day journey from Lhasa, to keep his date with the remains of the Himalayan master Santarakshita.

When Sankrityayan began his return journey to Kalimpong, he had to hire twenty-two mules to ferry manuscripts, paintings, and rare antiquities acquired during his stay.

Sankrityayan's second voyage to Tibet in 1934 was preceded by his ordainment as a bhikkhu in 1930. This, along with his fame as a scholar of the Tripitakas, the holy canon of the Theravada school of Buddhism, carried considerable weight with Tibetan monks, who unlocked the vaults of their monasteries. He threw all his time, energy and passion into his search for original palm-leaf manuscripts. His command over the languages used in the Buddhist canon helped in the quick assessment of their importance. These manuscripts had been taken from India to Tibet in the seventh century and from the ninth to thirteenth centuries. A serious study of these texts had the potential to not only open up new dimensions of Buddhist religion and philosophy, but also the Brahmanical and Jain traditions.

First, Sankrityayan set about searching for the Sanskrit manuscript of Dharmakirti's *Pramanavarttika*, considered the greatest Indian work on logic. He was aware that several European scholars were also interested in this rare manuscript. He managed to find only a fragmentary commentary on the text, but discovered forty volumes of other precious manuscripts. Sankrityayan used his Rolex camera to photograph them. He also copied many of them by hand, working at feverish pitch, sometimes for up to eighteen hours a day. Among the most poignant anecdotes in his travelogue *Yatra Ke Panne* is the recollection of a freezing winter day in Lhasa, when the ink in the inkwell froze, and another in Saskya when, while copying Asanga's *Yogacharbhumi*, his hands and fingers were so chilled that a brazier had to be kept lit to keep them moving.

There was an occasional windfall, as he notes delightedly in his book, 'Someone came all the way to Gyantse to sell a copy of the *Pragyaparamita* written in gold letters.' The Dalai Lama also sent him several rare volumes carefully wrapped in yellow brocade covers.

Sankrityayan's hunt for *Pramanavarttika* continued. He was told that Nepal's royal priest, Mahapandita Hemraj, possessed a copy, so he returned to India via Nepal to see if could borrow it. He managed to obtain it but was heartbroken when he discovered that it had a few pages missing. During his third and fourth trips to Tibet in 1936 and 1938 respectively, time seemed short and urgent. His travelogue, reminiscent, evocative and sharply alive to social cadences and cultural nuances unspools slowly, illuminating several significant moments of his Himalayan sojourn. He continued to remain hostage to the past, spending hours and hours in a time warp, photographing and copying manuscripts found in the monasteries of Saskya, Ngor and Shalu. The caches of manuscripts he copied included important works of philosophers and masters such as Nagarjuna, Asanga, Vasubandhu, Bhavya, Dharmakirti, Jnanasri, Ratnakar Sjanti, and Durvek Mishra. Finally, he managed to find the complete manuscript of the elusive *Pramanavarttika*.

Sankrityayan's friendship with Gendum Choephel, one of the most outstanding scholars and poets of twentieth-century Tibet, was legion. They were both inveterate travellers and sceptics, hardwired for uncertainty and seeking out the unfamiliar. They met in 1934 in Lhasa during Sankrityayan's second trip to Tibet. Choephel joined Sankrityayan's search for commentaries on the *Pramanavarttika*, and shared his excitement in discovering many more original Sanskrit palm-leaf manuscripts of lost Buddhist texts. They travelled across Tibet to monastic centres in Saskya, Pyokhang, Ngor, Shalu, Riphug, Narthang, Tsang Thupten and Zalu. Their journey through central Tibet in 1934 and 1938 was an odyssey, with moments of pain, privation and companionship. Choephel was in India from 1938 to 1946, visiting different parts of the country, spending time in old libraries and brothels, writing and sketching. He read a good deal of classical Sanskrit text, translating them into the Tibetan, including the *Kamasutra*. He also found common cause with the politics of the Tibetan Revolutionary Party, founded by a fiery group of exiled Tibetans. His return to Lhasa was fraught with dramatic moments. Accused of insurrection, he was incarcerated and died shortly after the occupation of Lhasa by the Chinese army in 1950.

Much like his friend, Sankrityayan acquired a revolutionary fervour in the 1930s. He translated the Communist Manifesto, was for a while closely associated with the Congress Socialist Party, and in 1938, became a prominent face of the peasants' movement and the Communist Party of Bihar. He was arrested in a crackdown on communists and spent two years in Hazaribagh jail and the Deoli Internment Camp. His monumental work *Darshan–Digdarshan*, a Marxist exposition on Greek, Islamic, European and Indian philosophy, was written during this period as was another masterpiece, *Volga se Ganga Tak*, stretching through 8,000 years of history.

Even though his politics was grounded in Marxism, he continued to be entranced by Buddhism and saw no contradiction between Marxism and the teachings of the Buddha. He kept travelling through the Himalaya and lived a major part of his last few years in Mussoorie and Darjeeling. His obsessive longing for Tibet had to be put on hold when he was completely debilitated after a couple of strokes. Tibetans continue to remember him as a man who in the words of K.P. Jayaswal, resembled the Buddha and, absorbed in scholarly pursuits, was universal in his outlook.

References

Sankrityayan, Rahul. *Tibbat Mēin Savā Varṣ*. New Delhi: Sharada Mandir, 1990.

Sankrityayan, Rahul. *Yātrā Ke Panne*. New Delhi: Bharatiya Prakashan Sansthan, 1995.

Sankrityayan, Rahul, *Merī Jīvan Yātrā*. Allahabad: Kitab Mahal, 1994.

Sankrityayan, Jaya. 'Rahul Sankrityayan: Mahapandit', Catalogue of Exhibition on Rahul Sankrityayan's Antiquities Collection organized by the Indira Gandhi National Centre for the Arts, New Delhi, 2018.

Jayaswal, K.P. 'Lost Sanskrit Works Recovered from Tibet', In *Selected Essays of Rahul Sankrityayan* (By Rahul Sankrityayan), pp. ix–xix. New Delhi: People's Publishing House, 1984.

Machwe, P. *Rahul Sankrityayan*. New Delhi: Sahitya Akademi, 1984.

Gerke, B. 'Rahulji's Quest for Tibet.' (Paper presented at the international seminar on the life and works of Rahul Sankrityayan at the University of St. Petersburg, Russia, October/November), 1995.

Chowdhory, H.B. ed. *Mahapandit Rahula Sankrityayana Birth Centenary Volume*. Calcutta: Buddha Dharmankur Sabha, 1994.

Chudal, A.A. 'A Freethinking Cultural Nationalist: Rahul Sankrityayan's Narrated Self in the Context of His Age'. PhD thesis, University of Vienna, 1994.

—

Romola Butalia's quest to search for and honour the adepts whose presence live on in the Himalaya is recorded in her books, which include In The Presence of the Masters *and* Sri Babaji: Immortal Yogi of the Himalayas.

In this intense and perceptive essay, 'Siddha Traditions: Dhuni and Chimta', she takes us on an experiential journey through the secretive rituals and meditative practices of the sages of the Siddha traditions. We learn of Haidakhan Baba, of Gorakh Baba and of the transformative role of the chimta and the dhuni in the custody of the knowledge holders of these ancient and sacred traditions. She talks about the sadhus and ascetics she has encountered, immersed in their meditative practice, and of the mysterious figure of Sri Haidakhan Baba, first written about by Paramhansa Yogananda in Autobiography of a Yogi.

Butalia's profound piece concludes with her walking away, as 'the invisible doors of siddhalok shut silently' behind her.

CHAPTER 11

Siddha Traditions

Dhuni and Chimta

ROMOLA BUTALIA

In the Uttarakhand Himalaya, the power of Sri Haidakhandi Babaji's dhuni and chimta are legendary.

In the nineteenth century at Nainital, an early encounter between Babaji and Commissioner of Kumaon, Sir Henry Ramsay, led to a close relationship between them. Ramsay was going to court on horseback along the cold narrow Thandi Sarak, alongside the lake. Near Pashan Devi temple, Babaji, who was sitting by the road, clicked the chimta clasped in his right hand. Distracted by the sound, Ramsay's horse reared suddenly. Annoyed, Ramsay had Babaji escorted to the local police station, where he was kept behind bars. A little later, riding further down the road, Ramsay saw Babaji ahead. Babaji clicked his chimta again. Ramsay is said to have headed straight to the police station to see why his orders had not been obeyed. He found Babaji in the lock-up, looking guilelessly at him.

Sri Haidakhandi Babaji and Sri Sombari Babaji, often seen together in the late nineteenth and early twentieth centuries, were household names in the Kumaon Himalaya. Many of the dhunis or sacred fire pits and gufas or caves, where they had done tapasya, spending time in austere asceticism, are still maintained in worship.

Most often, spiritual conversations of great depth have taken place beside a dhuni. There are different kinds of dhunis, related to rishi-munis, yogis and siddhas, knowledge holders and sanyasins or renunciates. Many dhunis, that have been used by a mystic, remain as akhanda dhunis, where continual worship is maintained. Several are now temples keeping adherence to the strict traditions associated with that particular dhuni. Throughout the Himalaya there are many siddha dhunis, and the local population is deeply aware of their power and energy.

> *Chakmak chimta dhuni pani*
> *Sab rakhiyo sath siddho ke bani…*
> (The gleaming tongs, the sacred fire and waters, remember the words of the siddhas)

For sanyasins, a dhuni is of vital and fundamental importance. It is protective, nurturing and the source of knowledge. A dhuni is the symbol of dhyana and gyana, or meditation and knowledge. In the Himalaya, and at all ancient places of siddha tapasya, the dhuni holds the key to sacred mystical knowledge. Both adept and practitioner alike, approach the dhuni with the deepest respect. Through this medium, rishis and siddhas have always revealed siddha vidya or mystic knowledge and practice. The dhuni is revered as the nirakar swaroop or formless form of the Absolute. Through it, the siddha gurus have taken this parampara or tradition ahead.

> *Bina dhuni dhyan nahin…*
> (Without dhuni there is no meditation)

Some of the well-known dhuni temples in the Uttarakhand Himalaya are those of Goljyu Deva, Harijyu Deva, Shyamnath, Siddhanath and the Narasimha avatar of Lord Vishnu. There are many dhunis in the names of rishis, like the Saptarishi dhuni, as well as Sri Dattatreya and Sri Gorakhnath's akhanda dhunis. Also, there are Katyuri dhunis in honour of the Katyuri dynasty that once ruled here. In Uttarakhand, householders also practice dhuni seva, maintaining tapasya and anushthan, or performance of austerities and ritual worship at the dhuni for a period of time, during which they maintain no connection with their homes.

The chimta is a divya astra or divine weapon of siddhas, which is believed to have been bestowed by the grace of the Alakh Purush, Lord Shiva, and through the siddhas to the yogis in the siddha lineage. The chimta in the hands of a knowledge-holder of these ancient traditions is the symbol of knowledge and wisdom, of transcending the tattwas or five elements of Earth, Water, Fire, Air and Space. The shakti or power of a chimta is energized through anusthan. It is a symbol of glory, like a crown associated with the glory of a king. A chimta should only be in the hands of a gyani, or one with the knowledge that it represents, as a crown befits a worthy king.

In a sacred dhuni the trishul or trident, and the chimta are ever present. The sanyasins of different traditions receive the chimta, along with the sacred mantra that holds its power, as a blessing. Within it remains the shakti or power of the spiritual wisdom associated with it, and it becomes the infinite source through which this knowledge and wisdom continues to flow.

Lohe ka chimta, Satguru ka gyan...
(The chimta of iron, the knowledge of Truth)

The two aspects of the chimta are Shiva and Shakti, with the pivotal ring as mahamaya, representing the Alakh Purush, symbolic of The One. Sri Gorakshanath is believed to have received this divine weapon from Lord Shiva himself, a weapon that had the power to create other divya astras. The trishul and chimta of Guru Dattatreya, Sri Matsyendranath and other saints, retain the shakti of these divine symbols received as boons from the Alakh Purush, with which all creation can be awakened.

Kailash parvat se Yogeshwar aaya
Alakh Purush se chimta paya...
(Yogeshwar Lord Shiva came from Mount Kailash
From Him was the chimta received)

Chimta Vidya or this sacred knowledge is maintained with utmost sanctity and secrecy. Reading about the philosophy brings academic knowledge. The deserving sadhaka receives it with the initiated mantra, specific performance of ritual worship, and the strict and austere sadhana associated with it. Thus is the power of the chimta activated, else it is a mere plaything, like fake currency that has no intrinsic value. In the case of divine weapons that have been received as a boon, these are only received by a siddha to fulfil divine will.

Teen loka nau khand mein chimte ki maya,
Chimte se Guru Datta, Machhendra, Goraksha,
Naun Nath, Churasi Siddho ne
Sare srishti ko jagaya...

> (In the three realms and nine planes, Guru Dattatreya, Matsyendranath, Gorakshanath, the nine Naths and eighty-four Siddhas have awakened creation with the power of the chimta)

In current times, some wandering ascetics can still be seen carrying a trishul and chimta in respect for the renunciate's path. The dhuni is, however, losing its relevance, especially among those who have moved away from the ancient traditions and practices and resorted to a modern version of sanyas. With this change, those aware of the depths of knowledge and sadhana that go with dhunis are few and far between, and much ancient wisdom and the power inherent, have become seemingly extinct. In reality, though, this wisdom is still known and maintained in sacred, unrevealed form at siddha dhunis, through which spiritual wisdom is kept kindled and revealed from time to time.

At the turn of this century, I began tracing Sri Haidakhandi Babaji's footsteps to his tapasya sthals and oft-visited places.

I took the road past Padampuri, enjoying hours of listening to the reminiscences of yogis and aged Kumaonis who had known him in their childhood and early youth. Leaving the metalled road and crossing the footbridge at Padampuri, I heard the familiar resonance of the river below as it tumbled over boulders, changing direction on its way downstream. As I turned the corner, my eyes went to a burning pyre and a handful of people quietly completing the final rites of a departed one. Till today, births, weddings, deaths and all related sanskars are conducted without fanfare, with a solemn dignity, a touching reminder of the hardship of everyday living in devaloka, or land of the gods as Uttarakhand is known as, where traditionally man did not add flourishes to divine will.

Walking up the short bridle path, I found Swami Parmananda Puriji sitting outdoors in the sun on his woollen asana or blanket, placed on a handwoven chatai, or mat. I sat on the folded blanket on the stone slabs of the courtyard and warmed my hands on the stainless steel glass filled with strong sweet tea with the taste of ginger and fragrance of wood-smoke.

As Swami Parmanandaji talked of his life, he showed me his voter card. Born in Varanasi on 10 October 1889 in a Kashmiri family that had migrated many generations ago, his grandfather was a Bar-at-law at the High Court. He had spent his childhood in Assam, completing his school education at Shillong, Meghalaya, before studying medicine from Nil Ratan Sircar Medical College, Kolkata, at the time called Campbell Medical School. He served in the eastern sector as a physician, posted in Bengal and Assam.

In 1933 or '34, Swami Parmanandaji first met his guru, Swami Vishuddhananda Puriji, the proponent of Surya Vigyan or solar science. He was a renowned adept whose guru was from the mystical Gyanganj, a name that is invariably whispered in silent awe as a space beyond physical dimensions. In 1937, he took sanyas diksha, spending the next five to seven years in bhraman as a wandering mendicant, followed by two years in Rishikesh, some twelve years in sadhana in Vrindavan, and over six decades in this region of Kumaon.

Swami Parmanandaji also spoke of his darshan of Sri Haidakhandi Babaji in 1938 or '39. Babaji was last seen publicly around 1920, when he is said to have taken living samadhi after a visit to Askot. Yet there are accounts of his having met devotees briefly till around 1940. It is generally stated by yogis that these brief appearances in the physical body were through his yogic powers. The historical personality, Sri Haidakhandi Babaji, was commonly associated by yogis of this region, with the mystical personality first written about by Paramhansa Yogananda in *Autobiography of a Yogi*.

Swami Parmanandaji spoke of the late evening when Babaji had given darshan to him. He recalled how he had asked Babaji, 'How do you recognize a tattwagyani, one who has overcome the elements, and an atmagyani, one who knows the Self?'

Sri Haidakhandi Babaji had replied that there was no tol or balance by which such a person could be measured. However, there were some lakshans or indications. An atmagyani saw no dosh or fault in anyone and spoke no ill of anyone.

Swami Paramanandaji continued, 'What can I speak of the gross? I will talk the language of the spirit.' He spoke of the Nada Brahma or transcendental vibration, in which I had been deeply absorbed in the wee hours of that morning at the Paharpani Gufa, where I had spent several days in sadhana. In sandhya bhasha, the twilight language of yogis that transcends time and space and individual consciousness, Swami Parmanandaji easily took me to that Highest Truth.

Swamiji said, 'In spiritual life, for a seeker of the Truth, atmagyan or self-realization is through tattwa darshan or transcending the elements of earth, water, fire, air and space, of which our gross bodies are composed. A mantra and a saffron cloth is given to the seeker and he is shown the expected behaviour which will form the lifestyle of the path. With that, japa or recitation of the mantra begins. When the mantra becomes jagrat or awakened, the initiation into spiritual life happens. There are different processes through which this is done.

'On the Bhakti Marg or path of devotion, naam-japa is the fulcrum. Yogic techniques are the process of purification on the Yoga and Gyana Margs. Through this medium, Anahat Nada or the cosmic vibration that is within us and without, which is the very basis of life, is awakened. At the time of awakening of the Anahat Nada and of the Kundalini, the guidance of an adept is required. In such a state, the sadhaka or practitioner keeps hearing the Nada, sometimes as the reverberation of a shankha or conch, a ghanta or bell, and other mystical vibrations. The sadhaka cannot understand where the sound is from, and can become confused. His attention is directed inwards. Within the Anahata Chakra, at the heart centre, the sadhaka finally recognizes his ishta deva or personal deity.

'Within the chida akasha or space of undivided consciousness, the Nada is left behind, and jyoti, light, is awakened. The jyoti becomes prakash or the light of knowledge. Beyond the jyoti, the sukshma or subtle realms are awakened. One becomes aware of pitrloka and devaloka, the realms of the ancestors and celestial beings. After this comes atman darshan or self-realization. Within atman darshan, too, there are stages of realization.

When one realizes the veda vakya, Aham Brahmasmi, I Am Brahman, ahamkar of atman darshan still remains.

'After this stage one realizes Sarvam Khalvidam Brahman, All Is Brahman, there is nought but Brahman. When one is immersed in this state of consciousness, one becomes fully sacrificed, completely surrendered. This is the state of wisdom consciousness. One no longer performs any personal work, one works for the welfare of all.

'Many remain in the state of duality, enjoying the bliss of dvaita, the Bhagawat lila or divine play of existence, and do not enter into the ananda of Nirvikalpa. The sadhaka who remains immersed in the purnananda of Consciousness, the pure bliss of Existence, does not return. Yet, only if he returns is this process possible.'

A few years later, Swami Parmanandaji was staying with some sanyasins at Palara, in a recently built room beside the gufa where Sombari Babaji had done tapasya. I spent several days in a newly built kutia, a hut at the entrance of the gufa, with a dhuni between the gufa and kutia. Walking into the bowels of the earth, over perilous damp boulders, leads to a natural formation where worship of Devi is conducted and a diya is kept lit. Turning left and moving upwards into the deep dark recesses of the gufa leads eventually to the sunlight outside. The path back from outside is over several large rock formations, emerging near a Shiva temple, built recently by Swamiji. Near the exit of the gufa is an alcove, where many a yogi has stayed in tapasya.

A few kilometres further from Palara, which is now an active village, I spent an afternoon looking across the wide valley at the mountain known as Chhota Kailash. I have approached this sacred mountain from different directions. It is one of the many places where Sri Haidakhandi Babaji had spent considerable time in tapasya. From there, when he came to the village of Haidakhan, situated along the Gola riverbed where the mountains descend into the plains, villagers had asked what they should call him. He replied simply that they could call him after the place. Thereafter, he came to be known as Haidakhan or Haidakhandi Babaji.

The road from Palara ends at Pata. Here, the little-known Devi temple and dhuni are reputed to have immense shakti or power. Etched in my mind are days in the shade of Sombari Babaji's gufa, walking to different places where footsteps have not yet obliterated a time passed.

Travelling in a hired car in dire need of servicing, along badly neglected winding roads not on the tourist map at the time, between Champawat and Lohaghat, I stopped to walk the last kilometre to Maneshwar along a paved path in the midst of oak, birch and fir trees. I was visiting Swami Shivendra Puri, known as Thanapatiji.

The lingam at the Maneshwar temple is swayambhu or self-manifested, not established by anyone. It is believed that the tapasya of some ancient rishi caused the manifestation of the lingam as a blessing of Lord Shiva. The temple was built by the Chand Rajas of Champawat.

Near the entrance to the complex was Thanapatiji's hut. Scattered around are huts for visiting saints and practitioners. There is a naula or underground source of water which leads to a kund, a reservoir, beside the temple. This kund is much like Badrinath, except that the water is icy cold. Dipping a metal bucket with a rope attached to it into the kund, I filled it, carrying it to a small 'bathing room' some distance away. The cold water led to a hurried bath, after which I went to the temple to offer worship.

Behind the temple are the samadhis of the different sanyasins who have lived here, including the live samadhi of Siddha Baba Bhairav Giriji, the first in a long line to head this ashram. A live samadhi is when an adept voluntarily gives up the body to merge with Universal Consciousness. This is a known practice among yogis, and there are several instances of living samadhis.

It is a rare adept, a siddha yogi, who takes living samadhi to dissolve the body. There have been historical instances where the body was not found. It is said that in place of the mystic Kabir's body, flowers were found. A siddha who merges with Universal Consciousness can take a body, as and when required, through the manifestation of divine will. The legends regarding Sri Gorakhshanath appearing as a young lad from the compost pit, where the vibhuti or sacred ash given in blessing by Sri Matsyendranath was discarded, is a well-known instance.

To take jal-samadhi or him-samadhi, to merge the elements of the body into water or in the Himalayan snows, is the way of rare Himalayan yogis. It is believed that Sri Haidakhandi Babaji, in the tradition of rishis and siddhas, did that. He is regarded by many yogis of this area as the Cheeranjivi Ashwatthama, immortal of the Mahabharat.

Among the authoritative scriptures, the Vishnu Purana states that Ashwatthama will be responsible for recording spiritual history and codifying the Srutis or revealed knowledge in the next Mahayuga, or period of four eras comprising the Satya, Treta, Dwapar and Kali Yugas. Ashwatthama will also be among the saptarishis responsible for evolution of human consciousness in the eighth, Savarni Manvantar, after the current Vaivaswat Manvantar of seventy-one Mahayugas.

The rishis have taken form throughout recorded Puranic history, and their names and lives are known. But siddhas are those supreme yogis about whom almost nothing is ever known. The mind cannot easily grasp their time frames, or context. In their presence, the limitations of possible and impossible disappear.

Sri Haidakhandi Babaji was a visitor at Maneshwar during the time of Siddha Baba Bhairav Giriji. It is said that he probably visited before and after as well. Since the time of Siddha Babaji, the priests of the temple at Maneshwar have been sanyasins. Thanapatiji lived in Siddha Babaji's mud-plastered hut, which was cleansed daily with gobar-mitti or cowdung-earth. It was a traditional sage's hut: austere, with the chief features being the ancient dhuni and an area of worship. A faint fragrance of dhoop or incense wafted occasionally from Thanapatiji's dhuni.

Thanapatiji had received darshan of Sri Haidakhandi Babaji in his childhood, in his ancestral village near Gangolihat. I wanted to know more about Babaji. There were only a handful of people remaining who had met him.

The difference between talking about Sri Haidakhandi Babaji to a sanyasin and to others, is that the sanyasin focuses on the wisdom he gained from the meeting, whereas others talk of miracles. Babaji's simplicity is well acclaimed. Once, while visiting a poor devotee, Babaji asked him whether he had completed the home he had intended to build for himself. The devotee said that since he was alone and didn't have the money to pay for the labour, he had been unable to build it. Babaji stayed on to carry slabs of stones and help his devotee build his home.

Thanapatiji said that two things stood out about Babaji. One was his attitude of 'mein hi mein'—absorbed in the Self, and the other was 'mein aur tu mein bhed nahin'—no difference between you and me. When he spoke, he did not try to create a sense of satisfaction in the other, but only expressed the gyana or wisdom of his being.

'Today, sadhus speak words that are pleasing to hear, catering to the audience they address; true saints only speak the Truth,' said Thanapatiji.

About Sri Haidakhandi Babaji, he said, 'He never saw any negative in anyone, he never saw the faults and blemishes. From him I learnt that God does not look at our paap and aparadh, or sins of omission and commission. We should not think "I have sinned" and remain in that negative. We should focus on how we can repair the damage done, how we can change our behaviour. We should atone for it through positive action, through remembering the name of God. When we remember our sins, which we will from time to time, we should replace the thought with that which will atone for the sin. "*Punya ke samne paap nahin rehta*—in the face of virtue, vice no longer remains."'

Thanapatiji further added, 'A human weakness that most of us suffer from is our need for appreciation, for status, for respect by the other. Sri Haidakhandi Babaji never had this trait. He respected the other so completely that there were occasions when he took the blame for something that was done by another, so that the other would not lose face. He believed that in respecting another, Narayan or the Lord Himself was being respected.' Saying this, Thanapatiji's voice broke and his eyes filled with tears. He said, 'I cannot speak of him or think of him without feeling great emotion. What a blessing it was to meet him as a child. If only I had known and understood the greatness of his being then.'

Many decades ago, on the walking trail to Pindari Glacier, at the village of Khati, 20 kilometres from the roadhead, several yogis had camped for the night. In a barren, gobar-mitti or mud-and-dung plastered room, by the light of a wood fire which took away the bitterness of the cold, I spent a long evening in conversation with two tapaswi yogis. Both of them were breaking the day's fast with a frugal phalahari or fruit-based meal, which they shared with me.

They confirmed my deep-rooted conviction that I would not have a guru or single spiritual teacher. Both said, 'Let life be your teacher, learn from everyone you meet.' Twelve years later, meeting them again, one yogi taught me some kriyas or practices as an effective way to detach from the external world. He said, 'You are not the body and you are not the mind. You are the Self beyond. Dive within yourself. Meditate and go into the darkness, expecting nothing. You will recognize yourself.'

The other yogi introduced me to the siddha marg through the dhuni and related tapasya. I asked him directly, 'Who are you?' He laughed and said, 'How can I tell you who I am? I cannot see my own face. We recognize ourselves when we see ourselves in a polished mirror. We live in different realms at different times. Who we are is a factor of time.'

Having done sadhana according to different mystical traditions, in my experience, knowledge is given wholeheartedly to the sincere aspirant, according to their yogyata or readiness to receive it.

In bhraman or spiritual wandering, I have done dhuni sadhana at innumerable places. Dhunis at which I have done considerable sadhana are in and near the Gabori Gufa at Paharpani, at Gethia in the Kumaon Himalaya, as well as at Vrindavan.

There are other places where I have lived in sadhana and met many great yogis and siddhas, in realms beyond the dimensions of the world. Each has been a treasured experience. What remains of them is the experience itself, integrated into a timeless knowing.

At the Kumbha, dhunis are maintained with strict adherence to the guru parampara. Not everyone has dhuni-adhikar, so when sanyasins come to the Kumbha, only one who has dhuni-vidya will maintain a dhuni. At places of public meeting, they will not have a dhuni unless they are versed in the practice and given the traditional protection and blessings that are associated with the teachings in the specific tradition. Having maintained a dhuni in the Akhada-kshetra for the entire period of the different Kumbhas at Ujjain, Haridwar and Prayagraj, practising austerities, like maintaining phalahari fast, through the entire period of forty days to three months, I have since continued to maintain a dhuni in the Kumaon Himalaya, where I live.

When I first visited Siddhashram, near Sitlakhet, with Sri Gorakh Babaji, he left, blessing me thus, 'May you have darshan of Sri Babaji.' I spent several days there, in solitude and meditation, staying in the main kutia, cooking a rudimentary meal in the adjoining kitchen. I had to cross the courtyard and traverse a considerable distance to a rustic toilet. I would carry water from a water source below the kutia some 100 metres away to have a cold water bath in a basic room with an outlet from where the waste water led into the fields below. I walked 3 kilometres through forested paths to get provisions and vegetables.

Sri Haidakhandi Babaji's kutia and dhuni no longer exist. The stone temple built by him has changed somewhat. Looking up at the original stonework of the temple, I was deeply aware of the energized space and the shakti of this siddha-sthan. I could envision the simple temple Sri Haidakhandi Babaji must have built to invoke the sacred energies. The vibrations here remain potent and palpable, despite the unfortunate attempts to modernize the temple, as is the trend with most old temples now.

The yagya kund in the stone courtyard outside the temple retains the power of the space, especially when the aahutis or offerings are made to Agni, the eternal witness, which receives the offerings of solids and liquids, and conveys them to space through the winds. The fragrance of ghee and samagri, offered into the fire, quickly sweeps through, seemingly reaching the Syahi Devi temple a couple of thousand feet above. The skies above are an unending blue. Where the eye wanders, there are wildflowers, native plants and overgrown beds of dahlias and gladioli scattered in disarray.

At Siddhashram, I was deeply aware of siddhalok. There was a wonder and joy of eternity that was ever present during the time I spent there alone. The days were spent in an entirely different realm of timelessness, of perfection, of infinite possibilities.

Sri Haidakhandi Babaji was a living presence at Siddhashram, more tangible and more real than flesh and blood. His presence was everywhere, within and without. I was in perfect tune with siddhalok, where all things are not only possible, but all thoughts are a reflection of what already is and what will be. The mind was so perfectly still that the smallest vibration could be traced back to aeons of living, and the ringing peals of an ever-widening circle could be heard till they faded into total silence. I could only hear the cosmic sound of being.

At nearby Sitlakhet, I had sat looking at the carefully preserved handwritten notes of Siromani Pathak, in mixed Kumaoni and Hindi in a school notebook, wrapped in a cloth. His son handed it to me to leaf through, and his grandson then read it out. It brought alive the magic of a lost time, of how Siddhashram came to be. The players had all left the stage. The answers to the present lie in the causes of the past, just as today we write our future in indelible ink. He who knows the cause no longer grieves, he is no longer bound to the chain of time. He can enjoy the lila, for that is all it is. Sri Haidakhandi Babaji reiterated through the yellowed pages of Siromani Pathak's writing, 'Ultimately, the victory is of Truth.'

I have returned to Siddhashram with different people at different times, watched the flames leap up as I worshipped at the yagya kund. Each time, I have returned briefly to that ever-present eternity, the doorway of which exists through many spaces in the Himalaya and elsewhere. Such a state of perfection lived in total awareness is by the grace of those beings who belong to that realm.

On Janamashthami, Sri Gorakh Babaji arrived at Siddhashram, and we celebrated the festival by maintaining a fast and offering aahutis or sacred offerings into the fire. Babaji was clad in a saffron cloth wrapped around the waist and another similar cloth carelessly draped like a shawl; the pujari who maintained morning and evening worship at the temple was in a well-worn white cotton dhoti-kurta; and I in an unbleached kora sari.

Who knows where the mantras and the invocations reached as they wafted through the stillness of the crystal clear air, a fragrance of deodar, oak and pine intermingled with ghee or clarified butter and samagri of sesame seeds, Himalayan millet, rice, dried fruits, Himalayan herbs and incenses.

When it was time to leave Siddhashram, I awoke pre-dawn, at Brahmamuhurta, to meditate. Through the small wooden window that I had kept ajar, I observed the stars fade in the inky sky as the dawn broke gradually, gently, and filled the tiny room with a suffused light. I went for an early morning walk along the forested paths, hearing the continuous call of the barbet and the fluttering wings of the magpie on its morning flight between perches; feeling the dampness of the misty dawn against my skin and watching the speckled dew on the ferns and grasses; hearing a pine cone fall to the ground on pine needles strewn below with a gentle rustle; seeing the light shimmering on a giant cobweb; aware of the cacophony of insects and the gently slanting dappled light through the foliage.

Returning, I quickly washed and cut the vegetables and kneaded dough. The priest knocked early at the kitchen door, suggesting that he cook the vegetables and make rotis while I prepared to leave. I slipped outdoors and quickly went to all the places grown familiar, as though I was leaving home. Sitting on a gunny sack in the veranda, now bathed in sunlight, stainless steel thali and glass in front of me, I sprinkled water cupped in the palm of my hand, invoked with mantras, and ate the prasad. I bid farewell to the pujari and his school-going son, whom I used to teach for an hour in the afternoons during my stay there, and who had now come with his father to say goodbye. I ran for a final thanksgiving to the temple and yagya kund. At the gate, I lightly touched the stone plaque that I had noticed when I first entered, with Siddhashram engraved on it. The winding roads were calling.

As I walked away, the invisible doors of siddhalok shut silently behind me again.

—

Madhu Tandan lived in the remote and idyllic Mirtola ashram in Uttarakhand for many long years before she returned to the world to write Faith and Fire: A Way Within. *She was twenty-six when she and her husband Rajeev left their settled daily existence in New Delhi to seek an alternative lifestyle and search for meaning amidst the chaos of living. Here, she shares an essay on their journey of faith.*

Their guru, Sri Madhav Ashish, (1920–1997), Ashishda to his devotees, was born Alexander Phipps in Edinburgh and posted in India as an aeronautical engineer during World War II. His travels led him to Ramana Maharshi and then to his guru, Sri Krishna Prem—also an Englishman and, by a karmic quirk of faith, himself once a fighter pilot in World War I.

Her piece explores the unique relationship between the guru and the devotee in Hindu thought and practice. She records the learnings, unlearnings and Awakenings on the thorny path of self-realization. 'Gradually, the old voices, which had not been silenced by my shift to the ashram, raised their head again—voices affirming personal identity. Juxtaposed against this were values from the Ashram where you try and self-remember, be watchful of yourself, still the mind and go beyond. In time I realized that the old voices need not be trampled underfoot but transformed.'

CHAPTER 12

Letting Go

MADHU TANDAN

The jeep was loaded. Just the wood-fired stove to be put in.

'I can't say we've done the right thing, but we'll share each step of the way,' Rajeev said as we covered the first mile of the journey. The soft January morning mist blurred the windscreen. I wanted desperately to look past the blur, wishing that the present would become transparent enough to show us the future. The swishing of the wipers echoed my father's words.

'Isn't this rather sudden?' he had said, putting down his newspaper. 'After five years, Rajeev has finally got his business on the rails.'

'He is pulling out, I'm quitting my job; we're leaving this house and selling most of our stuff,' I'd replied.

'To go as a visitor to the Ashram is one thing, to live there is another matter,' my mother had said gently.

Ashishda, our guru, had said very little and yet expressed everything as a prelude to what was, for us, a monumental decision to live in his Ashram in Mirtola in the Kumaon hills. 'Simplify the entire paraphernalia of living. Come with only the bare essentials. The important thing is the inner attitude, for you can't reduce the outer luggage without inwardly being prepared to do so. Remember, the Latin word for luggage is "impedimenta",' he had advised, coalescing his upper-class English upbringing with thirty-five years spent as a sadhu in India.

'You are barely twenty-six, far too young,' my father had continued. 'A remote wilderness, miles from the nearest town, no radio, no telephone, no television, no marketplace, no social life ... just ... an idea in your head. You don't know the reality of it!'

Reality. That's what I want to confront head-on, Dad! No philosophical wrangles, no second-hand versions, but a discovery reached through my own experience. This day-to-day reality we live in couldn't possibly be what life was all about. An incomplete poem, a knotted handkerchief as a reminder of a forgotten promise, age hardened by habit and marks on a page where the ink ran out ... There must be more to it.

This vague questioning had gradually found a focus through Ashishda, who had shared with us his vision of life. For over five years we had practised his teachings through meditation, self-reflection and dream interpretation. Twice a year we would visit the Ashram and try to live our lives according to both his and our ideals.

Long before we took this decision to move, Rajeev had asked him, 'Can we stay here?'

'No,' he had said. 'This is not a place to run away to. It's a place you finally come to, to face things.'

Two years later Rajeev had had a dream, powerful in symbolism. Ashishda's face had been flecked with feeling as he listened to the dream in which a question was being asked again and again. An answer had to be given, not tomorrow or the day after but now ... here ... in this room. I had looked for the answer in Ashishda's eyes—watchful, alert, held by a moment amplified by crucial choices about to be made.

He had stared at the cracks in the wooden floor, offering no detailed interpretation of the dream, which was very unusual for him. He looked at me with only the barest hint of a smile on his face. I felt a barrier of resistance rising within. He seemed to read me and had slowly shaken his head, as though to dispel my fears.

Rajeev had looked at me, seeking a confirmation I was still not prepared to give. Silence stretched back and forth like the shuttle of a weaver's loom. Ashishda stretched his long legs and leaned back against the wall, closing his eyes, waiting. My heart kept beating fast as though trying to keep pace with what might come to pass.

'Can we stay here, Ashishda?' Rajeev had asked again.

With a look of someone guarding ancient secrets, Ashishda replied, 'Yes, your time has come.'

Big changes happen when the time is right, or when the old seasons pass by. We were not like age-old trees that effortlessly shed their autumn leaves. In us the sap was still green, so that if we shook, perhaps not even a single leaf would fall on its own. But now, Rajeev and I felt we had to respond to a more urgent call. We were uprooting ourselves of our own free will to join Ashishda and meet the unfolding of a great challenge—wonderful, magical, all-consuming and even terrifying.

And for what? To give up material comforts. To distil our emotions and focus our mind on the inner enquiry. Finally, to surrender to a man, a guru, a belief, which demanded total submission of oneself. There was nothing to mark our intent: no bare feet, no shaven heads, nor the conventional saffron robes of renunciation.

'The ego has to go,' Ashishda had said, echoing what mystics the world over have written, from the anonymous authors of the Upanishads to the Neo-Platonists, the Christian saints, the Sufi poets. 'It is the one obstruction to perceiving Reality. When there is nothing left of you, something real will be born.'

Any transition we made would have to be done silently, inwardly. Ahead of us was the journey of a lifetime, behind us memories. And with us now were Ashishda's words, 'Don't leave any backdoors open. Burn every bridge as you walk across it, so that you give your all to the life you have chosen to live.'

In the lifestyle Ashishda had outlined, nothing was to be rejected; it would be a harmonious blending of the inner and outer life. Every experience would be part of the effort to produce wholeness. The body, the mind and the emotions would all be harnessed to serve a single intent—to find ourselves. Ashishda believed that a higher awareness was more easily achieved through a life lived close to nature. With his lifestyle, he had formed a bridge connecting soil to soul.

The Ashram aimed at self-sufficiency in food, which meant that our small community of fifteen or so would learn how to plant, weed and harvest crops and probably carry headloads of compost to fertilize the fields. We would milk cows, deliver calves, churn butter, bake our own brown bread and make our own jams and pickles. We would even have to build our own tiny cottages. Besides a few local masons, there were no carpenters, plumbers or electricians in that wilderness.

This would be no solitary contemplative life of the romantic kind. It was going to be a 'hands-on' spirituality. Twelve hours of manual work each day would be offered in selfless service to the Temple. This was intended to cut out the messy edges of gain and profit, and for the added dignity that comes from working for one's own food. The internal resistance to this gruelling labour would be tempered by introspection, while the complexities of our emotional nature would be clarified by dream analysis. Meditation would help to stop the internal chatter of thoughts so as to reach a 'still point' within. The attempt was to give recognition—through the body, mind and emotions—to that higher awareness. A letting go of our everyday self, a paradigm shift towards a new centre within and without.

In the evenings, everyone would come together to sit with Ashishda. He would provide a context to our questions by reading to us from a wide variety of books, including Plotinus, Meister Eckhart, Rumi, Ramana Maharshi, the Upanishads, Buddhist texts, Theosophy and the Zen masters. This would help us see the interconnectedness of the various paths that led to the Truth.

In this life of solitude, I kept no diary, no notes, only a record of my dreams. At one point during our years at the Ashram, I reached such an abyss of despair that I abandoned all hope. Then, totally unexpectedly, there was an affirmation. I was touched by something so profoundly beautiful that I dare not give it a name. It filled my being with an all-embracing experience of love that I have found difficult to replicate. Unobtrusively it taught me, guided me and sometimes gave me glimpses of a state of being against which the limitations of my everyday reality stood out clearly. It transformed my perceptions, for example, of the role of suffering in life. I do not pretend to understand the full scope of this mysterious force. What I pieced together of it was subject to my limitations. Yet, for a while, I felt the capacity to surrender all that was 'me' in order to meet this force wholeheartedly. Later, I wondered why I could not have made my surrender more willingly.

When I looked for causes or explanations, I found none. As Rajeev said later, 'To understand Grace, one life is not enough.' All I know is that when we felt we had lost everything, help had come and whispered its final assurance. In those moments, we felt that a gift had been given to us that would, in some small measure, be ours for the keeping.

Six and a half years in the Ashram had made us feel that we had no other life than the one we had lived here. All the days and months condensed to this point where, sitting in the sun, I seemed to be recovering from an exhausting climb. At the end of that year I recorded a dream:

A production of Shakespeare's *Macbeth* is underway. The finest actors and actresses from all over the world have gathered to rehearse.

I am standing in the shadows, watching the floodlights come on as Macbeth and Lady Macbeth appear in dazzling costumes. Suddenly the director appears and hands me a copy of the script, saying, 'Play Malcolm's role.'

I protest, 'I'm not an actress. I can't even audition, let alone play the role.'

My words remain unheard as the director vanishes. I read the lines of the part and feel at a loss. Days pass, months pass and I go on practising. Occasionally I manage to persuade someone to practise with me. One, two, three, maybe four years pass. Slowly I begin to get the hang of the role. There is activity all around me but I seem to sense it only through a peripheral vision. I am so involved with the role now that I rehearse it every spare moment I get.

One day someone announces, 'The day after tomorrow is opening night.'

There isn't an empty seat in the auditorium and the air is alive with expectations. The play begins. Malcolm is to appear towards the end of the play and I see myself coming onto the stage to fight Macbeth in a one-on-one combat. The next minute, Macbeth is lying dead even though I, as Malcolm, had made no move to kill him.

At this point, Malcolm makes an impassioned speech, and calls upon the powers above to protect, guide and nurture the highest in him so that he never comes to the same end as Macbeth. There is a moment's pause before the audience breaks into spontaneous applause. The curtain falls and I walk back unnoticed to the corridors behind the stage, tired but not unhappy. I suddenly sense the director behind me. I turn around and he smiles, saying, 'That was good. Remember what ultimately counts is the sincerity of the effort—the impassioned giving. The rest is immaterial.'

I had seen him so rarely throughout the production that I'm very pleased to be with him. He says, 'I am going to cast you in another role, another play.

'Oh no!' I protest. 'Not so soon.'

He just smiles indulgently and says, 'Another play, another role.'

Clearly, according to this dream, one phase of my life was over and another was due to begin. A surge of confidence flooded over me for I felt it signalled a new role within the Ashram. Was the dream confirming an internal process?

When I asked Ashishda, he did not say much except, 'It sounds very much like an archetypal dream. Why did you hesitate to say "yes" to the new role?'

Six months later, circumstances developed in such a way that we were caught in the eye of a storm. We were confronted with a choice—stay or leave—each difficult to abide by. How could we be sure when sometimes the most irrevocable decisions are made in a state of mind one might later regret?

Over seven years ago, we had sat before Ashishda and heard him say, 'Yes, your time has come.' Now we sat with him in silence. *Say it, say it*, the silence in the room seemed to goad us.

'Maybe we should leave?' Rajeev finally uttered the words, his eyes hoping Ashishda would contradict him.

'Think about it,' Ashishda said hesitantly. Then he changed his mind and said firmly, 'Maybe it's for the best, your moving on. Hold on to what has been given to you. Wherever you are, the Path will always be with you. The effort you make is never lost.'

We bent down and kissed his feet. He rose and hugged us.

'You've given us so much, Ashishda,' Rajeev said, his voice unsteady.

'When I am in Delhi next, come and see me.'

A curtain call had been made on this phase of our lives, as indicated by the words in my dream. I had not understood them then but realized now that we had to leave the Ashram and begin a 'role' set in radically different circumstances. Ashishda, it seems, had honoured the dream by not insisting we stay.

On our last evening in the Ashram, as we stood in the Temple anteroom, the circular ring of fire from the panchdeep seemed like a benediction on the past and the present. The conch, full of water, was being offered. My mind held on to each moment, unwilling to let it go. At the age of eighteen I had travelled to meet a tall Englishman who had helped shape more than fourteen years of my life. How was I to walk away from it all?

I felt as though a riptide was drawing me back into the sea of uncertainty. Without Ashishda as guru, without the centred atmosphere of the life he had designed and without the single-minded focus we had been afforded, where would I stand?

I was threatened by our return to city life. Without the alchemy of his presence, would I drift away from what I held so vital? Would I lose what I had gained? Or was another kind of letting go being demanded of us?

The service was almost over. The whisk was put away and the drumbeat ended on a sombre note.

What had life at the Ashram been? A pilgrimage, or a living out of emotions that hadn't run their full course? Or was it a seeking of a fresh canvas on which to repaint an old picture? When a canvas cannot be painted on any more, the eyes seem to memorize every detail so that its colours, lines and textures become the means to preserve its essence, like the blue shadows of the evening encircling a garden full of narcissi in bloom, against the long strips of silvery clouds in the sky. Why, even the tall deodars seemed to be pointing their green fingers at the first sprinkling of stars over the grey dome. I watched as the evening closed its drooping eyelids on much more than just the ending of a single day in our lives.

As I walked down the ramp towards the Samadhi, I knew that although I was leaving something behind, I was also carrying something away with me. What was mine was not only the conviction that there is a transcendental Reality, but also that there is a way through which we could meet that Reality.

And moreover, I knew that this 'way' is open to each one of us.

For on the Path, I now believe, we are never alone. The Inner Preceptor stands quietly in the wings, like the director in my dream, stepping into the light when his presence is most required. This Presence brings the reassurance that someone is always watching over our faltering attempts to play the role we have been given. Where the shadows stretch their arms to meet the light, where sleep struggles towards wakefulness, there 'He' sometimes smiles in wordless greeting.

Where does a story begin or end? Not only on the first and last pages of what is told, but in the echoes of what remains untold. We trap experience within words, when the real story of any individual life lies just below the threshold. What words can express is that we returned to Delhi in April when the first warm breath of summer was drying the last of the winter salvias and dahlias. We were like waves that had rolled on to other shores and returned to the old ones with a sense of bewilderment. Perhaps we needed these old shores to understand what had happened on the other shore. But suppose, in time, if we deeply regretted leaving the Ashram, would we be stranded in shallow waters, spending our life sighting ships at mid-ocean? Our raft was Ashishda's assurance: 'The true ashram is a state of mind, it doesn't belong to a particular geographical place. It stands for being united by love, for acceptance of suffering, not for escape into euphoria; for introspection, not for blaming things on others; for service, not for personal progress. Finally, for intelligent enquiry, not for unquestioning belief; for dedication, constant watchfulness, courage, vigour, fire ...'

Many years after my Guru's death I dreamt of him:

> I am on the banks of the Ganges, maybe in Benares. There is no one there but him. Tall, thin, with greying shoulder-length hair, his all-too familiar faded gerua robe tied with a similarly dyed cloth around his waist, his eyes shining with a light I had seen more than once when he was alive.
>
> In his hand he holds a cloth like the one he is wearing. He gives it to me and says, 'Wear it.' I climb the steps of the ghat and go to a room. First, I tie it as a lungi. It does not work. Then as a saree. That too does not work. Finally, I wear it as an alkhela (robe) and go down the steps to meet Ashishda. I think my head is shaven; maybe a stubble remains. The setting sun streaks the sky with orange and lights the waters. I touch

Ashishda's feet. He raises me by the shoulders and says, 'Remain still. Work unobtrusively and die to your former life.'

He looks at me for a long moment. I feel overwhelmed. The next moment, he has gone.

I sit on the banks of the river not knowing what to do. I watch the sun set.

And now, many, many years later the colours of renunciation appear once more before me—sanyas. Was the dream indicative of the future? If not, what could it be? A wish fulfilment? Sanyas represents a wandering mendicant detached from wealth, property, family—a wish many Hindus harbour as a cultural ideal.

The shade of the cloth given by my Teacher suggests that this may not be the meaning of the dream. It was not dyed in the usual saffron of a sadhu's garb. Could the dream be nudging me towards an aspect of his teachings, and not towards traditional sanyas? His own journey as a novice had begun with the death of the smaller self. Possibly, the dream was not about leaving the world, staff and bowl in hand, but about going 'still' on one's smaller self. A different order of letting go than the traditional one.

The manner in which I tried to wear the cloth also made me reflect. Not as a sari (feminine), nor as a lungi (masculine). It worked as an alkhela, devoid of gender distinctions. Mystics of every tradition assure us that in spiritual awareness, we gradually dis-identify from everything that normally constitutes identity—body, gender, mind, intellect, ego. It is said that by the time we reach the threshold of full spiritual potential, all dualities are left behind: no more are we black or white, old or young, learned or ignorant. No more you or me. So, was the reference to dying in the dream urging for the dissolution of all distinctions—the true sanyas?

But hadn't my entire life been a letting go, a relinquishment of one sort or another?

When we left our Delhi life for the Ashram, it was a letting go of all former representations of myself—work, family, a familiar lifestyle and all the aspirations of the culture we lived in.

But what we had relinquished outwardly had to be dealt with inwardly: the struggle to let go of the 'self'. In the Ashram, your personal identity or 'you' did not count, only service did. The constant submission was to the deities in the Temple, represented by surrendering to the will of the Teacher, seeking inspiration from who he was and which was often resisted by who I was. He maintained that for a new centre to form, the present integration needed to be dissolved. A shift away from one's desires, opinions and comforts. The existence of this new centre of consciousness had to be taken on trust. And a sustained effort had to be made to live by it. Perhaps the effort to sense it and live by it became an invocation. A renunciation of the personal so that Reality could reveal itself. Ashishda never failed to emphasize that the search is an enquiry and not merely a following of disciplines. 'Follow that enquiry back beyond your identifications,' he would urge us.

Yet another kind of renunciation followed when we left the Ashram. A reluctant leaving behind of a life that we had adopted, and more than that, the moving away from the Teacher.

Gradually, the old voices, which had not been silenced by my shift to the Ashram, raised their head again—voices affirming personal identity. Juxtaposed against this were values from the Ashram where we try and self-remember, be watchful of ourselves, still the mind and go beyond. In time I discovered that the old voices need not be trampled underfoot but transformed. A letting go of that which was unexamined. Time to seek the truth from an unborrowed self.

When I had first met Ashishda I asked him how I would find my true identity?

'By keeping still.'

'What does that mean?' I asked.

'Watch, observe, don't identify with your thoughts. The effort should be to try and stem the flow of thoughts. There is a quiet place within that is not fussed about by people, things, hurt feelings and unsatisfied desires. When the mind is quiet only then can the true identity be found.'

Was this what was being affirmed in the sanyas dream? Remain still.

And would remaining still lead to working unobtrusively? Perhaps each supports and fulfils the other. When we work unobtrusively, we let go of self-affirmation. And wouldn't that, in turn, help in remaining still? Half of one's life is spent in building up one's identity and the other half in defending it. Perhaps, this statement demanded a sloughing off of all that constituted 'me'.

And wouldn't that be linked to dying to my former life—my individual biography or the way I viewed it? After all, traditional sanyas hopes to find meaning by radically removing the structures of life. But before doing that, one has to develop a sufficient amount of personality to gain confidence. Ashishda had likened this dismantling to the scaffolding that must be removed once the building is complete. 'If one has worked on oneself, age helps one to see the scaffolding for what it is: a necessary but temporary structure.'

I did discover something. If I managed to stop my thoughts, even momentarily, in that infinitesimal pause the slate would be wiped clean, the person that I habitually was would become absent. In fact, for that duration, this untidy world would dissolve. Yet an awareness remained, an attentive awareness–self-existent, featureless, unbounded. It just was. Observation suggests some sort of involvement in what is observed. But this state is unconcerned with what it is observing. It felt like a presence, glimpsed when thoughts were not eclipsing it.

Was I being reminded by the dream of this state? Or was it asking for a more direct approach to the source of this awareness? Religious symbols stir feelings and act as vehicles to affirm the sacramental nature of that awareness. However, the rituals have to be internalized. One has to find within oneself the states of being which they outwardly represent.

Ashishda had once asked, 'Whose are these pleasures and pains?'

I felt the obvious answer was 'me'—what my body experiences.

He then said, 'It does not take very long to realize that the body is not the same as "me".'

'Why?'

'Because I observe the sensations provided to me by the body. So, the "I" or the "me" must be separate from the body. But what is the nature of this "me"?'

'Isn't the "I" my thoughts and feelings, my personality?'

'Again, you can be aware that you observe all your thoughts and feelings. Doesn't this suggest that the observing "I" is apart from the "me"?' he asked.

'Are you suggesting that the ability to see, hear, or sense cannot be the "I"?'

'You may have to enquire: Which "I"? The "I" that participates in activities, or the "I" that observes?'

I was silent, trying to digest his words.

'I am only suggesting an obvious fact, that the "mind" has two aspects—it can see objects in the outside world, and it can also see itself. This ability is possibly what distinguishes us from animals. But what is the nature of this observing "I"? Is it identical with the personality, or is it distinct?'

Was my dream a call to seek in the direction Ashishda was suggesting? From ordinary activities like cooking, cleaning and gardening, and from everyday emotions like anger, irritation, fear and pleasure, a secret could be coaxed out, a self-observing awareness discovered.

Perhaps it would be a dual relationship. I would begin to own myself, my thoughts, my perceptions. And in owning them, I would begin to watch them as though they were separate from 'me'. And maybe, just maybe, in the space between the two, I would begin the journey from the circumference to the centre.

A sanyas where the measure of one's absence reveals glimpses of an ever-present awareness.

Postscript

Mirtola Ashram is located in the Himalayan foothills of northern India. It has a lineage of three extraordinary teachers, Sri Yashoda Mai (1882–1944) who founded the Ashram in 1929 with Sri Krishna Prem (1898—1965) followed by Sri Madhava Ashish (1920—1997) who was known to his friends and pupils as Ashishda. Ashishda was our Teacher who, in his astonishingly integrated mountain Ashram, taught through personal guidance how every individual's inner search revolved around the life of the Spirit, and could find expression in the life that was lived there.

This essay is an extremely personal one where I try to understand the abiding enigma of Neem Karoli Baba, one of the greatest Himalayan masters, and someone who has touched and transformed my life. It is also a heartfelt tribute to the silent saint, Shri Siddhi Ma, who was Neem Karoli Baba's disciple and successor. I had the privilege of meeting and being blessed by Siddhi Ma in the later years of her life and owe much to her.

It was while writing this piece that I discovered that my other guru, Swami Chidanandaji of the Sivananda Ashram, Rishikesh, who had guided me at crucial phases of my life, was himself a friend and admirer of Neem Karoli Baba. I found this deeply reassuring and a validation of the pervading grace of the Himalayan Masters, whose all-knowing presences live on in the Dev Bhoomi, the land of the gods.

CHAPTER 13

Neem Karoli Baba and Siddhi Ma

NAMITA GOKHALE

Guru Sakshat Param Brahma, Tasmai Shri Guruveh Namah
(The embodied Guru is the highest and eternal godhead; salutations to that Guru)

Neem Karoli Baba's life was strewn with the miraculous at every step. The accepted laws of physics, and of time and space, did not seem to apply to him. He never employed these extraordinary powers for aggrandisement or gain. He was an emanation of many presences and personages whose spiritual seeking had come before him. I am personally both mystic and sceptic, reluctant to yield my rationality. Yet, there are mysteries that are best left alone, and so it is with my faith and belief in Maharajji.

Neem Karoli Baba, Maharajji to his bhaktas, was a puzzle and a paradox. He left no teachings, no formal legacy, and yet devotees around the world are constantly forging intense connections with him. The barriers of language, culture and religion break down before the compassion, love and sense of fellowship his followers continue to share.

I had the great privilege of meeting Neem Karoli Baba when I was a child of six. He appeared strange, as did the other grown-ups he was sitting and chatting with—except for my grandfather, Dr C.D. Pande, who was, as ever, comforting and loving.

This was probably around the year 1962. The Baba had established himself as a beloved, if mystifying, spiritual figure and presiding deity of Kumaon. His transformative presence imperceptibly changed the way a rigid, caste-bound and hierarchical society addressed its spiritual needs. He invoked the inner resources of agape, caritas and emotional generosity, and fused together a community of believers who continue to congregate and maintain the bond across generations. He was a renowned Himalayan seer with strong roots in Kumaon, but also someone who drew the devotion of disciples and devotees around the world, whose lives he had touched. He may no longer be in his body, but his spiritual energy continues to enlighten people.

Who was this personage whose living presence endures and irradiates the hearts of those he chooses to bless? To my mind, he is the essential Himalayan master, timeless, formless, informed by mysteries humans cannot seek to grasp. A friend once described him as the patron saint of Silicon Valley. It seems a moniker at odds with the frail, vibrant, often mischievous guru in his woollen plaid blanket. He is also described as the quantum saint, and he did indeed seem to have changed the trajectory of conventional linear thinking of an astonishing array of intellectual entrepreneurs. In my travels, I have encountered devotees of the Baba in distinct but scattered footprints across the United States, the United Kingdom and Europe. His spiritual aura found resonance with the dreaming minds of a new generation of techno-magicians, who imbibed a deep dose of his crazy wisdom in their youthful journeys to the East. His most well-known devotee in the US was Ram Dass (Richard Alpert), the Harvard psychologist, whose work created a bridge between Eastern and Western philosophies. Larry Brilliant, the inaugural director of Google.org, took Google's Larry Page and Jeffrey Skoll, co-founder of eBay, on a transformational pilgrimage to the Kainchi Ashram, nestled on the foothills of the Himalayas, to meet his guru. Steve Jobs arrived at the Ashram in 1974, too late to have a physical darshan of the saint, who had left his bodily form in 1973. Jobs was reported to have a photograph of Neem Karoli Baba beside him in his last days. Mark Zuckerberg spent time in the Ashram as well.

The living legacy of Neem Karoli Baba is perhaps best exemplified in the life and outstanding achievements of Larry Brilliant. Inspired by Maharajji, Larry and Elaine (Girija) Brilliant played a key role in the World Health Organization's (WHO) smallpox eradication programme. In the extract below from his book *Sometimes Brilliant*, Brilliant tells us of the arduous goal of seeking a job in the WHO at his guru's instructions:

> But I kept going back anyway, every time he asked me. Trips to Delhi from Kainchi were gruelling, a dozen hours if everything went right. Trains were late or cancelled regularly; bus rides on mountain roads were terrifying. Delhi was an obstacle course of beggars, with the craziest drivers in existence and cows and other animals wandering the streets. It would have been great if Maharajji could have sent me there just once, on the right day to see the right person so I could land the job.

> But mystical traditions are filled with stories of teachers testing and training and sometimes tormenting their students. A classic example is the story of Milarepa, the eleventh-century Tibetan saint Wavy had told us about, who subsisted on nettles during meditation. Milarepa had been a robber and a murderer, so his teacher, Marpa, made him build and tear down tower after tower—a humiliating process that lasted years, but would purify the obstacles to spiritual development, that is, Milarepa's inner stew of rage, violence, and revenge. I am not Milarepa and I am not a saint, but walking into the WHO office over and over again and explaining that my guru had told me to come work for them might have altered my biochemistry. I think Maharajji wanted me to achieve non-attachment to success. A spiritual apprenticeship can be confusing, even counterintuitive. Those long, exhausting trips, constant rejections, and the daily reminder of my unworthiness, the roller coaster of doubt and the balm of Maharajji's reassurance, were all part of the preparation. What developed in me at that time was faith—delicate, wavering, tenuous, but faith, nevertheless.
>
> Sometimes people say that faith is the opposite of doubt, but I don't think that is true. To me, the opposite of faith is rigid certainty. Doubt is the constant companion of true faith; like God, it is more verb than noun. Faith is the ride, not the station, as Indians describe it. No one can avoid doubt, scepticism, fear and uncertainty on the journey to faith if they are honest with themselves. Obstacles are the training ground.[50]

Indeed, faith is the journey, not the station. Faith is the step in the dark which is not there. After Brilliant joined the WHO, after he became a world-renowned epidemiologist and visionary philanthropist, he looked back and reflected on his journey in his book.

> At certain moments, the ordinary rules of cause and effect are suspended. Living in a sacred space, surrounded by sacred images, following a guru,

50 Larry Brilliant, *Sometimes Brilliant: The Impossible Adventure of a Spiritual Seeker and Visionary Physician Who Helped Conquer the Worst Disease in History* (New York: HarperOne, 2017), pp. 140-41.

> a teacher, or a prophet who seems prescient and nudges you towards a specific path—impossible things happen. Since you cannot explain them through reason, you must acquiesce to unreasonable theories. After that, everything begins to make sense again, but in an unexpected way: all impossible things begin to seem quite possible after all.[51]

Neem Karoli Baba's grace extended far beyond the celebrities he attracted. He was and is the spiritual head of countless Indian families, and his smiling face and blanket-clad form is prominent in framed photographs in homes and public places across Uttarakhand and the rest of northern India. Who was this saint who left such an ineradicable footprint in the hearts and minds of millions?

To begin at the beginning, let us follow the journey of a young seeker who left the life of a householder and set off on a religious quest that took him across the contours of the Indian heartland before he found his anchor in the mountains of Kumaon, in the central Himalaya. The known linear facts of Neem Karoli Baba's life are as follows: He was born at the cusp of the twentieth century on 11 September 1900, in the village of Akbarpur in Uttar Pradesh. His parents were Brahmins and he was given the birth name of Lakshman Das with the family surname, Sharma. The young boy was persuaded into an arranged marriage by his parents at the tender age of eleven, as was the custom then. However, his restless nature was not ready for household duties and he left home in search of spiritual knowledge, leaving his young wife behind. His father, Durga Prasad Sharma, appealed to him to return. He honoured his father's wishes and lived with his wife and family for several years. Two sons were born to him, Aneg Singh Sharma and Dharam Narayan Sharma, as well as a daughter, Girija. He was a loving husband and father, but the call remained within him and he set off on his wanderings again.

During his travels across India, Neem Karoli Baba's given name of Lakshman Das was replaced by a variety of different titles and sobriquets. Handi Wallah Baba, Tikonia Wallah Baba and Tallaiya Baba are just

51 Larry Brilliant, *Sometimes Brilliant*, p. 153.

some of these. He was also referred to as Chamatkari Baba—the Miracle Saint.

The title 'Neem Karoli Baba' was given to him in the aftermath of an astonishing episode that defies explanation. He was travelling on a train without a ticket. The conductor had the locomotive halted in the village of Neeb Karoli in Uttar Pradesh and forcibly evicted the holy man from the compartment. Neem Karoli Baba settled himself in the shade of a spreading tree, smiling beatifically. The train then prepared to resume its journey, but the engine driver could not get it to start, despite repeated attempts. After several futile efforts, somebody suggested that the holy man, who had been so unceremoniously pushed out, be placated. The railway officials went to him with folded hands and requested him to step onto the train again. Neem Karoli Baba smiled mischievously and agreed to return to his seat if they promised to establish a railway station in Neeb Karoli, and to be more respectful to holy men in the future. The train chugged off happily once he was on board.

Reports of this strange occurrence spread, and he became known thereafter as Neeb Karoli Baba, which over time became Neem Karoli Baba. This story is not apocryphal, although it may require a leap of the imagination to understand and accept it.

In the course of his frequent trips to the Kumaon Himalaya, Neem Karoli Baba established the Hanuman Garhi Temple on the outskirts of Nainital in 1950. Although he worshipped the gods and goddesses of the Hindu pantheon with equal devotion, Lord Hanuman, the symbol of strength and devotion, was ever and always his chosen deity. Many felt he was indeed an emanation, or incarnation, of Lord Hanuman.

Kumaon and Garhwal, in the state of Uttarakhand, comprise the Devbhoomi, the Land of the Gods. Religious traditions have converged there over millennia. It could be said that at least two deep spiritual lineages meet in the life and legacy of Neem Karoli Baba.

The ashrams in Kainchi (set up in 1962) and Kakarighat in Kumaon, were both built on spots sanctified by the meditative presence of the great Himalayan seer, Sombari Baba. This reclusive figure was amongst the saints blessed by the mysterious 'Babaji'—an immortal mystic who is said to roam the Himalaya, materializing and dematerializing at will. Babaji is said to exist outside the constraints of a physical 'Kayic' body and to manifest through the wanderers and seekers in the Devbhoomi. It is told that Lahiri Mahashaya, the guru of Swami Yogananda Paramhansa, received enlightenment from him.

It is significant that Neem Karoli Baba established two of his dhams and ashrams on spots sanctified by Sombari Baba. Even today, the sanctum sanctorum of the Kainchi Ashram is the small overhang of cliff where Sombari Baba had lit his dhuni, his sacred fire pit. Neem Karoli Baba also meditated on this spot and consecrated it. The vibrations of calm and pervading spirituality are palpable there, despite the throngs of visitors and devotees who tour the temple premises.

The Ashram at Kakrighat is similarly blessed with the footprints of many legendary saints and gurus. Sombari Baba meditated under the spreading banyan tree; Swami Vivekananda spent a night there. It is reported that he met Haidakhan Baba, and possibly Sombari Baba, during the visit.

Neem Karoli Baba's other converging lineage is also a Himalayan one. He was part of the so-called 'Crazy Wisdom' tradition of the Himalayan adepts, who refused to be constrained by narrow ritualistic interpretations of the path. Spontaneity, intuition and selflessness mark their attitude to enlightenment. They accept anomalous and eccentric behaviour as they search an experiential whole body understanding. The spiritual tests the masters of this tradition subject their disciples to are often allegorical and unorthodox.

This Tibetan 'Yeshi Cholwa' way included Masters such as Milarepa, his biographer Tsangyon Heruka—the self-proclaimed 'Madman of Central Tibet'—the Mahasiddha Saraha, and many others.

The 'Crazy Wisdom' is derived from Tibetan traditions and describes the state of being of those who have crossed the limits of conventional thinking to reach 'wisdom gone beyond'. It also devolved seamlessly as a form of Himalayan wisdom within those from the Indic tradition, including Guru Gorakhnath and the diverse tantric schools that followed. Neem Karoli Baba embraces both these streams, and many more, in his 'Be Here Now' teachings, which were never codified but always imparted with a mischievous playfulness.

The revered saint Swami Chidananda of the Divine Life Mission, Rishikesh, from whom I received many learnings and blessings, had a deep bond and kinship with Neem Karoli Baba. Chidananda-ji had a quiet demeanour with an intense spiritual aura and was a traditionalist, though not rigidly ritualistic. Maharajji, on the other hand, was effervescent and full of the unexpected. I am certain that they communicated deeply in Sandhya Bhasha, the 'Twilight Language' spoken only by adepts and the initiated.

This tribute from Swami Chidanandaji encapsulates their relationship:

> Salutations to the holy memory of worshipful and beloved Sri Baba Neem Karoli—the wonder mystic of northern India. He is one of the most unique phenomena among the religious fraternity of saints, sages and holy fakirs of northern India. It would not be a wonder to me, if, as I am sitting and dictating this article on a mildly warm summery afternoon in Jaipur, Rajasthan, at this moment Babaji is perfectly aware of this ... in spite of the fact that revered Baba Neem Karoli is physically no more amongst us and has left his body very recently, just about a couple of years back. Though this statement may seem rather extraordinary and would surprise many of the readers, yet, it is nevertheless true that many of Babaji's close disciples and devotees had personal experience of the fact that revered Babaji seemed to be aware of whatever they had been saying and doing in distant places, far away from him, and Babaji was actually in some other place at that moment. This has convinced most of his closest followers that Sri Baba Neem Karoli was a 'Siddha Purusha' (perfect being) and knower of the past, present as also of the future.
>
> —*Trikala Jnani*

Chidanandaji continues his reminiscences saying:

The last time I had the good fortune of meeting revered Baba Neem Karoli-ji was in the month of October 1973. This was when I visited him at his secluded Ashram at Kainchi near Nainital, in the Kumaon Hills. It was late evening and, when we arrived at Kainchi, it was dark.

I, with my companions, went down from the road with the help of flashlights and, crossing the little bridge that spans the mountain stream, we entered the Ashram. The entire place was totally deserted and absolute silence prevailed. The Temple pujari received us in the courtyard and conducted us into a little room. The revered Baba Neem Karoli was seated on a cot and was wrapped in a simple blanket. He received me and my party with a very kind and benign look and motioned us to take our seats on the carpet spread near the cot. I knelt down beside the cot and offered my homage, laying my head upon his lap where he had tucked up his foot, being seated cross-legged. Babaji softly said, *'All right, all right, very good'* and signed to me to be seated. One of our party, Sri Yogesh Bahuguna, had brought seven or eight oranges in a little towel. There was an empty basket by the side of Babaji and he placed these oranges in the basket as an offering. We then sang some Sankirtan and sat in silence for a couple of minutes. Babaji started to distribute the fruit as prasad to us. By this time, some other workers and devotees of the Ashram had gathered near the door. Sri Yogesh-ji was taken aback and overcome by surprise when he observed that Babaji continued taking oranges from the basket even after he had already given away eight oranges and went on distributing this prasad to all the members of our party, plus the assembled Ashram staff. Ultimately he had given eighteen fruits in all. From where the additional ten oranges came into the basket is something we could not explain. Perhaps only Babaji knows this.

> Babaji's unusual personality and extraordinary powers have been corroborated by certain other of his devotees whom I had the occasion to meet afterwards. Several times, close devotees of Baba Neem Karoli have seen him simultaneously at two different places, at one and the same time. In both places it was not merely a matter of just seeing him but Babaji was very much with them, talking to them and even partaking of some refreshments offered by them.
>
> It is believed that he had done Upasana (worship) of Sri Hanuman and attributed many of his miraculous deeds to siddhi (psychic power) through his Upasana.

This testimony from one of the most revered of Himalayan saints, who lived in the foothills of Rishikesh by the banks of the most sacred of rivers, the Ganga, indicates Neem Karoli Baba's standing in the hierarchy of spiritual masters.

Ram Dass's (Maharajji's devoted disciple who carried his legacy to the West) moving account of his first encounter with his guru also gives a sense of his charismatic and often contradictory personality.

> My encounters over the last two decades with the living presence of the Baba, despite his physical body passing over, can be considered only out of the realm of quotidian linear reality. This was … the monk who could lose his temper and express his anger, the mystic who could laugh and joke with the playfulness of a child. Yet his mastery over the mystical and magical was never used for shock and awe, but only to enable everyday acts of kindness and compassion. There is a shift of perspective in those who have received his grace. Magic is always around us, and many of his acolytes have indeed moved the boundaries of magic into the domain of technology.

Neem Karoli Baba was very well known in Kumaon, but we had also heard of Shri Siddhi Ma when I was growing up in Nainital in the 1960s. She was the pious daughter-in-law of the Sah family who owned the India Hotel, just down the hill from our house. My mother remembers seeing her as a young bride, and how she was beautiful and cheerful and pleasant and spent much of her time in the Naina Devi temple.

It was in the years that Neem Karoli Baba established his ashram at Kainchi that Shri Siddhi Ma, a close disciple and successor of Maharajji and a great yogini in her own right, as well as Jivanti Ma, her constant companion in devotion, became integral parts of his spiritual passage. Ma was the living Shakti of the Kainchi Dham, the feminine strength, who imparted harmony and purpose to the motley band of seekers who sought refuge there.

Although I had been blessed by him as a child, Neem Karoli Baba appeared before me as a guru and guide much after he had left his body, in a manner that was oblique, overwhelming and in retrospect, ordained. Shri Siddhi Ma wordlessly summoned me to sit at her feet and listen to her silence. Today, as I attempt to summon remembrance, I can feel the touch of her warm hand on my head and the soft tapping of her feet.

The few times—perhaps eight occasions—that I had the privilege to meet her are all encapsulated in a memory of calm and clarity. She would be sitting bolt upright on a chair in a white sari, the white of fresh, fluffy snow. She would appear still as a painted portrait, motionless as an alabaster statue, and yet a restless movement of her hands or the tapping of her feet would indicate the interior activity of that tranquil exterior.

She would be sitting in the veranda that overlooked the distant tear-shaped lake of Nainital, or in her bedroom, which opened into a prayer alcove that held the kambal, the blanket, a symbol of the living presence of Neem Karoli Baba. It is difficult to describe the power of Ma, her mystical presence and her radiant silence. There was something cosmic about that silence, as though she knew the hidden secrets of the earth and of the spheres beyond. Her eyes, when she opened them, indicated that she was perhaps amused by it all. There was joy and compassion in her glance, an understanding of pain as well as the ecstasy of spiritual experience.

It is difficult to understand the samskaras of sainthood, the karmic destiny that fulfils the quest for spiritual understanding. Siddhi Ma is alive in the hearts and minds of her devotees, surrounded by stories and mysteries. Along with Nanda and Sunanda, she has become one of the tutelary feminine deities of Kumaon. She is beyond words and adjectives and anecdotes, beyond the constraints of her physical body, an immortal who lives on in an eternal oneness.

Neem Karoli Baba did not propound a philosophy or credo, nor did he follow any elaborate rituals. He was dismissive of all that was grandiose or pretentious. He did not sit on a gilded throne (as many godmen are wont to), instead he half-reclined in an unusual yogic posture on his bare wooden takhat. He was usually draped in a black or blue plaid blanket and walked barefoot. He told his Christian devotees to follow Christ, although he gave them Hindu names while at the Ashram. There was no cult about him, but instead an intense sense of community, of belonging and being loved. There was also a sense of magic, of infinite possibility, and of grace. Maharajji could do anything, and one never knew what he might do next. He believed in prayer and laughter, music and mischief, and the importance of feeding and nurturing his devotees, as well as giving them spiritual sustenance. He spoke to those around him about their everyday concerns, about their jobs, their homes, their children, their health. He conjured up everyday miracles and guided them at every step.

The guru's disciples make the guru as much as the guru forms the disciple, in what is one of the most intense and symbiotic of all relationships. Neem Karoli Baba's disciples came from all strata of society and he reached out to them individually at the spiritual level they would best understand.

The spiritual experiences that Neem Karoli Baba provoked, and continues to provoke transformed those he blessed by breaking down the ego and by conferring infinite compassion and reservoirs of sustaining joy. He remains an embodiment of the Himalayan masters, of their secret knowledge, and mysteries.

After Siddhi Ma left her body in 2017, Ram Dass wrote, 'Since the time that Maharajji left His body, He started manifesting more and more through Ma's transmission. She connveyed the love that Maharajji is; she was a manifestation of that unconditional love.'

I return in memory to a misty morning, with the Nainital lake, shaped like a teardrop, where the eyes of Goddess Sati are said to have fallen, spread out far below me. There is a quality to the silence—it is sharp, almost piercing in its absence of sound. Siddhi Ma is silent too. She is seated in her customary chair by the corner of the veranda, with an enigmatic smile on her calm face. She is dressed, as always, in a handspun white sari. I carry the image of that last visit to Siddhi Ma at Jaya Prasada's home in Nainital as an amulet, a talisman to shield me and keep me in the cocoon of her grace.

Om Shri Hanumate Namah

—

René von Nebesky-Wojkowitz (1923–1959) was a Czech ethnologist and Tibetologist. His erudite and absorbing account of his encounters in Kalimpong, Sikkim and Nepal are recorded in Oracles and Demons of Tibet: The Cult and Iconography of the Tibetan Protective Deities. *His premature death at the age of thirty-six from pneumonia was attributed by many believers to the wrath of the protective deities whose esoteric and mystic secrets he had presumed to write about.*

Some dedicated European scholars of his generation sought to assiduously glean, garner and record what they could in what might be considered an aggressive territorial incursion into other systems of knowledge. The stories suffered a loss of nuance and meaning through their translations.

The following essay, taken from Where the Gods are Mountains, *follows the course of a ritual possession, where a Tibetan oracle enters into a trance. The tale has a twist in the end, as revealed in a later chapter in the book, which we have also excerpted.*

CHAPTER 14

Where the Gods Are Mountains

RENÉ VON NEBESKY-WOJKOWITZ

On the third day of every new moon the Mighty Thunderbolt entered the body of Lhagpa Tondup. Lhagpa Tondup was a pleasant young Tibetan I met in Kalimpong. Judging by his appearance, I originally took him for a well-to-do trader; until one day I learnt, to my surprise, that he was a very busy oracle-priest with a big clientele, notably among Tibetans passing through the town. He lived with his young wife in a house on the Tenth Mile, and it was there that I had my first long conversation with him.

The room in which he received me was more like a chapel than a living room. Against one wall stood an altar, against another a wooden throne with the sumptuous ritual garments worn by an oracle-priest during the soothsaying ceremony. The items of his costume were neatly sorted out in an order that never varied. At the bottom lay a long robe of yellow brocade reaching to the ground and half-concealing a pair of white, gold-trimmed boots such as the tulkus wear. An apron, patterned with dragons and trimmed with fringes, and a kind of cloak of brocade, had been spread out over the robe, and on top of these stood the oracle-priest's helmet. This consisted of a massive silver hoop encircling the lower edge of a tall brocade hat. The circlet was embellished with five small human skulls of silver; the hat bore on the front representations of three human eyes. In front of the helmet lay a small breastplate ornamented with mystic characters; beside it were a coil of red cord—a magic noose for catching demons—and the oracle-priest's great ceremonial ring.

The throne was flanked by two religious emblems: a trident bearing the model of a human skull and a spear with a triangular red pennant attached. Below the spearhead was a padded ring of material with three human eyes painted on it.

Next to the throne, over the entrance door, hung a most remarkable object. Fastened to a pair of black yak's horns by a dusty ceremonial scarf was a sword that had been twisted into a spiral. Lhagpa Tondup had once bent it in a trance. Swords twisted by oracle-priests are regarded in Tibet as an exceptionally potent defence against malignant demons. They are known as 'knotted thunderbolts' and hung beside doors to keep out evil spirits. An oracle-priest's ring—it was originally employed by mediums in bending the ritual bow—is also considered a powerful amulet; these rings are especially popular as travel charms among lamas, who carry them when on a journey.

The third day of the new moon, the day on which the Mighty Thunderbolt took monthly possession of his medium, fell just a week after my visit to Lhagpa Tondup. Although Lhagpa Tondup could go into a trance at any time his clients wished and, as he said, 'make the protective god speak out of his mouth', experience had shown that the seizure was always most intense on those days. On this occasion the séance was to be held in the Rimpoche's chapel, and there I had an opportunity of watching the ceremony.

When I entered the chapel that morning, around 10 a.m., some fifteen people were already in the room, amongst them my teacher Nyima. I sat down beside bins, and he whispered to me that I was just in time. The Rimpoche, who was to conduct the rite, had that moment opened proceedings by intoning a prayer.

Lhagpa Tondup was sitting on a throne-like seat specially erected for the purpose. I saw that he was wearing the heavy ceremonial garments over his everyday clothes; on his right hand glittered the sliver oracle-ring; the red demon-noose was attached to his left wrist. A broad khatag with its ends tied together hung round his neck, and the helmet on his head was fastened by a leather strap under his chin. The oracle-priest's legs were planted wide apart; his hands rested on his knees. Lhagpa Tondup's youthful face wore a tense expression, his eyes were closed.

Two of the Rimpoche's lama servants stood at the medium's side; a third servant, with an open censer in his band, was causing the aromatic smoke of burning juniper branches to drift into his face. The Rimpoche was sitting apart at a low table chanting an invocation, accompanying the rising and falling melody with a hand-bell. He was calling upon the tutelary divinity to leave his celestial palace and hasten here to receive the offerings laid out for him on the altar and then take possession of the body of the oracle-priest.

'Come hither, Mighty Thunderbolt, and take the tormas of meat and blood, the wooden platter with flour and butter and the drink-offerings—Tibetan beer, Chinese tea, fresh milk and sour milk—the "inner, outer and secret offerings" ... Fulfil the duties imposed upon thee: reveal the future, disclose false accusations, show what fruit the various actions will bear, protect the pious and aid them ...'

The continually accelerating rhythm of the chant seemed to be affecting the oracle-priest. He shifted restlessly this way and that on his seat and greedily inhaled the incense. The yellow butter lamps on the altar flickered dully through the dense clouds of juniper smoke; the figures of the priests in front of the altar looked like grotesque shadows. The penetrating odour and the shrill tinkle of the bells seemed to exercise an oppressive effect even on the spectators. I saw some of them retreat into the open air. Rivulets of sweat streamed down the pale face of the seer, who seemed on the point of fainting. From time to time his facial muscles twitched, and he buried his teeth in his lower lip as though he were in violent pain. Several times he lifted his hands nervously and tugged at the dangling khatag. His lips parted and the rapid breathing, keeping time with the singing, changed into hectic panting. Then he began to throw the upper part of his body quickly this way and that. Several times it looked as though he were going to leap into the air, but he got no farther than a clumsy attempt.

The two lamas beside the throne followed the medium's every movement intently, ready to spring forward at the first sign of collapse. The priest was still rocking to and fro, occasionally flinging himself backwards. Suddenly he bounded a good eighteen inches into the air and sank heavily down onto his cushion again. During the last few minute his face had undergone a terrifying change. It no longer bore the slightest resemblance to the familiar, friendly countenance of Lhagpa Tondup. The whole head seemed swollen, the skin of the face was dark red in colour, the thick blue lips were flecked with whitish-grey foam, and the saliva was dribbling from the corners of his mouth, which were drawn down in an repression of cruel contempt. The priest struck his metal breastplate with his clenched fist, until the skin tore and his knuckles were covered in blood. There could be no doubt that the medium was not simulating, but in a genuine and complete trance.

Now the oracle-priest's hands went up into the air as though trying to ward something off. The priest seemed close to suffocation; his panting changed into a deep, gurgling sound.

'That is the voice of the Mighty Thunderbolt,' whispered Nyima in my ear.

'Now he has entered his body, and therefore Lhagpa Tondup is undergoing the agony of Sonam Gragpa, who was killed by having a khatag thrust down his throat.'

The gurgling, snuffling noise gradually abated; the medium's movement grew calmer. His cramped hands, on which the veins stood out, rested again on his violently trembling knees. His eye remained closed, and his rigid, sweat-bathed face resembled a red demon mask contorted with rage.

I was really fortunate to be present at this soothsaying ceremony, for very few white people have previously had an opportunity of seeing a Tibetan oracle-priest at the height of his trance. The presence of unbelievers at such ceremonies is generally discouraged. The Tibetans believe that at this moment a divinity is in the body of the oracle-priest and might be angered at the sight of a foreigner. Moreover, it frequently happens that an oracle-priest seizes the ritual weapons that lie to hand, and rushes at the spectators with them. Tibetans had told me about séances of this nature in which members of the audience were injured or even killed; and once I heard that, in his frenzy, a medium slashed open his own belly, tore out his entrails and decorated the pictures of the gods with them. When such things happen the lamas say the protective god has punished a sinner or, as in the last case, the oracle-priest himself, for some serious transgression. I should now have liked to photograph the medium, but that was impossible—the Tibetans would have regarded it as sacrilege. Two years later, however, after protracted negotiations, I was able to take photographs of all the phases of Lhagpa Tondup's trance at a secret séance held specially for this purpose, and eventually also to make sound recordings of the hymns sung on thus occasions.

The Rimpoche ended his chant. He rose from his seat, straightened his cloak and approached the oracle-priest with reverently bowed head, to put a further ceremonial scarf round his neck. This act of veneration was not directed towards the seer himself, but to the protective deity now occupying his body. Then the Rimpoche picked up a porcelain bowl full of

China tea from a silver tray and raised it to the medium's lips, presenting the Mighty Thunderbolt with the prescribed drink-offering.

A servant pressed a short sword into the oracle-priest's tight hand. The seer placed the point against his hip, where a strong leather strap showed under his brightly coloured apron, and pushed on the handle until the blade doubled up. Then he wearily opened his hand, and the servant caught the falling sword.

Now the Rimpoche began the interrogation. He went up to the seer, laid a hand on his neck and whispered the questions into his ear. The answers were gasped out in isolated, almost unintelligible words. During other séances at which I was present in ensuing years he gave the answers loudly, and sometimes they positively gushed from his mouth, so that the lama whose job it was to put the prophecies down in writing could hardly keep pace with them.

On other occasions the medium made his pronouncements in well-rhymed verses and even repeated passages not clearly enunciated, at the request of the priest conducting the ceremony. It was often very difficult to extract any meaning from his prognostications; they seemed to me very vague and obscure. The lamas produced an interpretation, but even this could often be understood in more ways than one. The ecstatic babbling of the State Oracle was also, as a rule, taken down by his secretary in a kind of shorthand and later elucidated by a college of priests.

After about ten minutes the Rimpoche retired. The oracle-priest, seized with a sudden restlessness, began to breathe heavily again; he tugged at the tightly knotted khatag and rocked his body to and fro. Then he reared up, and fell heavily backwards into the arms of the servants, who sprang forward to catch him. His face turned deathly pale, and the whites of his eyes showed. The exhausted and prostrate body was shaken by convulsions; the hands were thrust forward several times with outspread fingers as though trying to push away some invisible object. Then the twitching subsided, the seer gradually recovered consciousness. Supported by the servants, he sat up with a groan and drank a mouthful of tea.

The séance was far from over. Whereas in his first trance, Nyima explained to me, the medium had been possessed by the Mighty Thunderbolt under his terrible aspect, the same protective deity would now enter into him under his peaceful aspect. The Rimpoche began once more to intone a litany, and the oracle-priest, who still looked thoroughly exhausted, resumed the posture prescribed by ritual, with legs wide apart. The period between the onset and the climax of the trance was much shorter on this occasion. As before, the seer began to gasp and tremble, but this time his movements were much less violent. His pale face wore a slight, friendly smile. Groaning, the oracle-priest gave the information he was asked for; but then he suddenly flung himself backwards with all his weight. Before the lamas who sprang forward had time to prevent it, the back of his head struck the stone wall with a resounding thud. One of the little skulls on his helmet snapped off and rattled to the ground. Eager hands raised up the unconscious seer and removed his helmet. His hair and the back of his neck were covered in blood, but closer examination revealed that the injury was only superficial, for the strong silver hoop and the leather bands inside it had absorbed most of the impact.

Tea and cold water brought the oracle-priest to his senses. After a quarter of an hour, when he had somewhat recovered, he declared that he was strong enough to go through with the rest of the ceremony. To my astonishment I learned from Nyima that two further divinities were to be called upon. The first was to be Namkha Bardzin, a lesser tutelary deity regarded as a kind of courtier to the Mighty Thunderbolt. On roll-paintings he is depicted as a red-coloured demon armed with a spear and a noose and standing on a decomposing corpse. While the lamas were preparing the oracle-priest for the next trance and piling up a mountain of cushions behind the throne, to prevent a repetition of the accident, Nyima gave me a brief outline of this demon's story. He was, he said, the spirit of a lama who had perished two decades ago during a snowstorm at Phari Dzong. The dead man was found by some shepherds, but instead of treating the corpse with respect, they made jokes about the unfortunate lama. His enraged spirit thereupon turned itself into a demon and slew the majority of the blasphemers together with their herds. Eventually the abbot of Dungkar Gompa in the Chumbi Valley succeeded in taming the evil spirit and transforming him into a protective deity of his monastery.

The Rimpoche's bell rang once more; the seer began to twist and turn, gasping, in the convulsion of a fresh seizure. His face turned red, and once again assumed the terrible demonic expression I knew from the first trance. No questions were put to him this time. The onlookers, led by the lama servants, now formed a long queue to be blessed by the medium—or rather, by the protective god that had taken possession of his body. With a deep bow the first priest approached the seer, into whose twitching hands one of the assistants pressed a long red silk ribbon. With some difficulty the medium tied a knot in the ribbon, raised it to his foam-flecked lips and then laid it on the bent neck of lama in front of him, who immediately stepped back and fastened the ribbon round his throat. These strips of silk with the breath of a tutelary deity clinging to them are thought to afford very effective protection against evil spirits.

I saw the Rimpoche, who had been standing near the oracle-priest with his back to me, suddenly turn round and peer about the room. When he caught sight of me he motioned to me—I could not believe my eyes—to take my place with the Tibetans in the queue and also receive an amulet. There might be some danger in approaching so close to the possessed medium, but I could not miss such an opportunity to observe him from close up. Besides, the invitation must be regarded as a great honour, and I could on no account refuse it.

The line moved slowly forward. Now it was my turn. I stepped to the front, bowed as I had seen the others do, and as I bent my head I tried to fix the magician's picture as precisely as possible in my mind—the red, sweat-drenched face with the convulsively closed eyes, the thick swollen veins on the temples … Out of the corner of my eye I watched the seer's restlessly fluttering hands—to my horror I saw they were obviously trying in vain to tie a knot in the silk ribbon. The breathing above my head grew more and more laboured. I felt intense fear—not of the weapons that stood within the oracle-priest's reach, but fear that he would perhaps refuse to put the red ribbon round my neck. I had attended several séances in Europe, and almost every time they had ended by the medium declaring in a reproachful voice that I was emitting a disturbing influence, which was defeating all his efforts. Was something similar going to happen here? Did the Tibetan medium, too, feel in his subconscious that a sceptical, coldly observant force was in his immediate vicinity? The seconds of waiting dragged on into endlessly long minutes. If I did not receive the consecrated ribbon, it might have unpredictable consequences for me. The superstitious Tibetans would certainty say that there was some evil spirit in me, and that the tutelary deity had therefore refused to bless me. No lama would ever lend me a book again or give me any information, much less allow me to take part in masher religious ceremony ... But I did not need to pursue these thoughts any farther, for now I felt the ribbon come to rest on my neck. I stepped back with a sigh of relief. Perhaps the slackening of my concentration had enabled the oracle-priest to execute the accustomed hand movements after all.

The blessing was scarcely over when the oracle-priest collapsed in a faint. Now the last divinity was to be called upon—Pawo Trombar, a red-coloured demon who holds a bleeding heart and a victory banner. He is said to be the spirit of a warlord who died in battle. Once more the rise and fall of the chant put the seer in a trance. He twisted convulsively for only a few minutes, then he suddenly opened his mouth and shouted in a guttural voice, 'O-ma, o-ma! . . . Milk, milk!' A servant hurried off to fulfil his request. He handed the oracle-priest the bowl, and again the onlookers filed past the throne. Each one bowed to the oracle-priest and held up his cupped hands, into which the trembling medium poured a little milk. I watched the people greedily drink the milk and even lick their fingers. The Rimpoche nodded to me encouragingly, so there was nothing for it but to take my place in the queue, which I did with very mixed feelings. But this time everything went off smoothly and I received my portion without a hitch. I drank the milk like the others. Afterwards I heard that this was no ordinary beverage, for the protective deity had turned the milk into an efficacious medicine that would ward off all ills. As before, the seer woke from his trance as soon as the last man in the line had passed him.

This was the end of the ceremony. The priest, who now looked utterly worn out, rose to his feet with a groan, and the lamas helped him take off the ceremonial garment. I could see that the thick everyday clothes he wore underneath were completely soaked with sweat. He staggered into a side-room, supported by two men, and there stretched out on an improvised bed. Meanwhile a lama ordered the garments and the rest of his outfit to be laid out on the chair in exactly the same order as I had seen them on the throne in Lhagpa Tondup's house. While this was going on, the Rimpoche intoned a prayer of thanksgiving to the tutelary deities who had today entered into the oracle-priest.

I left the chapel with Nyima in the early hours of the afternoon. As we strolled slowly towards the Tibetan quarter, I asked Nyima various questions about the spectacle we had witnessed. Above all, I wanted to know what the oracle-priest had said during the trances. Nyima was unable to tell me, however, for the seer's words had been unintelligible to him also. In any case, he informed me, the replies had not been intended for the ears of the audience as a whole. They concerned only certain private inquiries put by a Tibetan merchant, a friend of the Rimpoche, and his family.

As to the bent sword, he had often seen such things before. At the height of a trance the oracle-priest develops unusual physical strength and so has no difficulty in performing feats of this kind. A state of extreme exhaustion inevitably follows afterwards, however. Oracle-priests who are in great demand therefore die comparatively early as a rule. Amongst clairvoyant magicians of the lower grades there are some who try to impress the audience by various tricks, as Indian fakirs do. They transpierce their bodies with swords and spears, for example, without suffering any harm.

We had almost reached Nyima's house when I asked him a question, which had come to my mind several times that day.

'Do Tibetan oracle-priests make use of drugs in order to go into a trance?'

'Well no ... actually they don't ...' said Nyima, shaking his head. 'That would be trickery, for according to the doctrine of the Greater Vehicle it is the deity himself who descends into the priest and brings about this unaccustomed condition. But…' he stopped and let two approaching lamas go by before continuing in a low voice: 'There are some mediums who secretly take drugs to bring on the trance, for fear that it might not otherwise occur. But if the ecclesiastical authorities get wind of it, they can expect severe punishment. There are also oracle-priests—even among those of the highest rank—who take bribes. They then make predictions that advance the interests of those who have paid them.'

'And what drugs do the oracle-priests take?' I wanted to know.

Nyima shook his head with a smile. 'I know what they are, but I don't want to tell you yet. My countrymen would never forgive me, if they learned I had disclosed this secret to you. Be patient. On the day you leave Kalimpong I will tell you the names of these drugs.'

From time to time I heard some very strange stories from my Tibetan friends. Thus Lobsang Phuntsok, the son of a former State Prophet, told me of his experiences during the performance of the Cho ceremony. 'Cho', spelt *gcod* in Tibetan, means literally 'to cut in pieces', and the ceremony is called by this name because the meditant is alleged to offer his dismembered body for the gods, spirits and demons to eat. It is a very protracted ceremony, and Lobsang Phuntsok took many hours to describe it to me in detail. But in broad outline the Cho may be summarized as follows:

The meditant goes at night into a graveyard. First, he must recall the precepts given him by his teacher. Then he chants the introductory prayer, wielding a hand-bell and a skull-drum, and sinks into meditation. He conjures up before his spiritual eye his personal tutelary deity and unites his 'consciousness' with this divinity. Now it is as though he were floating in the air, and from his position within the deity he looks down upon his prostrate, lifeless body. A goddess of the order of the Heaven-Goers emerges from the body of the protective god and backs the meditant's body in piece. The latter immediately invites the whole Tibetan pantheon to a banquet and sets his own body before the countless hosts of his guests. To appease the hunger of the benign divinities, he turns his blood into nectar and his flesh into delicious ambrosia. The demonic Guardians of Religion and the evil spirits, whose turn comes next, greedily drink the blood of the corpse, devour the flesh and break the bones in order to suck out the marrow. During this orgy the 'consciousness' must seek to elucidate the causes and effects of fear. Once the banquet is finished the 'consciousness' discerns on the burying ground a radiantly new, godlike body. It leaves the security of the tutelary deity and enters into this new mortal frame, the meditant awakes from his trance and ends the Cho with a prayer.

The banquet of celestial beings is the climax of the Cho rite, but at the same time the hardest test for the meditant. If the 'consciousness' that has been absorbed in the tutelary deity is frightened by the gruesome spectacle, the whole hallucination is dissipated. Madness, or at least severe psychic damage, may result from a meditation that has gone wrong. Hence successful performance of this strange ceremony requires a slow and gradual introduction to the mysteries of the Cho by an experienced teacher. For those who master it, however, Lobsang Phuntsok assured me, the Cho is a refreshing source of mental and physical regeneration.

I also heard a great deal about Thumo, a combination of meditation and a particular breathing technique by means of which Tibetan yogis increase their bodily temperature. Thumo is supposed to render the yogi capable of meditating for days on end, almost naked, in a cold cell, or even in snow and ice, without any ill effects. Furthermore, so I was assured by Tibetans who had mastered this Yoga method, Thumo produces a gratifying sensation of lightness. Those who have learned the art of Thumo sometimes wear nothing but a single cotton garment known as a repa. Such yogis are called Repas after this garment; Mila Repa, the great poet, was one of them.

The Thumo training is concluded by a severe test. The testee, clad only in a loincloth, is wrapped in a large linen cloth soaked in ice-cold water. At the same time he eats a bowl of half-cooked tsampa. By means of Thumo he must dry the cloth, while he renders the half-cooked tsampa, which would otherwise cause him intense stomach pains, edible by generating heat. The testee has to dry twelve cloths in succession, and every time his body is wrapped in a fresh cloth he must eat another bowl of tsampa.

According to Tibetan assertions, many very learned priests, who have devoted themselves for decades to meditation and the study of the occult sciences, are able to make their bodies rise a short distance above the ground and float in the air. As a valuable preparation to this difficult art, the would-be levitationist is recommended to practise springing quickly to his feet from the posture of meditation without using his hands. This exercise, continued over a long period, renders the body exceptionally light. The highest degree of mastery has been attained when the levitationist can rest on the apex of a pyramid of corn without causing it to collapse. I was frequently told of priests alleged to be able to float in the air—but I never saw anyone do it …

I said goodbye to my teachers, the three Tibetan saints, and wondered to myself whether I should ever see them again. Then, late one afternoon, the time had come. I sat in a jeep that was to take me down to the plains, talking to Nyima, while the driver stowed my baggage. Good Nyima was determined to be present at my departure. We bade one another farewell. The driver had already started the engine, when Nyima leaned over to me and whispered: 'I promised that the day you left I would tell you what the oracle-priests take to induce a trance. It is … a mixture of hashish and red pepper!'

The vehicle jerked into motion. A wide curve, and then Kalimpong disappeared behind a spur of the mountain. The valleys were already beginning to fill with the pale mist of evening, but the icy strongholds of the gods stood cold and unapproachable on the horizon.

—

I have included two pieces in this anthology that bring out different aspects of the life and legacy of Swami Rama—that of the householder, the 'grahast', and that of the renunciate.

The first piece is written by Swami Rama himself. It is a lighthearted but deeply resonant record of his encounter with the Himalayan sage Gudari Baba during the course of a trek through the Valley of Flowers, which makes us relook at the linkages between the physical human body and the robes and accoutrements of the adepts, and the unlimited powers they can unleash from within themselves.

In the second essay, Devyani Mungali, renowned educationist and founder-principal of the Sanskriti group of schools in Pune, speaks of her father, Swami Rama, her relationship with him and the memories she carries in her heart. Born in the small hamlet of Toli in what is now Uttarakhand, he was lovingly named Kishori. After embarking on the spiritual life and being appointed shankaracharya of the Karvipeetham in South India, he returned to the mountains and married Lilu Pande, the daughter of a prominent Kumaoni family, and had two children with her. He then returned to the wandering life of a monk and became known to the world as Swami Rama. Mungali's moving and evocative piece is both a homage and a glimpse of personal history and memory.

CHAPTER 15

The Sage from the Valley of Flowers

SWAMI RAMA

There was not much literature on the flowers and ecology of the Himalayas, but I tried my best to go through whatever was available. One of the British writers wrote a book on 'the Valleys of Flowers of the Himalayas'. After reading this book, a flame of burning desire arose in my heart. In the Himalayas there are countless varieties of lilies, rhododendrons and other flowers, but I specifically was anxious to see one of the two valleys.

There lived a sage constantly travelling in that region of the Himalayas where this Valley of Flowers exists. I knew him well. He was very strong and healthy, about eighty years of age, but quite unusual. He used to carry a unique blanket all the time. It was very heavy. The weight of this blanket was approximately 80 to 100 pounds. You might wonder how he made this blanket so heavy. Any piece of cloth which he found during his wide travels, he would patch onto the blanket. It was a blanket of a thousand patches. He called it gudari, which means 'blanket of patches', and people called him Gudari Baba.

On my request he said, 'If you would really like to see the Valley of Flowers and want to follow me, you will have to carry this blanket.'

I agreed, but when I put the blanket on my shoulders I stumbled under its weight. He asked, 'How is it possible for a young man like you to be so weak when you are apparently so healthy?' He picked up the blanket and said, 'See how light it is?' Then he put it on my shoulders again. He knew my master and so he allowed me to follow him to the Valley of Flowers.

As I was following him this sage said, 'No one can retain his memory when he goes through the Valley of Flowers during the blooming season. We should bring all the obstinate kids like you here and set them right. Those who try to be intellectual and argue with us should be brought here so that they understand their worth.'

I said, 'But I am following you.'

He said, 'Oh yes. You argue all the time and don't listen attentively. You are very proud of your intellectual knowledge. I do not know how to read or write. You are more educated than I. You have education, but I have control of mind.'

I told him, 'I also have control.'

He replied, 'We shall see.'

I said, 'Sir, first of all, please take your blanket off my shoulders because it is difficult to carry.'

He lamented, 'Oh, the children of this modern age!'

He took his blanket from me and started conversing with it: 'O my beloved blanket, nobody understands anything about you. No one knows that you are a living blanket.'

I looked at him and thought, 'This man is really crazy!'

The next morning a Japanese monk joined us. He was equally anxious to see the Valley of Flowers. This Japanese monk also thought that Gudari Baba was a crazy man. He asked me, 'Rama, can you explain why this man is carrying such a heavy load?' We started talking and I thought it would be nice to share these experiences with each other.

This monk was afraid of going to the Valley of Flowers all alone. Someone had told him that if any traveller goes to see this valley, he forgets everything and his senses do not coordinate in perceiving sense objects. The traveller loses his memory and smiles all the time. He said that this baba was the right person to guide us because he travelled in this region and knew all the trails.

The next day this Japanese monk started shivering with fever. He had lived in the jungles of Burma and suffered from malaria. He had a temperature of 103 to 104 degrees and his pulse rate was very high. The baba said to him, 'You told this boy that I was crazy. Do you want to see the living power of my blanket? Do you know that this blanket is not a mere blanket, but a living force? Do you want to get well? Then kneel down and be humble!' The baba covered the Japanese monk with the blanket.

The monk said, 'I will be flattened! It's too heavy and I am a small man.'

The baba said, 'Keep quiet!' After a few minutes he took the blanket away from the monk. When he removed the blanket, it was shivering. The baba asked the monk, 'What happened to your fever?'

He said, 'Sir, I don't have a fever any more.'

The baba said, 'This blanket is very generous and kind and has taken away your fever.' The baba then looked at me and asked, 'Do you want his fever to be cured forever?'

I said, 'Yes, please.'

The baba said, 'But he calls me crazy. I don't think he deserves my help.'

I said, 'The sages are kind and great and they always forgive others.'

The baba smiled and said, 'Of course I will help him.' We travelled together for fifteen days and the Japanese monk did not suffer from the fever again.

Nine miles outside of Badrinath there is a side trail that leads to the Valley of Flowers where there is a small gurudwara (Sikh place of worship). We took our meal there. The people of this gurudwara knew Gudari Baba very well. We rested that whole day in the gurudwara and started our journey to the Valley of Flowers towards Hemkund the next day.

The flowers were in full bloom as far as the eye could see. For the first few hours it was soothing to the senses and stimulating to the mind. But slowly I started noticing that my memory was slipping away. After five or six hours the baba asked, 'Hey you! Can you tell me your name?'

We were both so disoriented that we could not remember our names. We had completely forgotten them. I was only aware of my existence and had a hazy idea that I was with two other people. That's all. The fragrance of those flowers was so strong that we could not think rationally. Our ability to reason wouldn't function. Our senses were anaesthetized. We had a faint idea of our existence and that of the things around us.

Our talk to each other did not make any sense. We lived in this valley for a week. It was highly enjoyable. The baba made fun of us all the time and said, 'Your education and strength have no value.'

After we came out of the Valley of Flowers, the baba said:

'Your joy was because of the influence of the fragrance of the flowers. You were not meditating. That's what marijuana and hashish do to people, and they think that they are in meditation. Look at me. I was not affected or influenced by the fragrance of those wild flowers. Ha, ha, ha! You have gone to college and have read many books. You have lived on the opinions of others so far. Today you had a good chance to understand and compare direct knowledge and the so-called knowledge that is really imitation. So far the opinions that you have are actually the opinions of others. Those who live on the opinions of others do not ever have the ability to decide and express their own opinions. Boys, this informative knowledge is not considered by us to be real knowledge. Even if you understand that direct knowledge alone is valid, you don't have control over the mind. The education given to modern children is very superficial. Without any discipline, control over the mind is not possible—and without control of the mind, direct experience is impossible.'

The Japanese monk left for Bodh Gaya, and I lived with the baba for another fifteen days. He is a free wanderer of this region, and all the pilgrims have heard about him. For practical schooling it is important for the renunciate to live with such sages who have direct knowledge of the values of life with its currents and crosscurrents.

CHAPTER 16

From Kishori to Swami Rama of the Himalayas

A Daughter's Tribute to Her Father's Spiritual Legacy

DEVYANI MUNGALI

On 26 October 1925, a boy was born to an extremely devout couple, Gaura Devi and Pandit Buddhi Ballabh Dhasmana, in the small hamlet of Toli in Pauri Garhwal. The baby arrived after his father's long and arduous tapasya at Mansadevi in Haridwar. He was doted on by his mother, an extremely kind, gentle and generous lady, and his sister-in-law (his elder brother's wife), in whose eyes he could do no wrong. He grew up in their loving care and was affectionately known as Kishori. Later on in life, he would be addressed by several names—Brij Kishor Kumar, Bhole Baba, Bhole Prabhu, Swami Ramdandi and finally Swami Rama. The last name would stay and it is under this name that he would find renown, not only in India but worldwide. But for me he was simply Babba—my father.

Babba's mother, my paternal grandmother, was renowned in the Pauri Garhwal region for having a mystical connection with the Almighty. The villagers sought her help in times of trouble, ill health, family discord or financial problems. She would just give them some mud from the walls of her dwelling, which the villagers would take home reverently and thus find solutions to their problems. Little did she know that her progeny's name and fame would spread far beyond this remote hamlet of Toli, where he would always be remembered as 'Kishori'.

Young Kishori started his spiritual quest under the tutelage and guidance of his guru and mentor, Bengali Baba, who was one of the sanyasis who had saved the Raja of Bhawal from his half-lit funeral pyre during the torrential rains in Darjeeling. This case became popular as the sensational Bhawal Sanyasi case, the longest-contested case during the British regime. Oblivious to the noise, Bengali Baba avoided the limelight after this and continued his spiritual pursuits.

Young Kishori spent several years wandering as an ascetic, in the region that is today known as Uttarakhand, gleaning as much knowledge as he could by learning yogic kriyas, doing meditation and studying the scriptures. He was blessed and privileged to have spent time with some acclaimed Indian sages—Neem Karoli Maharaj, Sri Aurobindo, Anandamayi Ma and Ramana Maharshi. Apart from this, he spent time with several recondite recluses, who spent their time praying and meditating in Himalayan caves and humble dwellings, far from the gaze of the mundane world. All those who knew him from that time—brother disciples, village folk and his relatives—remember him as an ebullient boy who had a keen intellect and an inquiring mind. He also seemed to have an almost preternatural ability to connect with animals. One of his unusual pets at that time was a bear.

Babba would often mention in private that the biggest gift of his life was the chance to spend time with so many learned sages. He also maintained that anyone who followed the path of meditation or pranayama consistently could achieve the same extraordinary state of mind that he was able to experience and demonstrate.

He was still a wandering ascetic when he was anointed as the shankaracharya of Karvipeetham, a golden opportunity at the age of twenty-eight. He succeeded Dr Kurtkoti, a leader of the learned monastic tradition. He held this position from 1949 to 1952. After returning to his master, Bengali Baba, in 1952 and practising yoga and meditation with him, he was encouraged to go to the West to spread yoga and the wisdom of the ancient Indian scriptures.

On 16 July 1960, he got married to my mother, Lilu Pande, in Mukteshwar, Uttarakhand. She was beautiful, cultured, intelligent and well-read, besides being a gifted artist, and belonged to a distinguished and renowned family of the region. She had completed her master's degree in English literature form Banaras Hindu University, and had been awarded a gold medal for her outstanding overall performance.

After living the life of a householder, husband and father for some years, Babba decided to embark on his spiritual pursuits again. Even when he chose his life partner, he was probably aware that he had found an exceptional woman who would face all of life's challenges with immense fortitude and equanimity. My mother spent her life single-handedly bringing up my brother and I with dignity and stoicism, working as a professor of English literature in Nainital. She retired as the principal of the Government Postgraduate College in Noida and is widely respected by friends, family, colleagues for her positivity, honesty, sincerity and sound value system. She is an anchor, the North Star, for us and we look up to her as our idol. This unsung hero's contribution to Swami Rama's spiritual journey and legacy is unfathomable and largely unknown. She silently supported her husband's varied spiritual and intellectual pursuits, always proud of his achievements. She sacrificed immensely in life and faced many challenges while bringing us up alone. She always urged us to love Babba and respect his work and achievements. She earned deep respect from Babba's family, especially his elder brother, my uncle Shri Prayagdutt Dhasmana, and her mother-in-law. My paternal grandmother was an extremely compassionate lady and my mother told me that whenever she would eat something, even if it were only a fruit, she would make it a point to share some of it with the birds. Babba also had a similar compassionate vein, but could be detached and loving in equal measure.

Not everybody is blessed to have a father with a glorious heritage, yet as a child it was bewildering and at times somewhat hurtful to not have a father physically present like those of my school friends. There were several occasions when I yearned for him to be around like other fathers—during school functions, festivals and birthdays. But Babba and I would regularly write letters to each other; those letters are my most prized heirlooms. The nickname he gave me, 'Bimbri', was a moniker that has remained with me till today. I would look forward to all the times he would visit but some of those memories are bittersweet. At times when I was questioned by my friends about my father's whereabouts and profession and would return home teary-eyed, my mother always told me that I shouldn't feel ashamed, instead I should be proud of what he was doing.

No matter how far and wide Babba wandered in his spiritual quest, his deep-rooted love for the Himalayas, drew him back to its feet. He not only came to be well-known as Swami Rama of the Himalaya, but was also named all of the institutes founded by him as Himalayan Institutes. His bestselling autobiography, translated into several languages, also bears the title *Living With the Himalayan Masters* and is testimony to the fact that he could never severe the umbilical cord that so deeply connected him to the Himalaya.

In 1969, Babba arrived in the US and was introduced to Elmer and Alyce Green of the Menninger Foundation in Topeka, Kansas, who had a well-equipped laboratory designed to investigate voluntary control of psychophysiological processes. He realized that this was the place where he could fulfil his master's ambitions to scientifically document the abilities manifested by masterful practice of yoga. He demonstrated an array of abilities, including simultaneously raising and lowering the temperature in adjacent muscles by 10 degrees Fahrenheit and placing his heart in such atrial fibrillation that it stopped pumping blood for several minutes. He manifested telekinesis in an environment carefully controlled for the motion of air and for electromagnetic forces. He spontaneously created deep non-REM cysts under his skin and also voluntarily entered into alpha, beta and delta brainwave states. He demonstrated a yogic practice called yoga 'nidra'—conscious entry into deep non-REM sleep. During the experiment, two technicians were quietly talking in the next room. When he resumed awareness, he recounted their conversation verbatim. He was not only focused on his inward state, but also remained aware of his external environment. There is no explanation in current neuroscience for his ability to do so. He performed these demonstrations to help the West understand that an individual's state of health and well-being was in their control.

The above demonstration of yogic kriyas merited him a mention in *The Britannica Yearbook of Science and the Future* in 1973.[52]

Babba didn't believe in impressing others with miracles, supernatural feats or by displaying his mastery over complex yogic kriyas. He had the rare ability to blend advanced spiritual practices with a regular lifestyle. Once, I inadvertently walked into Babba's room while he was engaged in his sadhana. He wasn't annoyed by this diversion; instead I witnessed an extraordinary yogic feat. He showed me how the temperature of his palm could differ to a great degree at two different spots simply by him controlling his breath and concentrating in a specific manner. On another occasion, I witnessed him channelling the flow of blood to one half of his body in such a manner that one half was absolutely ruddy and flushed and the other half was pale. I noticed that his energy level was depleted for some time after displaying these rare and complex yogic feats.

There were several other instances when I had the privilege to witness these kriyas, which defied regular explanation. In an almost self-effacing manner, he always emphasized to me that any practitioner who followed

52 *Encyclopaedia Britannica*, published by William Benton.

the yogic path, especially the science of breath control, could do similar things. He also stated that such siddhis were often the by-product of spiritual practice and should not be treated as an end goal or used as a barometer of true spiritual progress. On the contrary, he mentioned that frequently, these 'siddhis' could be major stumbling blocks to distract the practitioner.

He founded the Himalayan Institute of Yoga Science and Philosophy in Illinois, which was later moved to its current location in the Pocono Mountains of Honesdale in Pennsylvania. It became a centre for promoting yoga and holistic health through yoga retreats, residential programmes, workshops, seminars and publication of several books, journals and newsletters.

He was a man who wore many hats—he was a prolific writer and wrote more than ninety-three books on yoga, science and philosophy. He was a gifted poet whose love for rhyme and ability to play with words is evident in the beautiful verses that flow mellifluously in his compilation of poems, *Love Whispers*. He enjoyed playing tennis and dabbling with colours. His paintings were usually either abstract or realistic, based on nature. He had a fairly good knowledge of Hindustani classical music and apart from chanting mantras, he loved to sing. He invited several renowned singers and musicians to the Himalayan Institute in Honesdale for music concerts and retreats.

His labour of love, his swan song, was the Himalayan Institute Hospital and Medical College that he founded and built in Jolly Grant near Dehradun. He poured his heart, soul and resources into setting up this well-equipped hospital, the first medical college in Uttarakhand, which he envisioned would cater to the needs of the millions of less-privileged inhabitants from the far-flung villages of Garhwal. He was so enthused by this task that I recall seeing him lifting bricks along with the construction workers at the site. When I asked him why he was doing so, he said that this would motivate the labourers to work harder and accomplish the task at hand sooner. Even on the last day of his life, he was doing the rounds of the hospital to ensure that all was well.

When he sensed that his end was near, he sent a message through a common acquaintance that he wished to meet his family. All of us were there with him. He asked my mother whether she had visited the hospital and medical college, and seen what all had been accomplished under his guidance. It seemed as if he was waiting for her final stamp of approval. What was truly inspiring for me was how calm, composed and tranquil he was before he cast away his body. There was no fear or anxiety. It was amazing to see him embracing the unknown; comforting family, friends and followers around him, sharing his words of wisdom. He explained to everyone that his work was over and it was time for him to go; the body is just a garment but the soul is eternal. He said that his master would come to collect him and they would embark on a new journey together on 13 November 1996 at 11.08 p.m. My brother and my mother went to Tarkeshwar, the family deity's abode, to offer prayers for him. As soon as they finished offering prayers, he bid adieu to the material world on the day and time he had specified. He left his body with full awareness and control, true to the Himalayan tradition and its long lineage of adepts. He was cremated in Haridwar and his ashes were immersed in the holy Ganges river, which he fondly addressed as Gangaji or Ganga Ma.

There are a chosen few who leave their mark on this earth by rising above the humdrum existence of ordinary men and women. My father, Swami Rama, was one of these. He spent his life in the selfless service of humanity. He was a revered guru who provided guidance and succour to many. He was generous to a fault and had no attachment to worldly possessions. He wouldn't think twice before giving away his choicest possessions if anyone expressed appreciation for them. An expensive watch, a ring, a fine woollen shawl, on one occasion even a car, was gifted without a second thought. I recall that he once rolled down the car window and handed over a wad of currency notes from his wallet to an emaciated, half-clad beggar who had been seeking alms. The poor beggar stood dazed for a moment and then dashed off, zigzagging through the crowd, suspecting some mischief.

He is remembered with immense love and reverence by his family, disciples, fellow seers and young readers who have discovered his teachings and philosophy through his writings and lectures. In one of his last discourses he remarked:

> We have become a small family, the whole world is like a small family. But now we should learn how to live together with each other, how to behave with each other. It is love that will help, but a selfless person alone has the capacity to love others. Selflessness is the foundation stone of the entire life concept.

These words truly encapsulate his life's philosophy.

Babba was someone who treated prince and pauper alike. He had a childlike innocence, a remarkable zest for life and a wonderful sense of humour. His tall, regal bearing and self-assured demeanour made him stand out in a crowd. Worshipped by many, respected by most and adored by a legion of admirers, friends and family members, he lives enshrined in their hearts. His photos are devoutly displayed in several domestic shrines, temples and yoga institutes. His books continue to educate and inspire innumerable people.

It gives me great pride to know that he has positively impacted so many lives. One of his rare talents was the ability to meet his followers at their level of preparedness. He would encourage each person to follow the path which was best aligned with their innate nature, so for some he would encourage the path of Bhakti, for others it would be the Jnana Yoga path of self-inquiry and those who he felt were ready to learn would be initiated into the science of breath control and Raja Yoga.

I am blessed to have been his daughter in this lifetime and received his unconditional love and guidance. I am privileged to have known him not only as a sage, a Himalayan master, but as a father, friend, guide and grandfather to my brother's children and my children. I was privileged to have a glimpse of his knowledge, wisdom, humour and childlike traits.

The following lines from his beautiful collection of verses, *Love Whispers*, resonate in my mind even today:

Seer, O Seer, Stop for a moment;
Whisper thy secret with kind intent.
Are we only like seasonal flowers,
Or the travellers of endless hours?
You are like the eternal lotus that remains untouched
During the heavy shower of torrential rains.

—

This anthology is titled Mystics and Sceptics *because, for every true and discerning master and disciple, there is the dark mirror of ego-infused gurus and their vulnerable devotees.*

Bhushita Vasistha's painstaking re-examination of her eleven years in an Osho commune on the outskirts of Kathmandu, Nepal, spares no one, least of all herself. It documents her journey towards selfhood and self-assertion and the struggle to keep her individuality intact amidst community groupthink. 'This is a story of distortion, of god, of miasma, of the loss of a face.'

'It took me so long to realize that he, the leader, and us, the followers, had gravitated to each other because our pathologies complemented each other,' she concludes. Her hard-won learnings are more important than every platitude encountered along the path.

CHAPTER 17

In Search of the Miraculous

BHUSHITA VASISTHA

Every sentence I begin this story with feels wrong.

It feels wrong because I want to tell this story honestly. But honest storytelling is a miasma, isn't it? A claim to glean truth 'as it is' from the distorted interpretations we have made of our realities to stay sane. Perhaps to interpret is to distort. But I will try.

It was a July afternoon like any other. I had been assigned to interview the leader of an Osho commune on his views on vegetarianism. I could have simply interviewed him over the telephone, as I would usually do for such lifestyle stories. But this story was going to be my first byline article and I *was* intrigued by the commune. Osho had been dead for almost two decades; however, his reputation as the guru of the libertines was on the rise.

Could there really be a world where people loved as freely as he said humans should? Were there ways to avoid the stale certitude of marriage? Was sex as liberating and as poetic as Osho made it out to be?

I was seventeen and had started my first job as a stringer in a newspaper. I had far too many questions to let go of the opportunity to visit his commune and seek answers for myself. Besides, one of my fellow journalists lived full-time in the commune. I was drawn to his intellect and personality. So, the visit was promising on many fronts.

I caught a bus from outside my office in Subidhanagar.

I came from a small town where everyone knew everyone else. Everybody seemed to live similar lives. I didn't know then that humanity had systematically arrived at this monotony to avoid the anxiety of greeting the unexpected embedded within the everyday. If anyone had warned me that I would run out of my capacity to stomach the unexpected some day, I would have scorned them. I thought I was made for a better life—more adventurous, more thrilling, more ... just more than what I saw around me.

However, this undefined 'more' grew more intangible with time. I was increasingly haunted by the longing for something abstract. Of course, I was just seventeen. My body was becoming more perceptive to the calls of the sensual. I wasn't satisfied with life as it came to me. I was interested in my books, my work and men, whose attention I found very flattering. But I felt that the pleasure I sought lay beyond all these.

It was at this point that I had the opportunity to visit the Osho commune on the outskirts of Kathmandu. Nothing seemed out of the ordinary as I left; the bus took off, belching acidic fumes, depositing a layer of black soot and dust on the poplar leaves by the roadside. Outside, the city appeared dull and tired. Everyone seemed restless. I looked at their nameless existence and their seamless merging with the monotonous and ugly architecture of the city. The bus was full of passengers, and yet I knew no one. I found this crowd and this alienation stifling.

The bus stopped at the foothills of Nagarjuna mountain. I alighted to find my journalist friend waiting for me on his motorbike, smiling.

'Good ride?' he asked.

'Mm-hmm.' I smiled back. It was dignifying to become an identifiable person from a cog in the nameless crowd.

'We are not very far,' he said. We rode off on his bike.

The commune was perched on the tail end of the Nagarjuna national forest reserve. An unassuming cobbled pathway, weathered pleasantly with lichen and moss, spiralled down the hill. An occasional rush of breeze showered needlewood flowers on the stairs. I felt an expansion and calmness within and suddenly my reflexive aggressiveness, which one acquires from years of attempting to prove one's worth, seemed petty and meaningless. I wasn't prepared for this. We walked down stairs with bamboo gates, canopied with wild ivy and honeysuckle. I became aware of a shadow that fell over me like a crocheted veil. The spirit of the forest was seeping into me; I was melting from within.

I felt I had reached utopia. What I didn't know then, though, was that the word 'utopia' has a double meaning—a place to be in/a place that cannot be. Cartographers cannot locate utopias. They exist in the penumbra of reality, where poetry, gods and other maladies sprout. But I was only seventeen years old. Poetry and gods fascinated me endlessly. I was a willing captive.

I became an initiate at the ashram, a sanyasin. Of course, unlike the traditional Hindu sanyas tradition, Osho's doctrine allows sanyasins to have partners. In fact, as many as one wants.

I continued working outside as a journalist and going to college, but my life was gradually dictated by the activities in the commune. We would wake up and do intense cathartic meditation. We would howl and weep and scream and laugh. I wept over pain I had long forgotten. I screamed at people at whom I could never raise a voice in real life. I didn't know I had been so broken from the inside. The guru told us that we were beautiful innocent flowers, botched mercilessly by the cruel world outside. I was stunned by his acknowledgement. I felt validated and special. If the indifference of the city had frosted my soul, this close-knit community that ate together, danced together and showered each other with warm bear hugs after every meditation slowly thawed it back.

The community had around fifty inmates who lived there regularly and about a hundred others who joined for special retreats and celebrations. By South Asian standards, it was quite liberal and progressive. There were a few married couples, but many young people also lived together without bothering too much about the permanency of their affairs. Or, at least, they appeared unbothered to me then. The inmates contributed their labour and in return, the commune looked after their basic needs. There were many, like me, who worked outside and paid for their stay. I thrived in this community of young creative professionals, who were also exploring alternative lifestyles as spiritual practitioners.

Eventually I fell in love with the journalist friend who had taken me to the commune.

We were a family, replete with the all-powerful, omniscient Himalayan guru as the supreme father figure. Our Guru was a first-generation Osho disciple who was tirelessly involved in initiating people, giving discourses, leading meditation camps and overseeing the expansion of the commune. He had been a civil engineer and came from a family with credible political connections.

He was the most benign person I had ever known. His personal life wasn't perfect. He had had two unsuccessful marriages and lived all by himself in his bungalow; his second wife lived in the commune as well. He would encourage us to let go of our conditioning and jealousies and love 'without expectations'.

The word 'love' became expansive and multidimensional for me. I felt an all-pervading love for people, mountains and trees. I was getting there.

And then, one day, I caught my boyfriend clumsily making out with another female inmate.

Weren't we the chosen ones, who could love without expectation and jealousy? If so, why was my heart a sore wound?

I felt ashamed even as I protested to my boyfriend. This was the first steady relationship for both of us. Navigating intimacy in the nebulous, idealistic world, where love was supposed to be free of 'baser' emotions like jealousy, we felt like two lost souls, swimming in the fish bowl. Year after year, trying to find the new grounds of love, we found nothing but the same old fears. Neither of us realized then that we had chosen an ideal we could never live up to. And now we were forever bound to live the life of imposters.

Utopia was the place to be/the place that cannot be.

I felt foolish admitting my jealousies, my insecurities. My wails grew more heart-wrenching during the cathartic meditation. But otherwise, I was a happy, carefree sanyasin, untouched by the worries that plague mortals. In the process of perpetuating this pretence, I ended up hurting my boyfriend the way he hurt me. And like me, he too could never admit how much it pained. After all, we were Osho sanyasins—the harbingers of a new world order!

Months passed. My pretensions were weighing me down. I finally went to the Guru to ask for a way out, to learn ways to mitigate my jealousy and my pain. He listened attentively and lovingly. Bathed in the pale yellow tungsten light that illuminated the room, the tiny jasmine prints on his bedsheet appeared tender and fragrant. I broke down and started to weep. He patted my head gently and drew me to him. I felt protected. He told me to come to him whenever I felt troubled. With his silver beard and neatly trimmed silver hair, he appeared even more saintly in the tungsten light. I knelt at his feet in gratitude and then left.

'A guru is a father,' he told me. 'And a mother. A guru is everything.'

I had grown alienated from my family. My mother, in particular, was outraged at my audacity to live with a man out of wedlock. I regarded my family as perpetuators and defenders of attachment and jealousy, thus curbing the human capacity to 'love freely'. I was trying to rise above this pettiness. So, I had ruptured my attachment with my parents. And gradually, the Guru came to inhabit this void.

With each passing day, my idea of love became more volatile and unstable. I had willingly orphaned myself. But I was still a child. I looked around and saw that almost all of us in the commune were children trapped in the body of adults. We hadn't made peace with the dissolution of our childhood fantasies of serving an all-powerful father. We desperately tried to create a father figure who was omniscient and omnipotent. We pinned our hopes, dreams and illusions on him, our Guru. We wanted him to be infallible. To cover for his 'human weaknesses', we heaped generous sprinklings of metaphysical rationalizations. Sometimes we even marvelled at how human he was, after all.

His humanness started asserting itself more frequently. Looking back, I now understand how the followers in any cult are carefully taken through the process of self-effacement to the point that they are willing to submit to the most cruel and humiliating forms of servitude.

Every religious/spiritual group agrees that the individual ego is a hindrance to devotion. Burdened by our own miseries, disillusioned with the empty promise of success and happiness in the real world, we believe that the fault must lie within ourselves, that our ego must be our bondage. And in order to liberate ourselves of it, we let go of our personal boundaries. We become open and vulnerable. We want to submit to a higher consciousness that can liberate us from ourselves. When there is no self, you don't know the rules of the game any more. You can no longer decide what is wrong and right. Life becomes shrouded in miasma. Strange hands and mouths start sprouting out of this mist, groping you, caressing you, blessing you, appropriating you. *It must all be right*, you tell yourself. And keep collecting more pain. More shame.

On some nights, when everyone was asleep and the facade of spirituality eroded into the darkness, I tried to recoil into myself. But there was no self any more. I was just a phantom, an echo of something I didn't understand. I was a pliant part of a herd, but when left to myself, I was nobody. I was terrified of being alone.

One day, I dared to admit to myself that I was hurt. I went to the Guru and admitted to him that I was hurting. His utopia and his benevolence did nothing to eradicate my suffering, but I daresay, only added to it. When I finally accepted that the emperor was *indeed* naked, the masks were taken off our faces. And underneath our masks, each of us had a face the other couldn't recognize.

It took me so long to realize that he, the leader, and we, the followers, had gravitated to each other due to our complementing pathologies. We were desperately trying to recreate an idyllic childhood with our omnipotent father and he was as desperately seeking the childish, narcissistic comfort of being all-powerful. It was a grotesque game. None of us were who we pretended to be. We roleplayed this most ancient, archetypal and sinister fantasy of God-the-father and his begotten children.

Jorge Luis Borges once said, 'The worst labyrinth is not that intricate form that can entrap us forever, but a single and precise straight line.' He couldn't have been more accurate. I exhausted myself, my aesthetics, my intellect, my sensibility in trying to 'understand' life, groping for that abstract 'more'. Reading book after book, listening to endless discourses, watching documentaries, meditating for hours, I was walking down the path that promised to lead to understanding.

And yet I arrived nowhere.

I have come to understand that the only difference between a child and an adult is the intensity of the demand for meaning. A child can endure or even celebrate life without wanting to know its meaning. But for adults, life becomes predictable, routine automatizes, emotions become less overwhelming and death is a growing certainty that settles in our beings every morning when we wake up to draw the strength to play Sisyphus's game again. Defeated by this monotony, we seek refuge in God or in the notion of a Higher Purpose. How else can man endure death, poverty and suffering?

But is there a Higher Purpose?

One not-so-bright day, I just walked out of the commune, leaving behind everything I had built carefully for eleven years. I was on the road again, with nothing to call my own. I had awoken to the fact that there is no God, at least not in the sense that organized religions try to sell. There are no answers. There is anguish, there is suffering everywhere, and this is a precondition to being a human. One must find one's purpose amidst this chaos; not by projecting a pantheon of imaginary gods or gurus. Life is too vast for anyone to claim omniscience. We do not understand everything, nobody does, and it's perfectly all right.

Slowly, beauty has started speaking to me again. I could have never imagined how the breaking of the illusion of God would shatter me. For years, I meandered from place to place, weighed down by my own disbelief. The inability to trust is most anxiety-inducing and painful.

But slowly, wandering alone in the Himalayan valleys, listening to its rustles and moans, I am learning to become a devotee again. But this devotion is not for any one person any more. I submit to the tyranny and the beauty of life. I submit to the good and the evil she plants in each of us.

I submit to life itself, which is both ordinary and miraculous at once.

Sidharth is a painter, writer and mystic. His spiritual practice involves long treks in the high reaches of the Himalaya, where he searches for herbs, natural pigments and dyes for his artworks. It was in the course of such a journey that he first encountered the intriguing figure of Laal Baba and learnt from him his philosophy of colour, joy and freedom.

CHAPTER 18

Laal Baba

The Red Sage and the Secrets of the Life-Giving Herbs

SIDHARTH, TRANSLATED BY NIRUPAMA DUTT AND JASPREET MANDHER

In Tapovan, the brooding spiritual forest of life-giving herbs where sages sit in meditation for long years, the Rudra Ganga flows. Streams of different hues meet the eye—green, red, yellow, earthy brown—as they weave their way downstream, making such a din that one cannot hear even the sound of one's own breath.

Below Gaumukh, where the glacier pouts like the open mouth of a white cow, the Bhagirathi gushes out. Many streams meet there and waterfalls spring out of mountains. Rivulets are infused with Sanjivini herbs. The waters of the Vasundhara sparkle like gems and dance down in rapid steps.

Beyond stand the Shivalik Mountains in endless rows. The pilgrims walk in awed silence, aware of the murmur of the eternal silence.

Suddenly, someone prances down. He is wearing robes as red as his skin and his matted hair is rolled like roots. He stands, arms wide open, on a slender pathway of stones. 'Why have you come here to this Nandanvan, the picturesque Gangotri valley, to break the silence of the brooding forest,to break the tranquility of this land of Shiva and Vishnu?' he shouts. 'There is no place for you here, in the abode of my Laal Baba, in this garden of my Hanuman. Go back! Return to your own world far away from these life-giving herbs! Go back, I say.'

The lama stops in his tracks, mutters a prayer: 'O Laal Baba! You are right. What have we come here for? What business do we have here? Are we looking for something here? Beyond doubt, dear sage, you are absolutely right.'

Laal Baba calms down a little and then says softly, yet firmly: 'Do you think this forest will feel your presence, rid you of your turbulence and lack of peace? Or do you imagine this forest will deep-dye you in its varied colours and put you in rhythm with this infinite cosmos? Will you be able to become one with the Sanjivani herbs, banish pain and suffering, give peace and joy to humankind? At the moment, you are so disconnected! You do not even know how to walk peacefully on these pathways. You do not know how to step onto the forest paths with full consciousness. You meander around unseeing, unthinking, trampling over everyone and everything, crushing down buds and beetles! Your swagger says that you believe yourself to be the master of the universe!'

'O Laal Baba! Wherefore have you appointed yourself the lord and master of this place? Surely, you do not own this vibrant land, replete with utmost beauty and the original song of life! Living amidst these sylvan surroundings, why are you so angry?Seething in fury, how have you turned so red? O Sage! What is the reason behind your ruddy visage?'

Looking away, the sage speaks: 'Brother, the rivers here are red and have tinted my clothes and skin in their hue. Unlike you, I have not bought my clothes in the marketplace.

'These rivers flow past, singing and soothing the mind into a stillness undisturbed by even a ripple of thought. But just now I heard the piercing scream of the herb trampled under your foot. You have taken away the life of my little herb in this blessed heaven. Just look at the havoc you have caused here! This loss distressed me and I lost my calm for a moment. Wielding your stick, you make your way, crushing all that is in your path.

'The panacea of all ills, these Sanjivani butis, trees, birds, insects, all creatures big and small are the heartbeats of the universe and will remain so always. They are free of the human emotions of love, hate, animosity and rebellion—Satya, Sarva, Swayambhu (truthful, eternal, self-existing)—that you can never be!'

'O Sage! My gratitude to you for unveiling this truth! Seeped in our ego, we are like sleepwalkers treading this earth, unaware of its potential for sustenance, and our own too.

'I bow my head before you. I salute your awareness. O Laal Baba, I yearn for more communion with you, to gather insights from your enlightened mind. Please grant me this wish.'

The Baba laughs; pure laughter like that of a tinkling waterfall. 'Alright, you traveller, you have come to me and I have found you. All is preordained and coexistence is the truth of nature. One knows not who will be the taker and who the giver.

'To be self-aware and one's own master is the key to understanding nature. To be as natural as nature itself is the golden rule. Once you have mastered yourself only then will you be able to understand all else.'

Following the Baba's footsteps, we reach a cave. 'I live in the womb of this grotto,' he says. 'This shelter is as sacred to me as the womb of the divine Mother Goddess. Fold your hands, bow your head and step in as my guest. Do not mock at the dust, for it is the gift from Mother Earth which the pirouetting winds bring for us.

'I came here many years ago on a trek with my friends. I was a student of botany then in Delhi. It was here that I had an encounter with my guru, Laal Baba, and it was thanks to his largesse that I became one with nature. There was no going back. I stayed on, sleeping at the feet of my guru and never returning to the faraway material world.'

He continues, 'My Baba says:

In springtime, we all sleep off; simultaneously, somehow, the fire of hunger arises! Fires of suffering and flames of desire leap up!
The bodily flames go up all the while! What kind of fires are these?
Wake up and grow aware of all this—which fires and what awakening!
My dear, don't just slide off into non-awareness and sloth
the primeval naad has been playing—
the warp and weft of this life-flow—
the texture of this creation entire
was woven much before forms manifested
and time came up as a unit of life
every beetle, blade of grass and boulder in this vast and vaster cosmos
synchronizes with one elemental naad—
going on since no one knows when or for how long—
it is thus no surprise at all that every form in this cosmos
synergizes with the One primordial formlessness!
Every grain of sand, grotto and every galaxy
beams with the same agency and chimes with the One elemental sound
Clearly, it is the life splendourous exhibiting One in many
and manifold through Eternal Unity
Skies, earth, the netherworld
sun, moon, stars—all listen to the eternal naad
and move by its vibrations,
on similar lines, plants, trees and mountains tune into the primal notes
playing out since the beginning of the beginning

> water, fire and the body sacred sway midst one soulful naad
> that has been going on forever—sprinkling timelessness all around, hearing messages sublime—of oneness with the creation. In every breath of beings—resonating with the eternal naad—every bit and blade, bloom and fruit, every node and leaf, every seed, sapling, insect and moth, every millipede, banyan and mangrove, herbs, stalks and Sanjivani nectars—all talk wordlessly among themselves, harmonizing with the ever-present naad.'

Laal Baba continues, 'O curious one! O sensitive, inquisitive one! You can hear this consecration unto the sublime naad! Why don't you humans offer yourselves up to this all-enveloping naad? Dedicate yourselves to this symphony and witness the flowering of your life-breath, your being and the sprouting of the seedlings of beauty in your soul scape.'

The distant mountains glow in the light of the setting sun. Casting a stick in the incense fire, Laal Baba announces that it is time for supper. He asks for some red water in a pan, which he puts on the fire. Then he sets out a bowl each for everyone. He puts some dried herbs into the red water. The herbs unfurl in the boiling water, turn green and fill the pan. He continues praying with folded hands and then serves this evening meal to everyone. The fragrance and taste of the herbs fills the senses. It is a miracle, this food blessed by God.

'So you want to know my name?' he asks. 'I no longer have a name of my own. The name of my guru is now my name. The guru of my guru was called Laal Baba and I am Laal Baba too. We are known by the colour we are soaked in. The water in the stream is dyed red by herbs and flowers. Many are the miraculous features of these red waters. Three generations have lived in this cave, researching these herbs. Knowledge has also been gathered from the works of the sages of yore. Look, there, wrapped in a red cloth, lies the entire wealth of my Baba.

'We have acquainted ourselves with every herb that is to be found in these forests. We know their shape and size, the leaves they sprout, the blossoms they bear, the roots hidden in the earth and their taste. We have also experienced their outcome on our bodies, minds and souls.

'These have been documented on the bark leaves of the Himalayan birch tree and then sewn together, as did sages in ancient times. These bark pages have on them the research work done over two centuries.' Baba turned the leaves of the book as tenderly as one would hold a newborn.

'In deep meditation, we have chanted mantras over and again and then transcribed the same on each leaf. Each leaf we regard as divine communication. We cannot disrespect God, for who else would grant us the boon of salvation?'

Baba cautions us that to read these leaves, we have to be just as worthy as them. They demand the touch of purity.

'Listen, O Wanderer, seeking knowledge. Knowing these herbs and roots is no overnight task. To learn of their attributes, qualities and nature and the art of preparing them for consumption requires the persistence of Hatha Yoga that concerns itself with complete mastery of body, mind and soul.

'The shape of the herb—its beauty and glow, its texture and whether it rises skywards or spreads itself on the earth, whether it turns away from the setting sun or clings to crevices and climbs—is what needs constant and deep study. We have to know if it swims in flowing or still waters and how it stretches its roots beneath the earth. The colour of the leaves and shape of the thorns is important. All this takes a long time, and only then can one learn how it is consumed.

'There is a peculiar nutritional quality in herbs with sparkling, bright colours, while those bearing fruit may often be poisonous. But see the marvel of creation—just beneath the plants one finds the antidote in an accompanying healing herb.

'The smell of the herb is also a test to gauge if it can or cannot be used as food.

'O traveller! Try to understand and know each herb as one would know a human being. In silence and a deep, meditative state of mind, hear the first message and recognize it.'

The sky sparkles with stars and the snow-capped distant mountains shine in the moonlight. The song of the stream, rolling over the rocks and meandering through the forest fills the air with music. A soft scent wafts and fireflies play hide and seek, twinkling above the Bhagirathi flowing serenely below.

Sitting in deep meditation, Laal Baba softly recites his prayers. 'O Lord, bring peace to this earth and make it as pure as the dewdrop that falls at dawn.'

The twitter of the birds and the resonance of the red river herald the beginning of another sunlit, smiling day.

Washing the face in the red river, one begins to glow in its hue. Laal Baba laughs and says, 'So you too have turned red, at least for a day!'

Gifting the lama a necklace of twenty-seven seeds of different herbs, the Baba says, 'My love and blessings will stay with you always and stand by you forever more. We will meet again for sure, one more time! Go on, dear monk, your path awaits you; move ever onwards.'

Saying this, Laal Baba bursts out laughing—that loud, ringing laughter—and the tall mountains laugh along, in perfect unison.

—

Tsering Döndrup's 'The Handsome Monk', a contemporary Tibetan novella translated into English by Christopher Peacock, falls firmly into the 'sceptical' trope; or is Döndrup a sceptical believer? Delightfully witty, sharply ironic, darkly tragic, he tells of hypocrisies, synchronicities and epiphanies while providing a telling glimpse into a resilient and restless society.

Döndrup is a vastly popular and critically acclaimed writer who writes of traditional Tibetan life, set in the fictional county of Tsezhung. His work confronts the hypocrisies of organized religion, the indignities of Chinese rule and the universal absurdity of the human situation.

CHAPTER 19

The Handsome Monk

TSERING DÖNDRUP,
TRANSLATED BY CHRISTOPHER
PEACOCK

ONE

Towards the end of the tenth month of the Tibetan calendar it snowed, making it feel even colder than the middle of winter. It got colder still at dusk, when thick black clouds gathered in the sky. Watching the sky over his home as he took a piss, Gendün Gyatso shivered involuntarily. He fastened his maroon-colored satin and lambskin jacket, thrust his hands inside the sleeves, and carried himself back to the camp with ponderous steps. A couple of seven-, maybe eight-year-old kids, each chewing on some roasted barley ran over to greet him. 'Akhu is here! I'll take your bag.' Grabbing his yellow satchel, they wrestled and shoved their way inside.

With the exception of his sister-in-law, who was busy making tsampa by herself, there was no one at home. 'Where's Mom gone?' asked Gendün Gyatso.

'She went to your sister's. She said she won't be back for a few days.' His sister-in-law jumped up in a sudden fright. 'Akhu, you look awful. Are you ill?'

When he heard these words, Gendün Gyatso's pounding heart settled somewhat. 'No, no,' he said. As he was about to sit, he heard from outside the simultaneous sounds of a neighing horse and the thud of a descending rider. 'Dad's here,' cried the children in unison, wrestling and shoving their way out the door of the adobe house. His heart started pounding again.

'Ah tsi, you look terrible. Are you sick or something?' As soon as his brother, Gobha, saw him, he virtually yelled these words at Gendün Gyatso.

'No. I'm not … sick. I … you …'

'Me? I'm back from the front line to get provisions.'

'Oh, the front ...Was there an ambush?'

'Last night those bandits hit our second units camp again. By the grace of the Three Jewels, there were no casualties.' Gobha moved to sit. 'You really do look terrible. If you're not sick, then what's wrong?'

'There's ... there's something I need to tell you …'

'Is that Gobha? Oh! And Akhu Gendün's here too!' An elderly neighbour entered Gobha's house, leaning on his walking stick. Both brothers rose.

'Please sit, Akhu Gendün, both of you please sit,' urged the old man, himself taking a seat. From the way he tossed his walking stick to the floor with a clatter, you'd think he would never need it again. He seemed, however, to decide that this action was excessive, so he retrieved the stick and placed it in front of him. The walking stick made him seem very old, but he was in fact just over fifty, and his hair was still mostly black. Two years ago, during a pasture feud, he'd been shot in the calf, and because he couldn't get the wound treated right away, he'd been forced to rely on the walking stick ever since.

'Have the bandits hit again?'

'They hit our second units camp again last night. By the grace of Three Jewels, there were no casualties. A cadre and a detachment of armed police are coming from the county today. Seems like the fighting will have to stop.'

'Those bandits ...' The old man impulsively pounded a fist onto his knee. A sharp pain shot up his leg, forcing an 'Ow ow!' from his mouth. 'Isn't there anything you can do to hit them back?' he asked, after a moment had passed.

'If they're not attacking, then that's a good thing. How can we attack them? We move about in the trenches all hunched over; if you peek your head over the top even a little bit, a thousand guns go off at once, like peas popping in a pan! You know all too well how good the bandits' weapons are.' This last comment stirred in the old man feelings of terror, anguish, and hatred all at the same time. He bit his lip and fell silent. Gobha continued, 'We're on the high ground, but apart from the slight advantage of terrain we've got nothing. Winter's coming, and the wind on the mountaintop is unbearable. Forget about fighting back—the men won't even be able to stand on their own two feet when that cold comes. We're in a real tight spot.'

'Ah—it's not your fault. But those bandits have killed so many of our men. Even if we can't take revenge, we can't give them an inch of ground. If my leg wasn't like this, I'd throw these old bones into battle again! But without a penny, this is what happens...'

'How much are the yaks and sheep worth now?'

'Barely anything.'

'*Eh*—well anyhow, if we don't sell some, we won't even be able afford bullets.'

'Oh, yeah—I've still got a few here. Take them. Kill a few of their men and horses. Even if you can't get revenge for your dad, you can put the fear into those bandits. I heard a Muslim came to Spearhead Gönpo's place selling guns and ammo for cheap. Where is Alak Drong now?' The old man suddenly turned to Gendün Gyatso. 'It's your good karma that you monks don't have to lay eyes on the battlefield. It's no different from hell. If you hadn't taken your vows, you'd be out there now, feeling the terror and the pain—who knows, you might not even be alive. Ah tsi, our handsome monk is looking the worse for wear, is he unwell?'

Gendün Gyatso was a man with perfectly proportioned features. He had sleek black hair and a fair complexion. Just like in the Tibetan ode to Yangchen Lhamo, if you looked for a single fault on him, you'd simply be wasting your time. People called him 'the handsome monk'. His fellow monks had even said that as he possessed the thirty-two auspicious marks and the eighty excellent signs of the Buddha, he must be the reincarnation of a great lama, and they entreated him to give them his blessing. These later remarks may have been poking fun, but no one could deny the truth of the former. The women of Tsezhung joked about this topic in private: 'If I could get Akhu Gendün to break his vows with me, spending the next life burning on the copper horse would be a small price to pay!' After everyone had had a good laugh, penance would be added: 'Ah la, only kidding, om Vajrasattva.' When Gendün Gyatso was just six or seven years old, a lama visited his family. As soon as he saw Gendün Gyatso, he exclaimed in surprise, 'Ah tsi ah tsi, what a remarkable boy! You must keep this child clean and healthy ... Mmm ... it would be best if you have him enter the monkhood,' he said, patting the boy's head. His father was overjoyed and before long sent him off to take his vows, but at no point had Gendün Gyatso displayed any remarkable characteristics. In any case, his handsome appearance and gentle character made up for the fact that he wasn't all that bright or hardworking, and remained the object of people's desire and esteem.

Compared with those days, Gendün Gyatso really wasn't looking so good now. The most obvious change was in his face, which had completely lost its former lustre. It had become ashen and gloomy, like that of a man in very poor health. And the conversation his brother had had with that damn neighbour had heaped fresh suffering on his suffering, and fresh terror on his terror. He tried to get his emotions under control and calm himself down, but as soon as he stopped concentrating on it he began hyperventilating. That night he couldn't get to sleep at all, and the next day he looked even worse. 'You really do look terrible,' his brother said. 'Go and see Alak Drong, or a doctor. There's definitely something wrong.' He stuffed some money into his hand and left.

Gendün Gyatso put a hand to his face, then set out after his brother, who was already astride his horse.

'Oh, right,' said his brother, suddenly reining in his mount. 'Wasn't there something you wanted to tell me?'

Gendün Gyatso's heart almost leaped into his throat, and he felt like he could barely breathe. 'I ... I mean ... you ... you should ... be careful, be on your guard,' he said, swallowing repeatedly.

'That's it?'

'No, I mean, yes, ah ... that's it.'

'Don't worry yourself.'

As he watched his brother ride away, Gendün Gyatso thought, *It's best to just get it over with, like pulling a tooth—do it in one go. Worse comes to worst, I'd get a crack of his whip. And maybe I'd be feeling a bit better right now if I'd done it.* He sighed, regretting that he hadn't dared tell his brother what was really on his mind.

TWO

At dusk, Gendün Gyatso returned to the county seat. Wrapping his robe around his head, he wandered the streets aimlessly. That morning he'd eaten a simple breakfast, and though he hadn't had a bite to eat for lunch or dinner, he didn't feel hungry at all. When darkness fell, he found himself wandering unconsciously back into the Red Lantern Bar. Alcohol can relieve your troubles, they say, so maybe a drink would help.

A young woman came over and sat beside him. 'You're still wearing your monk's robes,' she whispered.

'Go away. Bring me a beer.'

The woman stood up, shocked. A moment later she sat again. 'If you want to drink, you can come to my place.'

Gendün Gyatso had no desire whatsoever to return to the woman's place, so he rose and walked out the door. When he came back to the bar some two or three hours later, he was more or less drunk. Not only had the alcohol failed to ease his pain, it had aroused in him a strong desire to be with the woman again. In fact, even in the midst of the intense anguish and fear of the last few days, he hadn't been able to put her out of his mind. Sometimes he hated the woman, sometimes he loved her. In the end, he himself couldn't say for sure; all he knew was that he had an irrepressible desire to be with her. The woman really seemed to like him too. At the start she'd told him, quite candidly, 'As a woman doing a job like this, I go with whoever pays me, but I've never met a man as handsome as you before. To tell you the truth, I really like you. But I've never made a monk break his vows, and there's no way I'm starting now. It looks to me like you're no ordinary monk. I think it'd be best if you just forgot all about this kind of thing.'

At that moment Gendün Gyatso had been overcome by a wave of desire, his sole wish being to bed the woman on the spot. Even if he'd had to die and go to hell as soon as he'd had her, it would have been worth it. 'I already gave up my vows,' he'd lied.

'Then what are you doing still wearing monk's robes?'

'I only gave them up yesterday. I don't have any other clothes right now. I'm planning to go home and get my lay clothes tomorrow.'

'Why don't you get some Chinese clothes? Aren't a lot of former monks wearing Chinese clothes these days?'

'I've never worn Chinese clothes in my life, and I don't intend to wear them now. Stop delaying.'

The woman had point-blank refused the money he'd offered, and Gendün Gyatso had felt moved. 'A pretty, nice girl like you shouldn't be working in a place like this. I hope you find yourself a husband and get on the right track,' he'd said then, and meant it.

'A girl who's done this job can never find a husband, especially a good one,' she'd said with a sigh.

'A monk and a prostitute. Aren't we the perfect match?' He'd then told her a true story about a monk from his monastery who went back to lay life. After giving up his vows, he married a prostitute, and they even had children.

'You're making fun of me.'

Even he hadn't known if he was kidding or being serious. Either way, he would have to return home the next day and get back into his fur jacket—there was no avoiding that. But he had gradually begun to feel a profound sense of regret, mostly because he hadn't considered that shedding his monk's robes meant he would have to go to the front line, where the most he had to look forward to was seeking revenge for his father. Ever since he was a child he'd been used to the warmth of the monks' quarters. Even when he returned to the family tent he lay in bed miserably, unable to stand the cold. If there was one thing more unbearable to him than fighting, it was sitting on a mountaintop thirteen thousand feet above sea level, getting blasted by freezing winds. What's more, even when the fighting was over, he'd still have to be out in the wind and the rain tending the cattle. He'd have to stalk about like a wolf just for the sake of keeping his belly full—this, like the breaking of his vows, was already a fact. When you think of it like that, how you can say all those clever people who leave their homes and renounce worldly affairs to pursue a life of solitude are doing it just for the welfare of sentient beings? And those soldiers who flee the battlefield and face disdain and ridicule, and then the next damn life ...

'Ah kha, what an idiot I am!' Gendün Gyatso had been tormented with regret. 'Demon, you wicked demon, look what you've done to me ...' He'd wept bitterly, striking himself in the chest over and over.

'Didn't you say you already gave up your vows?'

'I was lying to you. I was lying to myself.'

'Ah ho, you've ruined me! What will I do in the next life!?'

'Prostitutes don't have anything to look forward to in the next life anyway. You'll be spending the next life knee-deep in shit, piss, pus, and blood.'

The woman didn't get mad, she'd simply cried and leaned her head against Gendün Gyatso. 'I have no regrets. I have no regrets.'

'Me neither.' Gendün Gyatso had put his arm around her neck. These weren't just words, either. It was too late now anyway, he'd thought, there was no use in having regrets. He was by no means the only one to forsake his vows, and what's more, this woman was a real beauty—the most beautiful thing in the world is a woman, after all. *Haven't plenty of people given up their lives for the sake of a woman?* Despite this, it wasn't long before he felt regret again, and it came most notably whenever he sobered up—*What have I done*? he would chastise himself. Soon after that, the unstoppable regret and fear came back, so he kept drinking, trying his best to forget it all.

THREE

There's a new saying: 'Most men are called Tashi, and most Tashis are businessmen; most women are called Lhamo, and most Lhamos are prostitutes.' But the name of the woman Gendün Gyatso was in love with wasn't Lhamo, it was Lhatso. Lhatso rented a small room behind the Red Lantern Bar. Half of the room was taken up by a large bed, at the head of which was a cupboard. In addition to some makeup, the cupboard contained a yellow book called *The Lineage of Nyizer Monastery*. The book was distinctly out of place in that room, and it piqued Gendün Gyatso's curiosity. He asked Lhatso where it came from.

'A client left it here by accident a few days ago. Said he was a tourist. I was going to throw it out, but it's full of pictures of lamas and the monastery, so I kept it.'

Though the room looked very clean, it had a foul odour. Gendün Gyatso suspected that it might be the smell of semen. He lit incense again and again, but the smell proved hard to get rid of. For that reason, he spent less and less time in the little room and began to roam between other bars, clubs, and especially video stores. Though those places too had their share of pretty 'Lhamos', in his eyes none of them was as pretty or as kindhearted as Lhatso. Every evening, when he finished his drifting, he ended up back at Lhatso's, and he was usually drunk. At first he cursed her, calling her a 'black-hearted woman' and an 'evil woman', then he cried and struck himself in the chest with his fist. *I can't go on like this ... what's the point of living ...* he thought sometimes, and even considered suicide.

'If you want to die, do it somewhere else,' said Lhatso, at the end of her tether. Then she held him. 'Please, don't torture yourself like this. You're not the only one to break his vows. Even lamas break their vows, never mind ordinary monks. They don't have any regrets, so why should you? Get rid of your robes and give up the drink. We can open up a little store or a guest house together.' She tried to console him with these and other heartfelt words.

'No, no, you know nothing! If I give up my robes I'll be forced to get a gun and go to the front line, and the man who killed my father is there, so I'll have to be out in front, and those bandits have the better weapons ... oh—you know nothing ...'

'So ... it's like that.'

'It's like that. I'm not just a fallen monk, I'm a coward too. Now you know.'

'Then ... why don't we go to my hometown?'

'Didn't you say you're from Chukar County?'

'Yes.'

'Haha—that's exactly where the man who killed my father is. They're still fighting with our camp now.'

'Oh ... I see. Then why don't we go somewhere else?'

Gendün Gyatso shook his head, not wanting to talk any more, and went to sleep.

Every morning, Gendün Gyatso read *The Lineage of Nyizer Monaste*ry in bed, both to forget his troubles and to pass the day. The book documented a lineage of abbots from a Nyingma monastery in Kham. The photos of Nyizer Tsang, the great lama in charge of the monastery, looked just like him. Nyizer Tsang had died at the age of twenty-five, which, counting back from now, was twenty-five years ago—the year before Gendün Gyatso was born. The book said that the huge boulder into which he drove a ritual dagger was now the monastery's most precious religious artifact.

Though the features of the handsome monk Gendün Gyatso had lost their former lustre, his sleek, black hair had grown long, and anyone who saw him still felt that he was something special. When he was playing pool or watching a dirty movie at the video place, or whenever he was drunk, he always attracted a lot of attention. For that reason he didn't want to go out any more, and he kept swearing to himself that he wouldn't. Nevertheless, spending day and night in Lhatso's tiny, semen-stinking room was, to him, no different from being in prison. 'They say samsara is the prison of demons—how true,' he finally said to himself, and walked out the door. First he went to a pool courtyard—one of his old haunts from before he broke his vows. Hardly anyone in the little county seat was a match for him now, so he didn't even have to waste any money. He didn't give his opponent the slightest chance, and his mood lifted with the ringing clack of each potted ball. But soon a crowd of people gathered around him, staring in wonder. Feeling deeply uncomfortable, he quit his game, and wrapping his robe up over his head, left the courtyard. When he was drunk, however, he was never so cautious. He staggered about like the flame of a butter lamp in the wind, sometimes treading on his trailing robe and sending himself head over heels, after which he lay there, crawling about and rambling incomprehensibly. Sometimes he stuffed his fingers into his mouth, trying to make himself throw up. If not that, he moaned pitifully, or just lay flat on his back and passed out. If people gathered around to stare at him, he rolled about on the ground, shouting, 'What are you looking at? We're all people! Am I the only monk who drinks? Am I the only monk who's broken his vows? Ya, hic ... Alak Drong smokes, and drinks, and he's got a wife, and a kid, hic ... and he's still wearing the crown of the five Buddhas, and giving empowerments and transmissions and instructions! Ah, hic ... you want to see a show, go see that! Ah ... go on, go!' With that he flailed his arms, shooing them off.

'What a disgrace, what a fraud!' 'Outrageous, absolutely outrageous,' 'I swear on the *Kangyur*, if he wasn't wearing monk's robes, I'd sort him out'—the crowd cursed him with indignant oaths.

Luckily, Lhatso came running over at just that moment. She heaved Gendün Gyatso into her rented motor trike, got him home, and laid him on the bed. Not only did she clean the vomit off his clothes, she shook the dirt out of them too. His ice-cold heart was thawed by the warm tenderness of a woman, and he burst into tears. 'Let's get married, we have to get married!' he blurted out.

Lhatso was used to hearing such things. 'Go to sleep. We'll talk about marriage when you sober up,' she said.

In the morning, when Gendün Gyatso had sobered up, the foul odour of semen again drifted into his nostrils, and all talk of marriage was dropped. Feeling ashamed of his embarrassing behaviour the night before, he leafed through the pages of *The Lineage of Nyizer Monastery*. He more or less knew the slim volume by heart now and had no desire to read it in detail. He breathed a long sigh and finally got out of bed.

FOUR

The weather grew colder by the day, and now it was freezing even at noon. Sometimes a wind blew in from who knows where and tossed the white plastic trash discarded on the streets to and fro.

A young nomad who was revving the engine of his motorbike and charging aimlessly up and down the street suddenly collided with a pig, sending the bike skidding off a good ten paces. The rider, after flying five or six paces into the air, landed on the back of another pig that at that moment just happened to emerge from underneath the toilets. Happily, the man was unhurt and the bike undamaged, but the young man now smelled as unbearably awful as the pig he'd just hit. The onlookers, covering their noses with their hands, backed off as they burst into laughter.

Gendün Gyatso too chuckled to himself as he watched this spectacle. That was the first time he'd broken into a smile since forsaking his vows. Unfortunately, it only lasted for a moment, as a group of young monks—their robes wrapped over their heads, revealing only their eyes—was scrutinizing him suspiciously.

Since it was the cold season and the weather was so bad, Gendün Gyatso decided not to go to the pool courtyard and went straight into a bar instead. The monks who were tailing him didn't come into the bar but went to a restaurant across the road, where they looked in his direction through the window.

When Gendün Gyatso staggered out the door it was almost five in the morning. There was a fierce wind blowing and hardly anyone was around. The monks who had been watching him wrapped their robes over their heads, exited the restaurant, and blocked his path. 'Akhu, your robe has fallen on the floor,' said one of the monks as he picked up a corner of the robe and wrapped it over Gendün Gyatso's head, covering his face.

The bewildered Gendün Gyatso wanted to remove the robe from his eyes, but someone had his hands in a tight grip and he was unable to move. He hadn't a clue what was going on, and before he had the chance to react he was being dragged in an unknown direction. He shouted and screamed, but his voice was so inaudible in the harsh wind that he could barely hear it himself. He struggled as hard as he could, but the men holding him from either side were as firm as mountains, and he wasn't able to move them an inch.

The night before he had had a dream. Several monks took him by force to a large assembly hall, or maybe the residence of Alak Drong. They savagely stripped off his clothes, leaving him naked. Using a wooden spoon, Alak Drong inspected his genitals at great length, and finally, letting out a laugh, proclaimed, 'He hasn't broken his vows!'

The monks released him at once, and with exceptional reverence, begged his pardon as they re-dressed him.

He was overcome with joy and was so moved that he wept. Realizing that he really hadn't broken his vows, he became even more overjoyed. But he didn't want to leave Lhatso, so he hugged her tightly. This had woken her up, and she'd shouted in order to wake him. He'd been feverish and dripping with sweat, and had once more fallen into the abyss of suffering.

He'd been having so many dreams like this lately. Was this a dream too? Or had the Lord of Death's messengers already brought him to the next life? *No, no*, he thought once more, *even if I can't see it, I'm still in the human world, for sure. Maybe someone's playing a joke on me?* At that moment they stopped, and someone said to him, 'Hey—people break their vows, but who keeps on wearing monk's robes after they do? Why are you still dressed like a monk?'

The wind must have calmed down all of a sudden, as he could hear everything distinctly.

A man whose voice sounded just like that of a woman seized him by the scruff of the neck. 'What is the meaning of defiling the robes of the Buddhist order like this? Have you got some kind of problem with Buddhist robes?'

Gendün Gyatso, now even more convinced that this was neither a dream nor the afterlife, wanted to say something, but his assailant now grabbed him by the throat. 'You bastard, badmouthing Alak Drong! Let's see you get out of this!' With that the man punched him in the face. White, red, and yellow filled his vision all at once, and he tasted blood in his mouth.

'You still dare to slander Alak Drong now, huh?' said someone else as he punched him fiercely in the solar plexus. His whole body turned to jelly and he collapsed helplessly on the ground, feeling like his guts had been shredded.

'Take this, you fraud!' With a crack, a hard object connected with the back of Gendün Gyatso's head, and he passed out.

Although it was completely dark by the time Gendün Gyatso regained consciousness, he could tell by the faint moonlight that he was in a narrow alleyway. He felt cold, his head ached, he was thirsty, and his mouth tasted of blood. After a moment, he touched his hand to his head, and it came back covered in something wet and sticky—blood, of course—and he panicked. Mustering all his strength, he tried to get up, but his head felt even heavier than his body. In the end, his limbs unable to support him, he slumped back on the ground. He touched his hand to his head again. Blood was still trickling down the back of his neck from a wound the size of two fingers put together, causing him even greater alarm.

Going to the front line can't be any worse than this. I ought to just get rid of these robes now, thought Gendün Gyatso as he pressed his forehead to the ground and lay there moaning in pain. Hearing the sound of footsteps, he raised his head slightly with the aid of his hands. As the footsteps approached the beam of a flashlight fell on him, and a man cried out, 'Ah tsi! Someone's collapsed here!'

'Ah tsi ah tsi, it's a monk!' yelled the voice of a woman.

Gendün Gyatso told them that he'd been robbed and asked them to call a motor trike for him. Not only did they call one, they wanted to accompany him to the hospital as well, but he declined.

After they set off, Gendün Gyatso said to the trike driver, 'Take me to the Red Lantern Bar.'

'What? That's no place for a monk. I think you should go to the hospital.'

'Just do what I said.'

FIVE

Gendün Gyatso put on the Chinese clothes that Lhatso had bought for him and combed his hair, and he looked just as handsome as when he was a monk. But the pain in his head refused to go away, and sometimes he felt so dizzy he almost collapsed. Lhatso, helping to support him, took him to the hospital.

When they got to the hospital yard there were a lot more people than usual. Some were crying, some were standing in a daze, and some were pursuing the doctors who were rushing back and forth. Gendün Gyatso paid no attention to these people. Keeping his head lowered like a thief, he crept into the outpatient department. There were people lying left and right on the floor of the corridor, moaning horribly. An old man had been shot in the right side of his chest, and as he breathed red bubbles were sucked in and blown out of the hole. Near him was a man of about twenty with a wound bursting out of his left shoulder, like a blooming flower. The frozen hell where human beings split open like lotuses must be precisely like this, Gendün Gyatso thought. 'Blessed Three Jewels,' he murmured. This was the first prayer he had uttered since breaking his vows. A man with a belt bound around his head shivered fearfully and took a few gulps of air, as though he'd suddenly plunged into a freezing pool of water in the middle of winter, then fell still. The man who'd been holding his head in his lap shook him, calling out, 'Sangbha, Sangbha,' then, raising his voice, began to shout, 'Doctor! Ah ho! Doctor! Where's the doctor? Doctor—' but no one answered him. He leaned the man—or rather, corpse—against a wall, and after rushing from room to room finally managed to track down a doctor, whom he dragged over forcibly. The doctor, without removing his left hand from the pocket of his lab coat, used the thumb and index finger of his right hand to open the eyes of the man—whose head had by now slumped onto his shoulder—and gave him a quick glance. He put his fingers briefly to the man's neck and said, 'He's gone.'

The man seized the doctor. 'What do you mean?' he cried, wide-eyed.

'He's gone. Stopped breathing.'

The man slowly released the doctor and, as though he had suddenly thought of something, began to shout, 'Friends! Friends! Where is Alak Drong? Where is Alak Drong?' but no one answered him. Then a man whose voice sounded just like that of a woman ran over, crying, 'Doctor! Doctor! Come quick!' as he pulled and tugged at the doctor's sleeve. The man's unusual voice stirred something in Gendün Gyatso's memory. When he looked closely he discovered, as if awaking from a dream, that those people were in fact all from his camp. The man who had just died with his head slumped on his shoulder was Sanggyé Kyab, the boy who used to tend cattle with him when they were children.

Gendün Gyatso suddenly remembered his brother and began rushing madly about. The doctor from before was now in the middle of giving oxygen to a wounded man. The man was lying face up on a stretcher. As he was covered by a woolen coat, his wound couldn't be seen, but the whites of his rolled-back eyeballs were visible, and a coarse, drawn-out grunt was coming from his throat, just like that made by a cow when a Muslim butcher slits its throat.

Gendün Gyatso said another prayer, then continued to search each and every corridor and room. Much to his relief, not only was there no sign of his brother Gobha, he didn't find any of his other relatives either. He thought about checking whether anyone else had been wounded, but recalling his own circumstances, he decided this wasn't a place he should linger in and beat a hasty exit through the hospital doors. Outside, he let out a deep breath and finally slowed his pace.

'What's going on?' demanded a terrified Lhatso, planting herself in front of Gendün Gyatso.

'This is the work of your Chukar County.'

'Blessed Jetsün Drölma!'

'If they find out you're from Chukar County, they'll skin you alive.'

'And who could blame them? I'm scared.'

'I'm scared too. Really scared.'

'These pasture feuds are so horrible.'

'I guess this is what they call the cycle of samsara.'

After he'd received that beating, Gendün Gyatso had vowed that he would shed his monk's robes and give up the drink. *I may have broken my vows*, he'd thought, *but it's not right to defile the Buddhist garments, and I'd have fewer regrets going to the front line than living like this—neither monk nor layman, neither man nor demon.* So he'd removed his robes. But after he witnessed the terrifying scenes at the hospital, his courage again vanished. As soon as he got to Lhatso's place, he put his robes back on. Anxious about his brother and his family and disgusted by his own behaviour, his mind was beset as though by a storm and he couldn't calm down. Eventually, he called to Lhatso and asked her to go get him some beer.

'Shouldn't you not be drinking? And we don't have much money left, either.'

Gendün Gyatso knew that since Lhatso had met him she had of her own accord cut off all contact with other men, and she paid for the rent, the food, and moreover his booze and his clothes. With this in mind, he heaved a sigh. 'You're right. That damn money ...'

Lhatso seemingly wanted to give him some comfort. 'Oh well, there's still enough to buy a bit of beer. I'll go get some,' she said, rising to leave.

'No, no, I don't want any now. And I won't drink in the future either. Promise.'

SIX

Without his realizing it, the smell of semen completely disappeared, and he developed a sense of familiarity with and attachment to the room as if it were his own home.

As it happened, the cadre with a face whiter than paper, who came almost every week to the Red Lantern Bar and stayed there for free, was a policeman. At midday he came to the Red Lantern Bar in full policeman's uniform and whispered a few words into the ear of the woman who owned the place. After he left, the owner gathered all of the

'Lhamos' and announced, 'The police are going to raid us tonight. Be careful, and only standard services—no entertaining clients.' This forced Gendün Gyatso to go spend the night in a hotel.

When we Tibetans go to the city, the hotels put us all in the same room, and in the same way, the hotels in this county seat put monks in the same room. The room that Gendün Gyatso was put into contained two old monks. They said they were from Kham.

'Have you ever been to Nyizer Monastery?' asked Gendün Gyatso idly.

'We *are from* Nyizer Monastery, as it happens.'

Gendün Gyatso became immediately enthused. 'Oh! Tell me, is the boulder that Nyizer Tsang drove a ritual dagger into still there?'

One of the old monks leaped up all of a sudden, and whispered to his colleague, 'Hey, look closely. He …' Turning back to Gendün Gyatso, he asked, 'Have you ever been to Nyizer Monastery, sir?'

'No.'

'May we inquire as to your age, sir?'

'I'm twenty-five.'

The two old monks sat there agape, now glancing at each other, now staring at Gendün Gyatso. 'You …' said Gendün Gyatso, feeling somewhat uncomfortable. The two monks returned to their senses. One of them began to frantically search through his backpack, and after some time retrieved a photograph. He brought it over to Gendün Gyatso with extreme care.

Gendün Gyatso took a look at the photo and said, 'Yes, that's Nyizer Tsang.'

The two old monks gawked at each other and fell completely silent. After a moment the elder of the two began to babble incoherently, and upon failing to express anything resembling a point, awkwardly wiped the sweat dripping down his brow and the tip of his nose, after which he continued to babble even more incoherently than before. The other, slightly younger monk cut him off and got straight to the point. 'Would it be acceptable if we looked at the back of your head, sir?' he asked.

Gendün Gyatso wondered if he had fallen into one of those unpleasant illusions or dreams again. He unconsciously felt the scar on the back of his head and stared in amazement at the two monks sitting before him, one after the other.

'Um ... speaking plainly, the Nyizer incarnations all have a dragon pattern on the back of their heads.'

Gendün Gyatso felt the back of his head again, understanding everything clearly now. But strangely, he suddenly became even more flustered than the two old monks. 'No, no, it's not a dragon pattern!' he cried, jumping to his feet.

The two old monks nodded to each other and pounced on Gendün Gyatso like madmen. He wailed in anguish and struggled as hard as he could, but he fell into their grasp as if bound by the noose of the Dharma protectors. After they had taken a look at the back of his head, they suddenly let him go. 'Well, there's no doubt now,' said one to the other.

'Lamas, yidams, dakinis, and Dharma protectors! Our task is finally complete.' The slightly younger of the two monks prostrated to Gendün Gyatso three times, and as his head touched Gendün Gyatso's feet, he wept tears of joy.

The elder monk too prostrated three times, then placed a stack of money on top of a khata and brought it before Gendün Gyatso, who became even more flustered and terrified. 'No, no, you've made a mistake! I'm not a trülku, it's not possible!' he yelped. He went so far as to tell them, quite plainly, that he wasn't even a genuine monk. The two old monks didn't hear a word he said; instead they began to tell him about how before his death the previous Nyizer incarnation had composed a final testament, which clearly stated that there was no need to look for his reincarnation for twenty-five years, that his reincarnation would then be twenty-five years old, where they should search, and so on. 'Please, don't talk like that any more,' they said. 'Please come back to your monastery at once.'

Gendün Gyatso had no idea how to explain the situation to them, and it looked like the two monks were so insistent that they wouldn't give him the chance to do so anyway. 'Why don't you get up? We'll talk about this later,' he said with resignation, making them sit back on the bed. 'I've got a wife,' he added with a sigh.

The two monks took one look at each other and, almost in unison, replied, 'The Nyizer incarnations have always had consorts.'

'But my wife is a ... and I'm a drunk too.'

'The Nyizer incarnations have always partaken of the elixirs.'

Gendün Gyatso's mind was in turmoil. *What's going on*? he thought. *Is this all just a coincidence*? All of a sudden he thought of Lhatso and felt an irrepressible urge to see her. Hitching up his cassock, he bolted out the door and tore off. The two old monks went after him like cops chasing a criminal.

A crowd had gathered at the doorway of the Red Lantern Bar. Two policemen roughly shoved Lhatso into their car, then sped off to the piercing blare of the siren.

Gendün Gyatso stared after the police car, stupefied.

That day was the coldest of the year in the county seat. On the mountain peaks thirteen thousand feet above sea level, it was probably even colder.

Dr Jono Lineen has spent over twenty years travelling around the world as a geologist, deep-sea fisher, humanitarian relief worker, mountain guide and writer. His books include Into the Heart of the Himalayas *and* Perfect Motion.

This excerpt from Into the Heart of the Himalayas *takes us to Gangotri, the source of that most sacred of rivers, the Ganga. Even as the author is contemplating the all-too-familiar contradictions between the truc sadhus and the abundance of charlatans, he encounters an unusual sight. '... Three young men sitting at the far end of the deserted courtyard were tied together and the two burly, half naked, fully bearded sadhus standing by them were guarding them with sticks'.*

The twist in the tale, worthy of a Bollywood film, involves a kidnapping, a demand for ransom and a wild chase through a deserted village. Ah well.

CHAPTER 20

Into the Heart of the Himalayas

JONO LINEEN

8 November

I arrived at Gangotri in the early afternoon and the village was a welcome surprise. After Yamunotri I had expected a ramshackle assortment of disused chaff shops girdled by a wasteland of gunny-sack outhouses. I was wrong as the place was neat and tidy, like a European seaside resort in winter. The only inhabitants were a core of diehard sadhus—sincere Hindu holy men—and in this was another marvel for me.

Sadhus are Hindu ascetics who have taken vows to follow a strict path towards higher knowledge. They have given up the first three goals of Hindu life—kama, pleasure; artha, wealth and power; and dharma, duty—so as to concentrate wholly on the fourth: moksha, liberation. It is said that today, in India, there are between four and five million sadhus. Most of these men (and a lesser number of women) are dedicated to their path, but unfortunately there is a scattering of pretenders. Sadhus live on the charity of others. Indians in general are very generous towards their holy men and for the few less-than-authentic sadhus, donning robes guarantees them an income.

These false holy men have a tendency to congregate in areas frequented by Western tourists, I would guess because it is almost impossible for someone outside of Hindusim to tell the real from the imitation when it comes to holy men. In truth, I don't know whether in the previous five years in India I'd actually met a committed sadhu. But the holy men I met in Gangotri were a different breed because they were immersed in their religion. Unlike the sadhus I'd met in Delhi and Kolkata, they generally ignored me. By just going about their business, the sadhus gave me the impression that Gangotri was special, a place charged with religious energy. My expectations were heightened for the Ganga-Mai temple that is the centrepiece of the village.

Ganga-Mai means Mother Ganges, and this is how Hindus perceive the Goddess Ganga. She is all-giving but sometimes stern, an energy that is with you always. Almost every Hindu home will have a vial of Ganga water in their household shrine. Ganga water is the purest substance on earth and anything or anyone that comes in contact with it is cleansed. The goddess herself is portrayed as a beautiful, voluptuous woman who carries an overflowing Grecian-looking urn in her hands; she is the personification of abundance.

The myth of Ganga's appearance on earth is a great description of the peculiarly human qualities of the Hindu Gods. The legend goes something like this:

> King Sagara had two wives. One bore him sixty thousand sons while the other bore him only one, whose name was Asamanjas. The king once wanted to perform a religious ritual that involved a special horse, but the jealous Lord Indra stole the horse. King Sagara sent his sixty thousand sons to search for the animal. After digging up the entire earth's surface and then the underworld, they eventually found it in a cave close to where Sage Kapila was in retreat. Thinking that the learned man had stolen the horse, the sons hurled abuse at him. This brought the great master out of his meditation. He was angry and with one look instantly burned the sixty thousand sons to ash with his fiery gaze.
>
> The king heard of his sons' fate through Narada, the heavenly wanderer. He sent his grandson Ansuman, the son of Asamanjas, to undo the harm. The grandson met Kapila, who was pleased with the young man's tact. The sons could not be brought back to life, but Kapila granted that the souls of the sons could be released for reincarnation if touched by the waters of the Ganga. Ganga-Mai at this time resided in the heavens. However, it was many generations before Bhagirath, who was Sagara's great-great-grandson, was able to impress the goddess enough with his devotion that she agreed to come to earth. But Bhagirath knew that the impact of her fall to the planet's surface would destroy the world, and the blow could only be borne by Lord Shiva. Therefore, Bhagirath went into meditation again and obtained Shiva's agreement that he would cushion the fall. Finally, the river came down, the thundering descent was absorbed by Shiva's matted dreadlocks (when you look at images of Lord Shiva, you see in his hair a tiny waterfall of Ganga erupting from it) and thence it fell gently to earth. Where Shiva absorbed the flow's impact is the site of

> the present-day temple at Gangotri. Bhagirath then used his plow and dredged a course for the water to the south (the path of the present-day Bhagirath/Ganges River) and led the goddess to where the ashes of the sixty thousand sons lay. The souls of the sons were liberated and an ocean formed there. Today, this is Sagar Island in West Bengal where the Ganges flows into the Bay of Bengal.

The Ganga-Mai temple is simply designed, a pale stone square with four corner turrets and a central tower. It fits unassumingly into its surroundings. The current structure was built by the Gurkha general Amar Singh Thapa in the early seventeenth century.

When I was there, the lack of people and the white-noise rush of the Bhagirath River emphasized its tranquility. The temple was locked (it is closed for the season on the Indian holiday of Diwali around October-November each year and reopened in May), but I could see that the whitewashed walls of the inner shrine were covered with thousands of red dots—women's bindis or forehead markings. Bindis mark the area between the eyebrows that is said to be the sixth chakra, or energy centre. In Hinduism it is known as the seat of 'concealed wisdom'. In a way, each of these scores of women had placed a piece of their being in the guardianship of the goddess. The pattern created by the red marks was endless, like an Australian Aboriginal dot painting exposing a community's relationship with gods and the landscape.

Then, in true Indian form, reality shifted a little off to one side. I realized that three young men sitting at the far end of the otherwise-deserted courtyard were tied together and the two burly, half-naked, fully bearded sadhus standing by them were guarding them with sticks.

In Hindi, I asked what was going on and one of the guards explained the trio had kidnapped the teenage son of a wealthy Uttarkashi family and had been holding the boy for ransom in one of Gangotri's deserted shacks. The holy men had known nothing of this but had noticed smoke from the chimney of an empty hut. It would be unreasonable to expect that someone would take over an absent sadhu's hut without informing the others, so they knew something strange was going on. The holy men surrounded the hut and accosted the gang, who made a run for it. The monks went in pursuit and, after a wild chase through the deserted village, apprehended them. I like the image: a gang of ochre-robed, barefoot, dreadlocked sadhus pursuing a trio of knife-wielding gangsters. The kidnappers were being held until the police could arrive from Uttarkashi. I had a cup of tea with the sadhu guards; the captives stared at the ground.

I stayed the night in a deserted guest house. It wasn't officially open but after I enquired about the rooms, one of the sadhus, a heavyset man with dreadlocks that snaked down his back, touched me on the shoulder and silently indicated I should follow him. He didn't speak the entire time—maybe he had taken a vow of silence—but as we were walking he showed me a key and escorted me into the building and to a room. He didn't indicate that he wanted any money, but I gave him a donation, saying it was for the upkeep of the temple.

Tshering Tashi's piece is infused with a kinetic energy. It is about motion as a form of meditation, and the still centre within that fuels it. The author, researcher and festival director tells us of the adepts known as 'Lung Gompa' or 'Kang jor' in Bhutan and Tibet, 'Sen-nichi-kaihou' in Japan and trance runners to Western scholars.

Tshering Tashi introduces us to three monks he has personally encountered who have these mystical skills. The ways of these adepts and advanced spiritual practitioners involve a necessary degree of reserve in what must not be lightly shared or boasted about. The ability to run unfathomable distances at lightning speed is not to be subjected to casual curiosity—it remains in the realm of secret powers. Respecting these boundaries, the author gives us a glimpse of another world where physical and spiritual stamina coalesce and stretch to impossible boundaries as the body, mind and spirit become one.

We also have a valuable excerpt from René von Nebesky-Wojkowitz, where he writes about a kind of Mystic Marathon held in the snow every twelve years. This fascinating account reminds us of how much esoteric and also archival and material knowledge has been lost after the Chinese took over Tibet in 1959.

CHAPTER 21

Trance Runners

Riding the Wind

TSHERING TASHI

The Himalaya is a part of the world where many things mystical and inexplicable are possible. One such mystery is the belief in people with the skill to walk long distances in short periods of time, as if riding on the wind.

Adepts with this capability are known by different names. In Tibet and Bhutan, they are called Lung Gompa *(mediates on wind)*. In Tibet the common people also refer to this skill as Kang jor or 'fast legs'. Western scholars refer to them as trance runners.

Such adepts have been noted elsewhere. In Japan, they are highly revered and known as Sen-nichi-kaihou. Only serious ascetic practitioners earn this title after proving their ability to walk 8,400 km in 100 days. This is part of their 1,000-day retreat.

The School

If they are trance runners there surely must be a school for them. In my research, I have come across one such school.

In the book *Beyond Seven Years in Tibet*, author Heinrich Harrer talks about his visit to it. He describes the Shula Gompa monastery, which lies between Shigatse and Gyantse, as a peculiar monastery because it is a school for the famous Lung Gompa.

Harrer, who visited the monastery, noted that it was an exclusive school restricted only to a few chosen students. In this school, the monks trained in complete isolation. They did numerous exercises, 'built up their leg muscles by running on a pile of grain, while strict teachers provide the mental training'.

It was the tradition of the monastery to choose the ablest of all the students to represent the school. This monk had to prove to be mentally strong and physically able enough to run long distances.

Like the Sen-nichi-kaihou, the Tibetan monks had to run for long distances. Harrer notes that the monk has to run for a

> … hundred or more kilometres to Lhasa without food, drink or rest. On reaching the holy city, the runner is received with due reverence

> by a guard of honour. He then runs up the many stone steps of the Potala where the Dalai Lama presents him with a white silk scarf in recognition of his feat.

Then the monk is embraced as a member of the Tibetan nobility. 'He is rewarded and honoured as a yogi, a man who is able to free his soul from material things.'

Harrer further says,

> With exceptional skills such as these, the Tibetan trance runners would have achieved great success at the Olympic games and their country would have received widespread recognition. Even without their super sensory talents, living and training at altitudes between four and six-thousand metres alone would have given them a huge advantage over athletes from other nations.

Harrer was intrigued about them, but not too successful in extracting any information. He said that he was able to discuss it only with his closest friends.

The Tibetans regard trance running solely as a religious ceremony. Harrer says that the powerful Regent of the area would dispense severe punishment to anyone who tried to exploit these runners' almost supernatural abilities for non-religious reasons.

At the end of Harrer's seven years in the Forbidden City, he concluded that he did not 'ever seek to prove, or disprove, whether [the] Tibetan was really able to separate his spirit from his body'.

Tshampa

Bhutan has a few trance runners but unlike Tibet, there are no schools for training or festivals to showcase their running skills.

The three highly revered tshampa or hermits in the country who are believed to possess the skills to walk long distances in short time. Over the years I have met them many times and recorded their stories.

All three of them have spent most of their lives in solitary retreat. While they live illusive lives, most Bhutanese know about them and have high respect for them. Tsham Penjor is about seventy years old, Lopen Kado is over eighty and Lopen Chuki Lotay is eighty-two (at the time of writing). They are the greatest meditation masters in the country.

So far all three of them have evaded my question about the subject, but the other two adepts agree that the Lopen Chuki is an accomplished trance runner.

Lopen Chuki

I first met the master Lopen Chuki in 1995 in Paro, Bhutan, where he came to perform my grandfather's last funerary rites. My uncle and I were given the responsibility to drop him to Thimphu and then escort him to his monastery in Phajoding on top of the hill in Thimphu. The walk to the retreat house used to take over four hours of strenuous climbing.

At that time, I was twenty-two years old. Being a sportsman, I was fit, but the Lopen was about sixty-nine years old and looked frail. Yet he could walk effortlessly and my uncle and I found it hard to keep up with him.

The Lopen carried a cloth bag that he slung over his shoulder. He wore cheap Chinese plastic shoes with no socks. He pulled up his monk robe to his ankles and I did not hear him pant or short of breath even once.

During the four-hour climb, he would occasionally stop near a chorten and wait for us and offer us betel nuts, which he chewed rather aggressively.

Finally, when we reached his monastery, which is on the ridge on the mountain above 4,000 metres, I found that my shirt was completely drenched in sweat. I had to stay near the fire to dry my shirt and keep myself warm. As expected, at that altitude I was out of breath and it took a while before I could refill my lungs with air. But the Lopen did not show any of these signs. He quickly lit the fire and was busy preparing tea for us.

The Lopen is better known by his nickname, Lopen Boso Karp. He used to be the Yangbi Lopen, one of the top four spiritual masters of the Central Monk Body. After he retired, he chose to spend his time mediating in his retreat house in Phajoding above the Thimphu valley.

Like my family, many people invite him to their house and escort him back to the monastery. Over the years people started to realize his walking ability and soon word spread. It was only when his colleagues from the monk body confirmed this special ability that people started to associate him with the Lung Gompa.

Over the last five years, I have walked to the Phajoding monastery three times to meet him and try my luck in obtaining any information on trance runners, but have not been successful.

The closest I have come is in the winter of 2009 when I went with my cousin Sonam Nima. It had just snowed that Sunday, which slowed our pace. Unfortunately, when we reached the monastery we found that Lopen was in a year-long retreat.

So instead, we talked to his nephew Tshewang Norbu, a twenty-five-year-old monk who served as his attendant.

Norbu was friendly and offered us hot butter tea soon we started talking in his small kitchen.

I carefully broached the subject and did not expect to hear anything. Surprisingly, he had a few things to say about it.

He said that all his friends had told him that his master could ride the wind. He was also convinced of this because he had walked with the Lopen many times. When pressed for details he said that his master always carried bags of tea and packets of sugar and milk powder in his cloth shoulder bag. He walked comfortably even when wearing formal red leather shoes.

Norbu is from a farming village in Haa and was used to hardship. He was fit and could walk for many hours. He said that often during the climb from Thimphu to Phajoding, his master would wait for him, chewing betel nut, and would say in jest, 'The monks these days can't walk.'

He revealed, 'I once asked him to teach me to ride the wind.' In response his master looked at him and said, 'Don't be ridiculous.' Since then, he has not broached the subject.

Just before we left, he said, 'My master will complete his retreat in April, why don't you come back then and ask him the questions?'

As we got up to leave the kitchen, I looked out of the window and saw the Lopen with his upper torso bare, sitting in an upright position. I could notice his white hair.

It is said that Buddhist masters such as the Lopen Chuki are capable of suspending their state of mind. These esoteric forms the core of Tantric practices such as fast walking, and because it is considered to be secret, it is the least studied and most liable to be misunderstood. In the words of Dutch Buddhalogist J.W. de Jong, 'Tantrism is still the most neglected branch of Buddhist text studies.'

Esoteric Buddhism radically reinterprets the journey of spiritual enlightenment. It assumes that everybody is capable of embarking on this great journey but our weak psychological and unclear sensory foundations delays or prevents us from experiencing this bliss.

Trance runners are never discussed in public. The monks consider it a Tantric, secret practice but it's been said that if you prove your motivation, they are willing to teach. Over the years, accomplished Buddhist masters have passed down these teachings through intellectual discourse. Hermits in Bhutan say that these teachings are mostly oral and confirmed that they are passed down from masters to only those deserving monks who have attained an advanced level of meditation.

Lopen Chuki is now ninety-six years old and still lives in Phajoding monastery above Thimphu, and his nephew continues to struggles to keep up with one of the world's last-known trance runners.

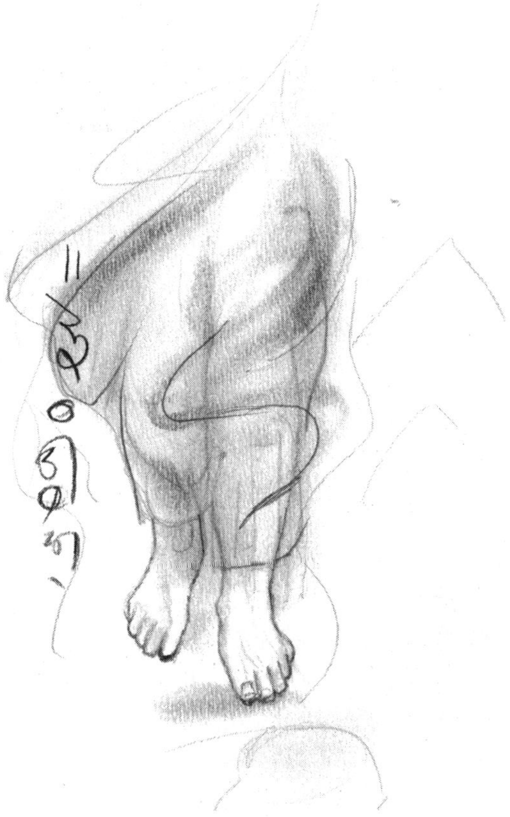

CHAPTER 22

Mystic Marathon

RENÉ VON NEBESKY-WOJKOWITZ

I heard a great deal about a kind of mystic marathon held in the Land of Snow every twelve years. The reports of some travellers in Tibet contained references, echoing Tibetan descriptions, of mysterious runners who are said to cross the country running for days on end without a pause, in a kind of ecstasy. There was also talk of a Tibetan yogi alleged to have covered the distance between the capital and a group of monasteries in Central Tibet, for some special purpose, in an incredibly short time. The West received these meagre and often very confused accounts with understandable scepticism. But my conversations with Tibetans convinced me that these fantastic-sounding stories contained a hard core of truth. Priests and laymen, officials and merchants assured me that every twelve years, one of the Snow Land's two most important yogis, accompanied by two of his pupils, passed through Lhasa on a cross-country run. They called this mysterious personage Mahaketongwa, the 'Great Caller'.

Rimpoche Dando Tulku told me the same thing about the Great Caller as the Summit-Secretary Lobsang Phuntsok, and my friend Nyima had even been blessed by him once in Lhasa at the home of Minister Kabshopa. When I asked him what impression the Great Caller had made on him, be shrugged hit shoulders and said: 'A lama like any other. What stuck in my memory most was the fact that his clothes stank horribly of rancid butter.'

My main source of information about this mystic runner was Phunkhang Se, the husband of the Sikkimese Princess Kukula; a brother of Phunkhang Se is the highest incarnate priest in the monastery in which one of the two Mahaketongwas resides. The name of this monastery is Nagto Kyiphug, 'Upper Forest, Cave of Joy'. Its inmates, like those of the Thelchog Ling monastery, the abode of the second Mahaketongwa, belong to the Kagyupa sect. These two monasteries situated in the Central Tibetan province of Tsang are regarded as the strongholds of Tibetan Yoga. All the monks living in them are given a thorough training in be various Yoga exercises lasting three years, three months and three days. Anyone who wishes to deepen his knowledge receives additional instruction covering six, seven or even twelve years.

The best of the approximately two hundred monks numbered by each of these monasteries is elected Mahaketongwa when a new one is required.

The choice depends primarily on his capacities, but the advice of an oracle-priest is also obtained. Every twelve years, always in a Bird Year by the Tibetan calendar, one of the two Mahaketongwas in turn sets out on the mystic Marathon with his two most experienced pupils.

Eleven years before this severe test—which is supposed to demonstrate the high art of Tibetan Yoga—on an astrologically auspicious day, the three yogis are walled up in separate cells. Their contact with the outside world is limited to a tiny window, through which they receive food and fuel for their lamps—for the Yoga exercises they must perform during these years of solitude include the study of occult writings.

At the beginning of the eleventh month of the Bird Year, the cells are opened. The monks accompany the three yogis to Shalu, an important monastery in the neighbourhood of Shigatse, where the Great Caller undergoes a trial. He is brought into a lofty subterranean room, the roof of which contains a square hole leading directly into the open air—it is the exit through which he will leave the cell again a week later. During this period the Mahaketongwa receives neither food nor drink, and in spite of the icy cold he is left only a loincloth.

On the day on which he is to leave the cell, visitors from far and wide gather at Shalu to see this spectacle. The two governors of the provincial capital, Shigatse, also come to watch the trial as representatives of the Tibetan Government. They take up a position immediately beside the orifice leading into the cell, and at a sign from them the Mahaketongwa has to 'float' up to the ceiling and force himself through the opening. If he succeeds in doing this, his body is wrapped in a yak-skin soaked in icy water, which he has to dry by Thumo. After he has done this the Mahaketangwa and his two pupils make ready for the journey.

They put on the normal lama's garments and around each of them is wrapped a silk scarf, to which both the governors affix their seals. These seals are to prove that the yogis have not taken off their clothes to rest on the way. All three wear large shell earrings. Their long hair hangs loose on their shoulders, apart from the fact that a few of the Mahaketongwa's locks are bound, on the crown of his head, into a knot from which a thunderbolt protrudes. On their brows they wear magical blinkers, whose long black fringes of bears hair hang down as far as the nose and obscure the eyes. The Great Caller's pupils are armed with long staves; he himself holds in his right hand a trident decorated with silk ribbons, and in his left a bone trumpet. In addition, a rosary is hung round his neck and he carries in his belt a phurbu, a magic dagger for fighting demons.

Accompanied by servants and officials on horseback, the three yogis set out on their long run. As soon as they have disappeared over the horizon the govenors begin to write a detailed report on the trial held at Shalu, which is immediately forwarded to the Government in Lhasa.

Running tirelessly, the yogis approach the capital. Couriers ride on ahead to inform the people of the Great Caller's arrival. The route is lined with people in gala dress waking to receive the Mahaketongwa's blessing by touching the ribbons on his trident.

Eyewitnesses who had met the Great Caller and his pupils told me that the three yogis did not actually run, but walked in a quick, rhythmic step. There are always young men who, believing that the mystic runners speed is not really so great, try to race them. But they invariably lose, because they have not the same endurance.

The yogis are allowed to rest for three or four hours at night. They take some food, and spend the rest of the time in meditation. During these pauses, the accompanying officials have to take care that the three runners do not fall asleep. The yogis probably derive far more benefit from these few hours of contemplation than if they spent the same time in sleeping.

The Great Caller's first objective in Lhasa is the Potala. At the foot of the Dalai Lama's residence he blows a bone trumpet: at this sign the servants standing in readiness have to open all the doors of the palace and light joss-sticks in every room. As the Mahaketongwa begins to mount the broad flight of steps leading up to the Potala, he blows a second blast on his trumpet, and then a third as he goes through the doorway. He runs through the rooms of the Potala scattering consecrated rice as he goes, to scare away the evil spirits that may have settled in the dark corners.

After a brief audience with the Dalai Lama, the Mahaketongwa and his pupils repair to the houses of various noblemen, who have invited the yogis to bless themselves and their dependants. Then the three runners leave the capital and visit Samye monastery, whence they return via the province of Lhokha to their starting point. They are said to cover this distance, which would take a fast-moving caravan many weeks, in just a fortnight.

Many Tibetans believe that the three yogis do the run in a semi-trance, or that they know magic formulas which give them 'fleetness of foot'. Most of those whom I questioned, however, had a simpler explanation. In their opinion the fabulous performance of the Great Caller and his pupils is due primarily to perfect bodily control, acquired by years of strenuous exercise, and the development of certain powers that are actually latent in everyone.

—

Writer, artist and former beauty queen Bijoya Sawian takes us to the Shillong of her childhood where, at the age of eleven, she first encountered a priest dismembering a hen and examining the entrails. Sawian's family was of the Khasi faith and followed the old ways of the Niam Khasi. Her grandmother, however, discouraged the traditional practice of divination within the family.

The Khasi religion invokes an imageless god, U Blei, everywhere—within and without. Every home is a temple and every place in the world prayer-worthy.

Sawian tells us of the ancient arts of divination, prophecy and soothsaying as practised in the verdant Khasi hills, and of the rituals employed to unravel the will of divine forces. The wrath of ancestors, transgressions and curses, and negative energies transmitted by jealous family members are combated in the psychic dimension through the intercession of priests and exorcists. We also learn of U Thlen, the snake vampire, believed to exist to this day in the Khasi hills, to be fed once a year with human blood so as to grant immeasurable wealth to the family that harbours him.

On reflection, U Thlen seems an apt metaphor for so much of the evil rampant in the world today.

CHAPTER 23

Divination

The Art of Foretelling in Meghalaya

BIJOYA SAWIAN

As a child of the mountains, I have traversed many frontiers known and unknown, real and perhaps unreal.

Shillong,the capital of the state of Meghalaya in the Khasi Hills where I grew up, spreads out on a plateau rimmed by mountain ranges clad in forests of pine. In the higher reaches, which men have left untouched, they say spirits reside and at night, the tiger-men prowl, leaving their human forms in their beds at home.

I was eleven. It was mid-morning, a Sunday and playtime. I walked, as usual, to the tall hedge at the western end of our compound and called out to my friend who lived in the room below her aunt's apartments. That day, she came running towards me with her finger on her lips and asked me to come over. It was not the normal practice and I was not sure if my mother would allow me to. Something, however, propelled me to comply. I went.

What I witnessed was something I had never seen before and was beyond my imagination: a priest sitting on a cane stool, had dismembered a hen and was pulling out the entrails. He was holding them up against the light and inspecting them intently, while my friend's family members sat completely still. Horrified, I ran out of their gate straight to my grandmother's room and told her about it in gasps and stutters.

She calmed me down and then talked about divination and the fact that she disapproved of it, which was why I had not seen the ritual ever performed in our house. A cousin of hers had been told by a diviner that she would die during childbirth and there was no remedy for her unfortunate fate. My grandmother and her family suffered for the entire period of nine months till the inevitable happened as predicted by the diviner: her cousin died after giving birth to an infant. Since then, she forbade any such divination practice in our home.

I grew up in a traditional Khasi family where we lived strictly according to our ancient indigenous culture and tradition. We practised the native faith, Ñiam Khasi. Prayer to us meant a direct communication with the imageless God, U Blei, who is everywhere and within us. Every home is a temple and every piece of the earth is prayer-worthy. Rituals are performed during the main ceremonies of naming the newborn, marriage and death. The smaller pujas are performed before the commencement of festivals, when the foundation of a house is laid, on birthdays,at the beginning of each year and on other occasions, according to the wishes of the family.

The priest begins his prayer by invoking U Blei to come and assist and bless the prayer meeting. He throws some rice into a container filled with water. Some rice grains sink and some float and, accordingly, he reads and interprets the signs to the family. Another way is to toss some rice onto a brass plate and read what is in store by noting the pattern formed by the scattered rice grains. He then prays for peace, good health and prosperity, and the ritual ends there.

In cases where a person or an entire family is suffering from some inexplicable affliction, impediment or disease and remedies are sought through divination, the process is more complicated; although this was never practised in our home.

With the passing of time, people who fell sick would first consult a conventional allopathic or homeopathic doctor or one from the more traditional disciplines such as Ayurveda or traditional medicine men who brewed herbal concoctions and lived in rural areas. If there was no respite and the malady they suffered from had no logical medical explanation, they would turn to the diviners. The more complicated divination rites and rituals are performed only when required, entirely by one's choice, never compulsory.

Divination is generally regarded as the practice of seeking knowledge, answers and solutions through supernatural ways. It is known and believed that divination has revealed, for instance, the wrath of an unhappy ancestor, secret crimes in a family such as murder, as well as unnatural practices gone wrong. Moreover, remedies for these have also been found through divination.

The process begins with shat pylleng when signs are read in eggs and rice. The priest sits on a mula (cane stool) and faces east. The family sits behind him or on either side, making sure that the east is not blocked. In front of him he places the dieng shat, a wooden tray, and on it he puts a small mound of rice and an egg on top. He then picks up the egg and prays to U Blei, the deities and ancestors to assist him and reveal the reason behind the misfortunes that have befallen the concerned family. When he feels that divine energy has intervened and the egg has become heavy, he smashes it on the dieng shat.

The signs are read by the way the ka kem/jingkem (the eggshells on the left) and the ka lar/jinglar (eggshells on the right) have fallen; how the yolk, the lieng, is splattered on the dieng shat, the condition of the broken shells whether they are facing downwards (lup) or upwards (leim) and by how much of the yolk or the white they contain; how much of the yolk or white on the tray do they cover if they are facing downwards. All these details have hidden meanings which only the priest can decipher. He has either inherited the gift from his ancestors or has learned the art from practitioners.

The signs in this process reveal numerous things. It could be the wrath of an ancestor (pitri dosh), a transgression that has to be remedied, negative energy transmitted by relatives and others and why they have resorted to witchcraft or whether the family has unwittingly disturbed the spirits in the forest while travelling. In some cases, they could be victims of a black-tongued person or one with an evil eye (nazar). Some may have erred and crossed limits with others through their words and deeds, or sometimes a promise to a deity, while supplicating for a favour, has been forgotten.

If the cleansing prayers after the reading are not successful, a ritual which involves animal sacrifice is advised. The animals used in these sacrifices are hens, goats, pigs and cows. The parts of the animal used depend on the advice of the priest or are in keeping with the customs of the particular clan involved. Usually, signs and omens are read in parts of the stomach (intestines), liver, spine, kidney, lungs and the spleen.

Hens are the most popular for sacrifices, unless otherwise advised or shown in the signs in the initial puja. The priest holds the hen with both hands after sprinkling some rice and water on it, prays for the well-being of the family and for signs that indicate the root of the problem. Once the prayer is complete and he feels that all is ready for the sacrifice, he symbolically bathes the hen and slaughters it by cutting the neck with a sharp knife. The blood is emptied out in a container, after which he takes out the entrails till he reaches the 'nierlang', the small intestine. He checks for knots and tears and any abnormalities, which foretell illness, loss and death—natural or unnatural. If any are found, it means that further pujas must be done. Each abnormality is interpreted to the family. At the end of the 'nierlang', there is a little swollen spot, the navel. The navel should also be in perfect condition and there should be no spot or dent on it. Two intestines, big and small, will be visible and measure about four to five inches. The intestine that hangs on the left represents man. The intestine that hangs on the right represents God and should be longer. This is a good sign and it means that the prayers and sacrifices will work and that good will triumph over evil.

However, if there are indications that the family is in the wrong, then divine intervention is clearly denied. In such cases, the priest has to first ascertain that the family is repentant for the transgression they are guilty of and appropriate rituals are performed in accordance to the rules before the remedial puja.

The priest is able to tell what exactly is going to happen—how, where, why and when. The revelations are startling and more often than not completely unknown to the people concerned. It could be a crime committed which had been kept secret. The people concerned may no longer be alive, but the anger and resentment remain in some form of negative energy that either possesses a member of the family or clings to the house and weakens the aura of the descendants, causing untold misery of all sorts. All this is clearly visible to the diviner.

The advice that is given, if there is hope for averting the tragedies, is to sacrifice another hen, one after another, and carry on thus till one finds entrails that are completely clear of spots, knots and tears. In the case of families on who black magic has been performed to bring them to ruin, it could take a long time and up to a dozen or more hens are sacrificed, with the prayers getting longer and more intense. There are occasions when the priest succeeds and there are times when he does not. In the latter case, another day is fixed. Sadly, sometimes the priests fail and the tragedy foretold befalls the family. This tragedy is then simply accepted as destiny.

It is a mystery to those who are not versed in this art how these details are clearly visible in the different parts of the animal's body. A crime such as murder has been unravelled and every single step leading to it has been read and interpreted through divination. If one asks a diviner, he will explain his method, but it is never easy to understand, and from my personal experience, I agree that there is a psychic dimension to the whole process. The priest will simply say, 'I can see the victim and murderer', 'I can see the crime being committed and why', 'This illness has been brought about by a close relative because of ...' and will continue to describe the relative and even the location of his/her home.

In one instance, a family was suffering misfortune in all areas of their lives. Their daughters were either barren or unmarried, which in a matrilineal society such as ours is the biggest curse. Through divination the family discovered that two generations ago, a maternal uncle died soon after he forbade the marriage of his niece to a man he considered unsuitable. (We do not marry into the same sub-clan and clan, and a certain amount of background checks are done to ensure that the couple is not related in any way). The uncle was believed to have been secretly poisoned and the marriage took place after his death. Nobody suspected the crime, but one whole generation suffered major losses in health and wealth. The daughters were born with physical defects such as a limp, a squint, a speech impediment and even blindness and major heart problems.

It was only in the next generation when some of the children, nieces and nephews suffered early and unnatural deaths that one of the sisters, innocent and completely distraught, sought the help of a diviner. The crime was finally revealed and remedies found.

It is never easy to appease an ancestor and it took months of prayer and sacrifices to communicate with the spirit. Finally, when the uncle relented, he promised that the children will not be harmed, but did not yield as far as new marriages and progeny were concerned. It was discovered that this maternal great-grand uncle had objected to the match because the boy his niece wanted to marry belonged to a family that was suspected of keeping U Thlen, the snake vampire believed to exist to this day in the Khasi Hills. U Thlen is to be fed once a year with human blood so that he may grant immeasurable wealth to the family that keeps him.

The legend of the Thlen is, to this day, shrouded in mystery. I have never seen one nor met anyone who has, although there are people who confirm its existence through personal experiences. It is believed that it still exists in the Khasi Hills.

The keepers of U Thlen cut a piece of cloth from a person's attire, or steal a whole item of clothing, or they cut a bit of the hair or steal some strands. The cloth or hair is kept by the family members till the appointed date when they are meant to feed the Thlen. On that day, the family gathers and a particular beat of the drum is played. The snake comes out from its hiding place, and as the prayers intensify, the cloth or hair turns to blood, which the snake sucks up. The person from whom the hair or cloth has been taken inevitably starts to wilt, i.e. lose his or her life force. If the victim's family discovers in time what is happening, he or she might be saved, but if not, the victim succumbs to the illness and the Thlen, thus appeased, bestows the promised wealth on the family that fed him.

Many lives have been saved by diviners who, through their skill, diagnosed and cured the victims of the Thlen-keepers.

Divination is also done before a hunt, a sporting event, a journey and in olden times, before going to war. U Blei is invoked in different manifestations—both male and female, according to the occasion. During a housewarming or the usual yearly prayer, we invoke Ka'leiïng, the goddess of the house; before a hunt, Mei Ramew, Mother Earth; before war, Ka'leikhyrdop, the goddess of war.

However, there are many sceptics. I too was one for the first twenty years of my life, having been told by my grandmother that we must simply pray and seek God's blessings and accept life as it unfolds.

Then I had a life-changing experience. Someone very close to me was indirectly involved in a tragic incident involving a firing by the police in which several young people died. His junior officer fired into the crowd in panic instead of up in the air, as had been directed by the senior. The senior officer was completely shattered and took full responsibility. Soon after, he fell seriously ill and his illness could not be diagnosed even by the best doctors in the region. He ate and drank with difficulty, became alarmingly listless and began to slowly wither away. As a last resort, his brother-in-law decided to consult a diviner. It was a long process as the signs showed that all remedies were blocked and no supplications worked.

Finally, an answer came on the sixth day of the puja. I remember that day clearly as we all awaited the return of the relatives who had gone to visit the diviner. The night before, everyone had prayed fervently and kept some rice under their pillow for the diviner to study. After the usual procedure of prayers and entreaties, the priest divined the answer in the specific positions of the rice grains. He prayed to God for forgiveness, pleading that the victims of the firing had been predestined to die a violent death and the officers involved were but agents of the victims' fate. It worked.

The same doctor and pathologist, who were not able to diagnose the illness earlier, miraculously found out it was hypothyroidism. Medicines were prescribed and a precious life was saved.

Once you delve into the magic of the Unknown, you realize how little one is in control of things. Or is it that we are actually in control, but do not accept the answers? The questions are endless and in this search we sometimes find answers we would have never imagined, which, in turn, are preceded by questions we never knew existed.

The rituals in this chapter are also referenced in Rabon Singh Kharsuka, *Ka Kitab Niam-khein ki Khasi* (Shillong: Fair Beaulah Lyngdoh), chapters 5, 6 and 7.

Academic, author and museum curator Dr Alka Pande's essay is a deeply personal one dedicated to the sacred geography of the Himalaya. When Sati, the feminine principle incarnate, immolated herself in the sacrificial fire after her father did not invite her to the ceremony, Lord Shiva, master of both creation and destruction, held her charred body aloft on his shoulders and lost himself in the cosmic dance of the Tandava, which could have led to the dissolution of the world. When the gods conspired to halt his dance of death, dismembered parts of Sati's body blessed the earth, giving strength and feminine sustenance where they fell.

In this essay, Dr Pande speaks of the sacred feminine and of the three Shakti peethas, situated in mountain terrain, to which she owes an intense emotional allegiance. She invokes the Naina Devi temple in Nainital, Uttarakhand, where the eyes of the goddess are supposed to have fallen, and the Jwalamukhi temple in Kangra, Himachal—revered as 'She of the Flaming Mouth'—which received her tongue. The third shrine, of Goddess Kamakhya in Guwahati, Assam, is dedicated to the spot where the Nilachal hill received Sati's yoni, her womb and sacred womanhood.

Drawn from Shruti (heard wisdom) and Smriti (memory), Dr Pande's piece takes us into the intersectionality of faith and belief, and the towering presence of the Himalaya.

CHAPTER 24

My Devi, My Shakti

ALKA PANDE

या देवी सर्वभूतेषु माँ शांति रूपेण संस्थिता।
या देवी सर्वभूतेषु माँ शक्ति रूपेण संस्थिता।
या देवी सर्वभूतेषु माँ सिद्धिदात्री रूपेण संस्थिता।
नमस्तस्यै नमस्तस्यै नमस्तस्यै नमो नमः।
या देवी सर्वभूतेषु माँ बुधि रूपेण संस्थिता।
नमस्तस्यै नमस्तस्यै नमस्तस्यै नमो नमः।

O Goddess omnipresent as the personification of peace
O Goddess omnipresent as the embodiment of power
O Goddess who gifts accomplishments and understanding
I bow to you, I bow to you, I bow to you again and again.
O Devi who resides everywhere in all living beings as intelligence and beauty
I bow to you.
Accept my salutations again and again.

—*Devi Mahatmya*[53]

My mother, who was from the mountains of Kumaon, epitomized my personal Shakti. In her, I experienced the personification of the universal mother.

I grew up in a deeply religious and traditional household, where the rituals of prayer were followed mostly by my father, with my mother not much a stickler for the 'taam jhaam' of pooja. The 1960s and '70s were extremely challenging for women in India. While modernity was part of life, women in traditionally bound modern families faced myriad challenges of taking care of the home and the hearth, as well as a desire to be economically independent. In upper-class professional households, they had an extremely heavy cross to bear.

I saw my mother and her ilk struggle with the demands of these asymmetries. She balanced the house, dealt with a successful yet patriarchal

53 Kartikey Tiwari. 'Navratri 2019 Nine Mantras for Maa Durga Puja: नवरात्रि में 9 दुर्गा को इन ९ मंत्रों से करें प्रसन्न, हर मनोकामना होगी पूर्ण.' *Dainik Jagran*, 30 September 2019, https://www.jagran.com/spiritual/puja-path-navratri-2019-mantras-for-maa-durga-puja-nine-mantras-for-nine-devis-19626749.html

husband, brought up four daughters and instilled in them a great sense of self-pride, respect and even a certain push to achieve. She was herself a trained musician and wrote evocative poetry amidst the relentless routine of raising her children, a dog and an often-insufferable husband.

Once I became a wife and mother myself, I realized the extent of her quiet sacrifice and her untold repression of personal desires without the aggressive resentment of many contemporary women. I truly did a 'namatasya namastasye' to her in all humility.

I was proud to be the daughter of such a strong and powerful woman who held the family together in her loving yet powerful grip of emotional strength. And it is from her that I seamlessly absorbed my deep adoration and veneration of the 'devi'. She read the Devi Bhagvatam conscientiously and would exclaim that each and every aspect of human nature is displayed in the many stories which string the text together. My father, on the other hand, would recite the Chandi Path and wake us up at 4 a.m. a day before Navratri to listen to the Chandi Path 'mahalaya' from Calcutta radio, marking the day of the descent of the goddess after she has vanquished the demon Mahisasura. For my father, this ritual was a reinforcement of his faith, but for my mother it was about actually living the faith.

I come from the Kumaon hills in Uttarakhand, at the foothills of the Himalaya, literally the land of the Devi. In fact, I regard these mountains as the abode of Shiva and Shakti. Although Shiva is supposed to reside with his consort Parvati at Mansarovar, I refer here instead to Devi who is all-powerful, often daunting, at times terrifying and chilling. She is the mother who nurtures and the goddess who combats the most frightening of demons. Devi lives and roams in the mountains and the mountains, in turn, are alive to the powerful goddess.

As I develop and disclose my understanding of the Devi, both from my personal beliefs and my deep theoretical study, I feel blessed to have been born into a household where scientific reason was tempered with religious belief. It is because of this hybrid, fecund soil in which I was nurtured that the Devi has made a deep incision in my psyche.

The word 'myth' can be traced back to imply 'a story that is a product of words'.[54] With its millennia-long existence, the Indian subcontinent abounds in myth. Stories that mix the mundane with the fantastical have been handed down orally as well through hand-inscribed verse. The Sanskrit works of such kind are mainly recognized today in two major series of works, the Vedas and Puranas.

What is identified as 'Hindu' tradition today comes down from Sanatana Dharma, a deeply interpretive way of life and belief that requires no codification and no book.[55] It is a tradition that conjectures temporary forms to ultimately bring us to a formless reality. 'Religion to the Hindu is the eternal search for the divine *Brahman*, the search to find the One truth that in actuality never was lost ...'[56]

Thus, the multitude of mythological characters and the fanciful, even mutating nature of each one's imagery represents the essence of life itself. 'The embodied soul (*jivatman*) comes from the Brahman, goes through the dramas of its many lives, and then at last desires to return to its origin. All Hindu scriptures, epics, ceremonies, and festivals are charged with this spiritual connotation.'[57]

One of the many rupa/svarupa/manifestations of the Devi is that of Sati or the daughter of the mind born son of Brahma, Daksha. As Daksha's daughter Sati is also known as Daksyani. She is married to Shiva.

'Devi', from the Sanskrit word 'div' meaning 'to shine', is the luminescent one. 'Sakti means power, force, the feminine energy, for she represents the primal creative principle underlying the universe.'[58] Crucially, the primordial truth that precedes the existence of everything is the mother goddess, Devi. This doctrine of conceiving of God as 'Mother' is one of the

54 David Leeming, *Oxford Companion to World Mythology* (Illustrated ed.). (Oxford: Oxford University Press, 2009).

55 Alka Pande, 'Shakti: 51 Sacred Peethas of the Goddess', in Arputha Rani Sengupta (ed.), *Cult of the Goddess* (D.K. Printworld, 2015).

56 Ibid.

57 V. (2008). *Shakti: Realm of the Divine Mother* (Illustrated ed.). Inner Traditions.

58 Alka Pande, 'Shakti: 51 Sacred Peethas of the Goddess', in Arputha Rani Sengupta (ed.), *Cult of the Goddess* (D.K. Printworld, 2015).

outstanding characteristics of Hinduism and is not to be confused with the more widely prevalent practice of worshipping a feminine deity as a guardian of a particular sphere. In Hinduism, Devi, when conceived of in all her completeness and not merely in one of her manifestations, is revered as 'the source of sustenance as the supreme cosmic force'.[59]

As Lord Shiva's consort, Goddess Sati was the precursor to Parvati. The story goes that Sati's father, Daksha, once held a yagna—a ceremony—to which Shiva (and in extension, Sati) was not invited. This story, as well as Shiva and Sati's marriage, goes back to even older myths of a continued animosity between Daksha and Shiva.[60]

When Sati realized that they were not invited to the ceremony, she was furious. She marched to her father's house and immolated herself in the sacrificial fire of the yagna. The grieving Shiva is then said to have lost himself in a cosmic dance of destruction—the Rudra Tandava—with her charred body on his shoulders. The tandava is the dance of Shiva and has a number of manifestations. It is a dance of creation, preservation and destruction. The intensity of Shiva's grief coupled with anger led him to dance the vigorous and horrific dance of destruction, which would lead to the dissolution of the world. Worried, the gods looked to Vishnu to find a solution to this chaos. Vishnu then employed his rotating disc weapon, the sudarshan chakra, which sliced through Sati's body.

So vigorous was Shiva's dance that the angas (dismembered parts) of Sati's corpse were scattered across the land from the north to the south and the east to the west. The sites where the angas fell are revered across the Indian subcontinent today as the Shakti peethas, meaning the seat of the divine entity, Shakti or Devi.

The Bhagavat Purana, according to which Sati self-combusts, lists 108 'siddhapeets' where her ashes fell to the ground. After her departure from the realms of existence, seeing the dishevelled order of things, the gods and

59 C.L. Bharany, 'The Supreme Is Female', in Arputha Rani Sengupta (ed.), *Cult of the Goddess* (D.K. Printworld, 2015).

60 David R. Kinsley, *Hindu Goddesses: Visions of the Divine Feminine in the Hindu Religious Tradition (Volume 12) (Hermeneutics: Studies in the History of Religions)* (First ed.), (California: University of California Press, 1988).

sages prayed to Devi. Pleased, Devi appeared as blinding iridescence and promised to return as Shiva's wife and Himalaya's daughter.

Folklore was associated with certain locations on earth that became holy at the touch of Sati's severed body parts and ornaments as they detached from her being. These were intertwined with the sacred geography of various rivers and ancient consecrated spots. They evoke the Mother Goddess as both nourishing and destructive aspects of the earth and the divine force behind the existence of the cosmos.

> There are thousands of *tirthas* in India, some well-known across the country, and some only locally. The great *tirtha* cycles include the seven sacred cities (*saptapuri*); the four divine abodes (*char dham*), one at each compass point; and the 'seats' (*pithas*) of the goddess, each corresponding to a part of the body of the goddess Sati. The whole of India adds up to a body cosmos.[61]

Myths are situated within historical periods. The same myth told in the medieval period of India as articulated in the Puranas (a body of scriptures of later Hinduism) may differ from earlier contexts and meanings. The nature of legends associated with Devi worship changes across time and space. She has been revered both independently as well as in relation to iconic male deities such as Shiva, Vishnu and Brahma.

Folklore has a unique place in the Indian context because the traditional way of passing down knowledge from generation to generation has mostly been oral. 'Even after scripts had evolved there was always a preference for the transmission of knowledge through oral rather than written means,'[62] as stated by Lolitha Vardharajan. Additionally, much exchange took place between oral and written transmission: '... the ongoing interaction of the

---

61 John Stratton Hawley and Donna Marie Wulff, *DEVI: The Goddesses of India*, (New Delhi: Aleph Book Company, 2017).

62 Lotika Varadarajan, 'Oral Testimony as Historical Source Material for Traditional and Modern India', *Economic and Political Weekly*, 1979.

oral and the literate constitutes one of the most remarkable and unique features of Indian literary culture.'[63]

The *Devi Mahatmya* of the Markandeya Purana (a sixth-century section) provides the central premise of the myths explored in our journey through the Peeths. According to this milestone text, the divine feminine, Devi, is a sovereign power free of (male) partners, superiors and inferiors.

> For the *Devi Mahatmya*, *maya* is not complementary or subordinate to Visnu, as other texts would have it. Nor is *prakrti* balanced—or superseded—by the principle of maleness, *purusa*, with which it is so often paired. Nor is *sakti* paired with, or subsumed in, the male god Siva. In Devi, these qualities stand on their own, constituting reality in a manner that is independently female.[64]

She, in fact, has female counterparts equally representing her in areas such as the battlefield; for instance, the ten Mahavidyas and the seven Matrikas. In the *Devi Mahatmya*, Shakti 'is a singular and universal phenomenon—as a phenomenon that Devi simply *is*'.[65]

There are three Shakti peethas (manifestations of the Devi Shakti) with which I have a deep personal engagement. These are: the Naina Devi temple in Nainital, Uttarakhand the Jwalamukhi temple in Kangra, Himachal Pradesh; and the Kamakhya temple in Guwahati, Assam. These three temples not only represent three very different aspects of the Devi, they have also manifested their deep presence in my life. As with most Shakti

63 Sheldon Pollock, *The Language of the Gods in the World of Men: Sanskrit, Culture, and Power in Premodern India* (First ed.) (California: University of California Press, 2009).

64 John Stratton Hawley and Donna Marie Wulff, *DEVI: The Goddesses of India*, (New Delhi: Aleph Book Company, 2017).

65 Ibid.

peethas, these three Devis also reside in the Himalayas, encompassing a sacred geography within it.

Every time I go to my home in Nainital I always visit the Naina Devi temple, which I have been visiting since I was a young child, clinging to my mother's saree pallu as she paid homage to the Devi, who was part of our 'ishta' deva. The Naina Devi image overlooked the beautiful Naini lake and was close to the mysterious Paashan Devi temple, which supposedly draws a death by drowning every year to propitiate the goddess.

In the 'pahads' or the hills of Kumaon, Naina Devi is not just part of everyday prayers but is also associated with the local ritual of ancestor worship known as the 'jaagar'. The jaagar is a local festival celebrated in each village with its typical flavour, where alcohol is very much part of what we would today probably call pagan rites associated with the Devi. It is consumed while watching the jagaria—who is supposed to be the receptacle for the local god or goddess who has entered his body.

The Jwalamukhi temple is dedicated to Jwalamukhi, the Goddess of Light, also known as the Flaming Goddess or 'She of the Flaming Mouth'. She is also the kula devi of the Pande community of the remote Paliyun village off Barechinna on Almora Road.

An ugra peetha, with 'tantric' overtones in the rituals of worship, Jwala Devi is not worshipped in the form of the Devi, but in the flames which emerge from different caverns at this temple site. The temple is known for its huge havan/yagna kund, where the rituals of fire worship are conducted with honey, ghee and foxtail nuts, sans black til or jaun, which are essential ingredients in havan samagri otherwise.

Over the years, as I continued my engagement with my everyday rituals, I started believing in the power of the Devi, and the powerful women whom I saw around me, particularly my mother, seemed to be the embodiment of the primordial goddess.

One day, Kamakhya effortlessly entered my mind space and, lo and behold, I found myself at her temple! My last visit to the Kamakhya temple was an unforgettable one. I was invited by my friend Mala Barua, who was writing a book on the temple and also capturing the visual history of the temple through photography.

Seeing the temple through the lens of another powerful woman was an unusual and insightful experience for me. As I went down the narrow, dark staircase, I finally reached the sanctum sanctorum where the mountain cleft submerged in cool dark waters that symbolize the yoni of the great goddess. I dipped my fingers in the holy water and brought it to my forehead and a cool calm descended on me. It was as dark and mysterious as the energy of Kamakhya.

Mala took me on a round of the Dus Mahavidya Temples, which are all situated in and around the Kamakhya Temple precincts. However, as I was entering the temple of Tara, I suddenly got a phone call that my eighty-nine-year-old father had been rushed to the ICU at a hospital in Delhi. I was quite startled and troubled, as I had lost my mother to lung cancer seventeen months prior. And there was my father having a huge ruptured ulcer, bleeding profusely. But I knew in my heart that he was protected by the powerful Devi. My father's second name being Tara, I wondered how the goddess would not protect him.

My understanding of the Devi is intuitive and emerges from witnessing my parents' adoration of her. My father, from a Shakt background, and my mother, from a Vaishnava background, both venerated and believed in the power of the Devi Maa. Over the years, as I trained to be an art historian and completed my doctoral work on Shiva and Shakti in the form of Ardhanarisva, the knowledge I piece together on Devi was gathered from multiple sources: the Puranas (Devi Bhagavat Purana, Shiva Purana, Skanda Purana, Kalika Purana, Vishnu Purana, Matsya Purana, etc.); local and cultic folklore; Shaivite and Shakta texts (Shakti Peetham Stotram by Adi Shankaracharya is significant); and studies on Tantra along with Tantric texts (most importantly, the *Tantra Chudamani*).

For believers like me, both the rational and irrational belief in the power of the Devi, drawn from the multitude of legends and myths, are testimony to India's vast heritage of received knowledge from shruti (heard wisdom) and smriti (memory). This is probably the essence of Sanatana Dharma, and how it operates.

mahā-vidyā mahā-māyā mahā-medhā mahā-smrtih,
mahā-mohā ca bhavati mahā-devi mahā-asuri.
prakritis tvam ca sarvasya gunatraya-vibhāvini
kāla-rātrir mahā rātrir mohā-rātris ca dāruṇā.

—*Devi Mahatmya*[66]

You are the supreme knowledge as well as the great nescience,
The great intellect and contemplation,
As also the great delusion,
The great goddess as also the great demon
You are the primordial cause of everything
Bringing into force the three qualities (sattva, rajas and tamas)
You are the dark night of periodic dissolution
You are the great night of final dissolution and the terrible night of delusion

66 Devi Mahatmyram: Sri Durga Saptasaṭi, available at https://www.anandamayi.org/ashram/Durga.pdf

—

This enigmatic piece by mountain geographer and multidisciplinary artist Vaibhav Kaul is difficult to decrypt, as it operates at so many planes and levels of meaning. Is it an unembellished factual recountal? Is it an allegory? A hallucinogen-induced fantasy?

The many mysteries of the high Himalayan reaches converge in this simply told yet deeply complex tale of Kaul's visit to the sprawling valley of Thanggu in the Sikkim Himalaya. Two headstreams of the turbulent Teesta river meet nearby; they will later join the mighty Brahmaputra.

The geomorphologist in Vaibhav Kaul seeks to assess and understand the geohazards of the terrain around him, even as his philosophical interests lead him to listen in to other whispers and reverberations. The local community of nomads and pastoralists follow Tibetan Vajrayana Buddhism and are steeped in Nyingma Buddhist animist folklore. It is through this prism and perspective that he writes about his encounter with the wrathful goddess Palden Lhamo.

This concluding essay brings together the many strands of magic and mystery that have found their way into this anthology.

As climate change devastates the ecology and fragile environmental balance of the Himalayas, the wrath of Palden Lhamo or Palden Lhamo, as well as her benevolent, nurturing aspect, becomes both a grim reminder of what may come and a redeeming portent of hope and faith.

CHAPTER 25

Terrains of Transcendence: An Inner Geography

VAIBHAV KAUL

I wake up shivering. My quilt is covered in snow, and so is the bedroom floor. The improvised polythene-bag windowpanes have been ripped apart by the piercing wind. My solar lantern is out of power, but luckily, the snow glow has made the incipient pre-dawn twilight bright enough to show me the way to the kitchen downstairs. There, the middle-aged lodge owner, Pemba,[67] has already started to cook salty, oily yak-milk tea and instant Maggi noodles on his enormous woodstove. 'The polythene must've given way?' he asks blithely whilst plucking two shrivelled wads of yak meat off a garland hanging from the crumbling ceiling.

'Yes, and there is snow in the room ... I am freezing!' I reply in a very grim tone. 'Sit down, my friend, and enjoy a cup of Pemba Special!' he exclaims rather mischievously as he pours equal quantities of salty tea and rum into my cup, absolutely refusing to understand that alcohol is not my cup of tea.

Noon arrives rather soon, or so claims Pemba's rickety, frostbitten Ajanta wall clock. I switch on my even frostier mobile phone, which has had no signal for a fortnight. '09:09, Friday, 16 October 2015' reads the screen before dying from battery exhaustion. Outside, a faint, haloed sun has begun to emerge from behind the low snow clouds. Hundreds of multihued Buddhist prayer flags are fluttering in the wind like butterflies–a welcome contrast to the bleak white landscape. I am in in the sprawling valley of Thanggu in the majestic Sikkim Himalaya, nearly 4,000 metres above the sultry plains of Bengal and not far from the frigid, arid plateau of Tibet. This is the first snow of the season, and it has come quite early. It will ultimately nourish the Teesta river, a major tributary of the mighty Brahmaputra, two of whose many icy headstreams unite right here.

The larger of the two rivers is known as Lachen Chu, after La-chen ('great pass' in Tibetan), a historic village located some 30 kilometres downstream. The smaller river—Jachu or Lashar Chu—flows southwestwards through the heart of the hamlet of Thanggu and right past my lodge. It is fed by three sacred bodies of glacial meltwater–Shaka Cho (the most voluminous), Yulha Khangsa (three little pools), and Sherabu Cho, all of which sit precariously between the snouts of rapidly shrinking glaciers

67 All personal names have been replaced with pseudonyms.

and loose moraines (ridges of glacially deposited rock debris) along the southwestern flank of the deeply glacierized 6,889-metre-tall giant that is the Kangchengyao Mountain.

For today, the geomorphologist in me had planned my second and most crucial geohazard assessment trek up the Jachu to the 5,000-metre-high, dangerously moraine-dammed proglacial lake of Shaka Cho. The lake appears quite capable—on being exposed to a major shock such as a cloudburst-induced landslide or avalanche in the monsoon—of suddenly bursting its bounds, discharging more than ten billion litres of water in a couple of hours' time, and wreaking havoc on the hamlet community. That journey into the icy realm of hazards will now have to wait until the sky is blue again. Nonetheless, I can still walk around the frozen hamlet and continue to break the ice (mostly figuratively) with the two dozen local families that have still not gone away, along with their countless priceless yaks, to various less snowy places for the harsh winter months that lie ahead.

Over the past week, I have learnt that the local community in Thanggu comprises two yak-dependent groups of people—the Lachenpa from the moist, forested subalpine valley of Lachen in northern Sikkim, and the traditionally nomadic Dokpa from the arid, treeless alpine plateau of Central Tibet. The former are ethnic Sikkimese Bhutia agro-pastoralists who speak a friendly-sounding dialect of the Tibetic Drenjongke language, whilst the latter are ethnic Tibetan transhumant pastoralists who speak a quaint, rustic dialect of the Central Tibetan language. Both groups practise esoteric Tibetan Vajrayana Buddhism.

I have also discovered that most people in the hamlet are acutely aware of the dynamics of rainfall-triggered geohazards such as landslides and flash floods, including those that involve sudden extreme discharges from glacial lakes that have been expanding as the glaciers behind them have been shrinking due to climate warming. Interestingly, a significant part of this awareness seems to come through the community's Nyingma Buddhist-animist folklore, in which geophysical entities are often personified. Nyingma, meaning 'ancient', refers to the oldest of the four schools of Tibetan Buddhism (the other three being Kagyu, Sakya and Gelug). Founded by the venerated eighth-century mystic-sage Guru

Rinpoche (Padmasambhava) during the reign of the Tibetan Emperor Trisong Detsen, it drew upon the very earliest translations of Buddhist scriptures, particularly the esoteric tantric ones, from Sanskrit into Old Tibetan.

I have come to realize that it is only by engaging with local geographical legends that some insight can be gained into the deep, behaviourally potent cultural meanings that seemed to underlie the community's everyday experiences of the physical environment, including the hazards present in it. The most widely invoked of such legends was that of Guru Rinpoche's quest for the beyul or 'hidden lands' (a term associated with Sikkim's medieval Tibetan name, Beyul Drenjong, meaning 'the hidden valley of rice'). The predominant local version of that story, which I have tried to construct from several local accounts, is as follows:

> After completing a mystical mission in Tibet, Guru Rinpoche, along with his retinue of disciples, arrived in and blessed the snowy highlands of present-day North Sikkim. Here, he sowed many seeds of virtue and concealed (within the earth, rocks, vegetation, glacial lakes and even in the sky) many sacred metaphysical teachings that were esoterically embodied and encrypted in treasures known as terma. He exorcised many demons and appointed them to the role of nyedag chosung or 'guardians of sacred places and defenders of righteousness'.
>
> Upon entering the region from the direction of the snowy sin-extinguishing site of Chorten Nyima (the North), Guru Rinpoche flicked a stone across the valley to test the auspiciousness of the landscape. The stone hit the foot of the Kangchengyao mountain and swelled into an enormous boulder (a present-day sacred site). The expansive blessed lake of Guru-dongma, 'the teacher and the pioneer', emerged at this site, just northeast of Kangchengyao.
>
> According to another account, Guru Rinpoche arrived in the region via Kyithang, 'the happy plain' blessed with his footprint, and assumed the form of Guru-dragmar or Guru-dong-mar, 'the red-faced teacher', to overcome a wrathful spirit at whom he hurled his vajra or indestructible thunderbolt weapon. After blinding the wrathful spirit, the thunderbolt

> landed at the site of the present-day sacred boulder, and the blessed lake of Gurudongmar came into being.
>
> The nearby Kangchengyao mountain either came to embody or house that thunderbolt-subdued, purified spirit. It became sacred in that Guru Rinpoche made it the local protector of morality (by blessing it with retributive powers, which could generate extreme geophysical events) and the custodian of the landscape, especially the Gurudongmar lake and several other scattered waters (glacial lakes and meltwater pools—108 in all, representing the auspicious number of beads in a Tibetan Buddhist rosary), including the 'female', moraine-impounded Shaka Cho on its southern side. All streams that emanated from these blessed pools came to be regarded as dutsi, the death-conquering elixir. Besides, Kang-chen-dzo-nga ('the great snows of five hidden treasures', aka Kangchenjunga), a mighty deity-mountain that lived not far away, was made the guardian of the wider landscape (of present-day Sikkim and Darjeeling). He was to be regarded as supremely sacred.

With legendary spiritual treasures hidden beneath mountainsides and in the immortality-giving (read: invulnerability-inducing) glacial meltwaters scattered all over them, the glacierized Kangchengyao landscape is accorded sacred status with a central role in the community's mystical model of geophysical dynamics. Glacial lakes, in particular, evoke in the community a numinous sense of quiet, humbling awe. Consequently, local glacier-related hazards, such as the widely known possibility of a catastrophic glacial lake outburst flood and debris flow from Shaka Cho, tend to be perceived not only as undesirable sources of material (including bodily) loss but also as enigmatic sources of transcendental insight into otherwise obscure metaphysicalities.

A few nights ago, by his woodstove, my rum-mongering friend Pemba introduced me to several elders who claimed to know the mind of every lake in the sacred realm of Kangchengyao. Ana ('Granny') Rinchen, a retired yak herder, expressed great faith in the noble intentions of the dutsi contained in Shaka Cho, which is 'diligently' carried to her doorstep in Thanggu by the Jachu river. She seemed to conceive of the local hydrogeomorphic system as a conscious and inherently good and just supra-organism, ethicizing its interactions with her community by making it a moral medium through which the law of karma operates: 'Till the age of eighteen, I used to spend my summers with my parents and yaks in the Lashar Valley, not far from Shaka Cho. People say the lake will burst one day, but there's water peacefully flowing out from underneath the debris [moraine]... That water is dutsi, the nectar of immortality ... I believe in its goodness; I don't think such holy water will want to smash the wall of debris and kill us, unless that is what we truly deserve ... unless that is the fate that our past thoughts and deeds have earned!'

Pemba himself presented another karmic (but much more humanized) conception of landscape processes, which arose from the many geographically referenced folk tales he had heard decades earlier from his 'wise elders': 'I've never seen a destructive flood here, but the Jachu river becomes rather aggressive in the monsoon. It even comes into our backyard. And when the bridge rattles in the middle of the night, we know that it's time to leave the house and run uphill, towards the monastery. But by the grace of Guru Rinpoche, our house has never been damaged ... Among the many lakes up there, Shaka Cho is the biggest and the deepest. I know her. She's sitting in Kangchengyao's lap, just above our yak pastures. She's tilting his lap towards us because she wants to leap out and come to us. But, by the grace of Guru Rinpoche, Kangchengyao holds her back. Kangchengyao likes to feed her ice. Every now and then, a huge chunk of ice plunges into the water, making a thunderous sound and sending ripples, even waves, right across the lake. Our wise elders have told us that the benevolent Kangchengyao will hold Shaka Cho in his lap only as long as we maintain an atmosphere of piety through our thoughts and actions ... I think Shaka Cho will surely come down one day, but I can't say when ... You see, karma acts through the sky, the earth, everything ... If human beings mindlessly keep on eating into nature to satiate the endless urges of their senses ... and they are foolish enough to forget that they themselves are part of nature ... they will really be eating into themselves, into their own survival, happiness and freedom! These disasters are fruits of our own karma.'

By imagining Shaka Cho as a restless girl sitting in the lap of Kangchengyao, a caring father figure who nourishes her and promises to hold her back until the time is ripe for her to leave him, Pemba's elders ascribed to the mountain regulatory powers over the operation of the law of karma via the lake. In their eyes, it was the influence of the collective bad karma generated by the community that made the lake want to 'leap out' by tilting the lap of the mountain outwards, and the effect of good karma that made the mountain restrain the lake. Just as atmospheric ('sky') and geological ('earth') forces governed the interactions between the mountain (including the glacier, scree slopes and moraines that descend into the lake) and the lakewaters on the earthly plane, karmic forces were thought to control them on some ethereal plane. In fact, potentially destructive natural events such as climate change-related extreme rainfall, floods and landslides were regarded as physical manifestations of essentially karmic causation. Karma was invoked also to make a more universal point about the inseparability of human consumptive activity from nature's dynamics, which placed the moral responsibility for environmental extremes and disasters collectively on appetitively driven human beings who tended to 'eat into themselves' by insatiably 'eating into nature', both in terms of environmental unsustainability and in the context of spiritual ill-being.

Shifting the emphasis away from human responsibility, Lama Dorje, a high-ranking monastic teacher, underlined the guardian mountain Kangchengyao's divinely appointed agency: 'Kangchengyao has been made so powerful by Guru Rinpoche that he can end war, disease and famine. But if he is not happy with us, he may decide to destroy us. And that is when Shaka Cho will be freed and sent to us ... For nearly thirty years, people have been saying that Shaka Cho is about to come down ... We are still waiting for the divine command.'

Another articulate elder, Aju ('Grandpa') Tashi, reiterated that the superior gods and the subordinate landform might have conflicting desires, but ultimately it was the gods' will that prevailed: 'I've been hearing since my childhood that Shaka Cho will come down one day ... that she will explode, her wall will crumble, and her water will take us away. But that has not happened yet, because the gods have not wanted it to happen. The lake has tilted herself very sharply towards us, and she aspires to come to us despite her attachment to Kangchengyao, of whom she was born. But the gods won't let her come ... until that is what they want. I can't say when the tussle will end ... Sherabu Cho is another one like Shaka, but she is much smaller and not yet eager or even prepared to leave her home. Whatever happens to them and to us will be the will of the gods.'

Grandpa Tashi went on to explain that the will of the gods was not autonomous; it was determined by the fruits of the affected beings' collective karma. However, if earnest prayers and other atonement efforts were made with a truly pure heart, it would become possible for the gods to grant sin-offsetting moral boons that could cause the course of one's life (or destiny) to circumvent the sorrow-causing effects of previous bad karma. 'The great secret is that even deities and demons are creations of karma,' he added, highlighting the paramountcy of karma and the ultimately atheist metaphysics that seemed to underlie it.

Remarkably, the community also demonstrated sophisticated, nuanced physical process-based understandings of the glacial lake outburst flood hazard, which seemed to be operating in unison with its folkloristically embodied karmic consciousness. Nourished by decades of lived experience, that local geographical knowledge (albeit not necessarily the underlying metaphysics) was comparable and fairly congruent with Western scientific geotechnical hazard assessments, including my own—both in terms of its appreciation of landscape dynamics and as a resource for practical disaster reduction.

Whilst the depth of the yak herders' experiential knowledge of geological principles was surprising, what absolutely stunned me was that, despite expressing unequivocal concern over the possibility of large-scale destruction, many of them spoke of the lake outburst hazard with breathless eagerness, smiling somewhat triumphantly afterwards. 'Mark my words, a monsoon storm will suddenly throw all of that stony garbage right into the soup bowl [glacial lake],' one herdsman proclaimed quite prophetically, 'and the soup will go "boom" ... haha, and we'll all go "zoom"!' Another herdsman added in a celebratory tone, 'Mud, stones and water will come down like a fire on kerosene.'

I began to see that there existed deep within certain people's minds a parallel and arguably perverse aspiration—to experience extreme, life-threatening geophysical phenomena as some sort of emancipatory escape to extramundaneity, perhaps as a spiritual adventure. In fact, many of the inhabitants presented a decidedly incorporeal worldview, which seemed to render material vulnerability and the risk of material loss quite redundant. They expressed a deep, affectionate faith in the physical landscape, its agency, and its 'intent'; natural hazards seemed to evoke little or no fear (even of death), panic or distress in them. They dismissed the fear of death with such philosophical statements as: 'Haha, death is the end of a great mystery—shouldn't you be looking forward to it?' and 'Life is full of risks, and that is what makes it worth living; the biggest risk is that of death—but what is life without death?'

Grandpa Tashi's words elucidated that sentiment: 'Don't you see how benevolent our mountains are? By the grace of the gods and the great Guru Rinpoche, they have given us all we have. They will never fail their own people, animals, trees ... And if they do something terrible to us, there will be a good reason for that ... The mountains have borne the weight of our wrongdoings for centuries ... Their rocks, snows and waters have been absorbing all the bad karma, and that bad karma has been fuelling the wrath of the great deities that dwell inside them ... There will come a time when all the wrath must erupt and reveal itself, and that revelation will cleanse us from all that ails us. At that moment, you and I will be breathing the same breath as the mountains, the rivers, and the great birds in flight... To live through the fury or be killed by it will be the ultimate experience, a great transformation, a glimpse of the "truth" that frees all minds from the tribulations of this illusory samsara ['world'] and its recursive loop of birth and death... Don't fear death; it is part of life, the gateway to the next life... or the window to parinirvana ['the ultimate extinguishment']!'

Grandpa Tashi's notion that the mountains 'have borne the weight of our wrongdoings for centuries' reflected his cultural and moral-spiritual association with the geophysical landscape as a medium for the administration of karmically retributive justice and as an instrument of salvation and liberation. It pointed to a perceived transformation of karmic energy into geophysical energy such that a materially catastrophic event such as a flash flood represented a morally purgative spiritual climax. This 'geo-cathartic' consciousness, in fact, seemed to pervade a significant part of the community, as if it had always been embedded in the local culture. Nearly every person I spoke with expressed intense emotional associations with the sacred mountain landscape even in casual conversations about everyday life, often effusing a faith in some kind of deep, dynamic unity between the psychological and the geological.

According to the Buddhist (and Hindu) view of reality, the material world is maya, an illusory experience of phenomena that do not exist independently of one's consciousness of them. Maya interferes with prajna-paramita ('wisdom perfection') or the attainment of a perfectly clear transcendental understanding of reality, which is the primary mechanism for dispelling all duhkha (worldly pain, suffering, grief and unfulfilledness, ranging in emotional expression from an elusive sense of existential unease to cataclysmic anguish) and achieving the ultimate ontological goal of nirvana (the 'extinguishment' of the three fires that sustain the sense of self—raga or sensory attachment, dvesha or sensory aversion, and moha or the delusory sensory acceptance of the temporal world as reality).

Over the course of my conversations with the community elders, I found that episodes of acute, devastating duhkha were understood to have the potential to inspire deep awe and trigger spontaneous maya-shattering 'awakenings' marked by surges of overwhelming compassion even in the most materialistic of experiencers. When not regarded as psychotic and actively suppressed, such emotional arousals were believed to act as opportunities for necessary shifts of consciousness that transformed the reality of one's existence. (Any interference with Nature to deprive fellow sentient beings of such redemptive opportunities was to be regarded as extremely uncompassionate and a crime against their consciousness.)

The elders explained that occasionally, a catastrophic event might spark mass eruptions of acute duhkha throughout a community. The genesis of such duhkha might be geo-psycho-cultural, i.e. it might involve the release of geophysical energy and its destructive interaction with humans and other beings in a landscape that has certain culturally assigned metaphysical meanings. In such a situation, synchronous climactic emotional states in experiencers of the duhkha would be capable of producing a powerful collective sense of bodily (material) oneness with the finite, evanescent earthly elements in action and a simultaneous self-annihilating realization of incorporeal absorption into the infinite, timeless cosmos. This, the elders asserted, would provide the experiencers with transcendental insight into shunyata ('zero-ness', nothingness, or total emptiness) or anatman, the absence and therefore the absolute invulnerability of the self in the face of any hazard. The disaster-risk-extinguishing idea of an invincible 'non-self' is embodied by the vajra, the legendary weapon—unrepulsable as a thunderbolt and indestructible as a diamond—from which the locally practised Buddhist tradition of Vajrayana derives its name.

The above metaphysical lens allowed at least some members of the community to rationalize natural disasters and indeed all kinds of intense suffering by gratefully accepting them as sacred gifts bestowed upon them by the cosmos. It certainly made them honour the 'hazards' present in their geophysical environment as contemplative instruments that had the power to bring about positive spiritual transformation (potentially in the form of what psychologists describe as post-traumatic growth). The sense of psychological invulnerability and fortitude fostered by eco-metaphysical affirmations within the traditional Vajrayana Buddhist cultural context seemed to be a powerful adaptive force that arguably challenged interventionist, materialist disaster risk reduction practices initiated by the rational, civilizing modern state and its 'scientific' knowledge machinery. On a deeper, more systemic level, it seemed to project metaphysical realization, as opposed to economic growth or 'development', as the fundamental means and measure of human progress and well-being.

Distraught about modernist-materialist onslaughts on the mighty vajra weapon that symbolizes traditional spiritual conviction, some elders took solace in an abstraction from the Prajna-paramita-hridaya ('wisdom perfection heart') or Heart Sutra, an early medieval Buddhist text that describes how Avalokiteshvara, the compassion-embodying bodhisattva ('enlightened being'), meditated and perfected transcendental consciousness to attain liberation from the world and all its suffering:

'*Gate gate paragate parasamgate bodhi svaha!*' ('Gone, gone; gone across; gone completely beyond! An awakening! So it goes!'). This innate human capacity to 'make the ego go away' and 'awaken the consciousness from the slumber of worldly attachment', the elders argued, must be the ultimate source of resilience.

Even though their deepest metaphysical convictions did seem to reflect the traditional spiritual emphasis on liberating the self from materiality, the vast majority of the people I spoke with exhibited a considerable degree of attachment to the material world and a clear indisposition towards death and material loss; they were quite eager to reduce risk by physically adapting to natural hazards. In fact, many of them regarded the extensive local presence of the Indian Army and the Indo-Tibetan Border Police Force (ITBP, a specialist high-mountain paramilitary agency)—both of which had conducted successful rescue and relief operations in the aftermath of a major earthquake in September 2011—as a source of great security and strength in the face of hazards. However, all of them showed fatalistic attitudes in that they insisted that it was impossible to subdue Nature (i.e. mitigate natural hazards) and imprudent to attempt to do so, for example, by means of extensive engineering works. I was particularly struck by Pemba's submissiveness vis-à-vis natural hazards: 'If we are to be killed, clouds will burst and entire mountains will come down with this river and that river. These embankments, bridges, roads, houses and trucks are just toys; they will be wiped out ... Nothing will remain—only mud and boulders! We can't overpower Nature; we shouldn't even try! If you think otherwise, just look at these mountains, this valley ... Can any engineer in the world build something like this?'

Pemba and everyone else seemed to cherish the idea that contently embracing all of Nature's offerings—pleasurable and painful alike—was the key to a peaceful and happy existence. Well, that brings my cold, hungry self back to Pemba's rum-scented kitchen, where a surprise offering might be waiting for me!

Pemba's woodstove is the largest, so there are more people in his kitchen than anywhere else. Urging me to join in, Pemba pulls out another yak-hair-topped stool from under his quilt stack and ceremoniously opens another bottle of rum. Staring at my slightly disgusted face, his tipsy young nephew begins to chuckle like a fox. All the men burst into laughter, and the women into song. The harmony is quite extraordinary—jolly and coquettish but somehow deeply meditative. My disgust turns into wonder.

As I loosen up a bit, a middle-aged woman—stone-faced and mysterious-looking—marches into the kitchen with some things in her hands. The singing stops. She comes up to me and places in my lap a cup of hot milk and two twirly pieces of khabze, my favourite local fried snack. 'Have it!' she commands rather hypnotically in Drenjongke. '… *shi she be!*' another woman murmurs. I have no idea what those three words mean, but I can sense that something is off. Everyone is staring at me—'all eyes poppin' out like chapel hat pegs', as my neighbour in Yorkshire might say—as if to witness the aftermath of my first bite or sip.

I am immediately reminded of the chilling warning that a dear friend whispered into my ears before I left his home in Lachen to come to Thanggu: 'Be very suspicious when a stranger offers you something to eat or drink. They may wish to poison you and offer you as a sacrifice to the wrathful goddess, Palden Lhamo. Many herbal poisons only cause severe food poisoning, but some can induce cardiac arrest within minutes of being ingested. The post-mortem will not reveal anything, so the authorities will conclude that it was the high altitude that killed you … Mind you, the practice has absolutely nothing to do with our ancient Nyingma Buddhist beliefs or any of the noble Vajrayana teachings of our great Guru Rinpoche. It is not tantra but crazy superstition. Those deluded maniacs think the goddess will shower them with good fortune and wealth if they sacrifice a man to satiate her bloodthirst. By the grace of Guru Rinpoche, there aren't many of them. But they do exist; they live among us.'

My mind also goes back to the sensational summer of 2012, when I was doing geological fieldwork in the accidental company of a scantily clad nonagenarian on the icy, windswept knife-edge shoulder of the 6,053-metre-high deity-mountain Gyephang (aka Raja or 'King' Ghepan), high above the ecclesiastical refuge of Labrang in the Lahaul Himalaya—an equally enthralling realm that lies some 1,200 kilometres away as the crow flies.

The aged Lahauli was a 'disgraced' Vajrayana monk-turned-shaman and a seasoned, death-obsessed practitioner of the eleventh-century Buddhist mahasiddha ('great enlightened being') Naropa's Chos-drug or Shad-dharma ('Six Doctrines'). In his day, he had been a scholar of bardo at certain Inner Himalayan monasteries associated with the Drukpa Kagyu and Gelug orders of Tibetan Buddhism, which he described as the liminal states of being between death and rebirth, rebirth and redeath, wakefulness and slumber, near-death and post-death, and past-consciousness and future-consciousness. It was there, under the spell of that bewitching old shaman who sang strange songs in the otherworldly Tinan tongue, that I first (nearly) encountered—both conceptually and practically (read: neurochemically)—the force embodied by the psycho-culturally potent deity and contemplative instrument that is Palden Lhamo ('the glorious goddess').

The shaman had, in all likelihood, mastered the power-packed esoteric yogas of Tummo (Tibetan for the fierce feminine embodiment of the blazing psychic 'inner fire') and Dzog-chen (Tibetan for 'great completion', the superlative ontological union that leads to rigpa, the transcendental knowledge of gzhi, the ultimate basis or 'primordial ground' of existence). As soon as his piercing eyes met mine, I was completely mesmerized and, like an artless child, began learning from him what later turned out to be some sixteen 'inner dances' of the rlung or prana—a sort of wind-like psycho-spiritual life-force that connects one's deep psyche to one's physiology, and is bodily expressed and experienced through the breath. Those inner dances—whether fiery/fierce or cool/gentle—appeared to generate distinctive 'psychic personalities' or chemical signatures inside my central nervous system, one of which belonged to the raging Palden Lhamo. On one occasion, they almost coerced my frenzied, overheated brain into drowning my body in the half-frozen, precariously moraine-impounded glacial lake that sits at the sacred 'lotus feet' of the towering Gyephang mountain.

To my surprise, the shaman interpreted my ability to survive that deadly advanced-level inner dance exercise as a sign of spiritual (read: neurochemical) progress in the direction of becoming 'fortified and fearless' enough to face and spontaneously unite with Palden Lhamo at absolutely any given moment, especially when I needed the power to 'stare the goriest of deaths in the eye, and turn them away'. He therefore entrusted me with the task of surviving a second, even more crazed day-long inner dance exercise aimed at taking me another step closer to a mystical rendezvous with the dread-destroying goddess. As I closed my eyes to begin the exercise, he reminded me that Palden Lhamo had once slaughtered her own son, devoured his flesh, drunk all his blood using his skull as a chalice, and stripped his skin off and toughened it to make a donkey saddle out of it.

During that inwardly emancipatory, supra-sexually rousing dance of the mind and the breath, my outward being manically sprinted down to the bed of the fast-flowing Chandra river (a headstream of the Chenab) near the village of Sissu, magically swam over to the other side without a rope, jogged up a series of freshly cultivated terraces (in what had been a ghost hamlet since being ravaged by a glacial flood in the 1830s), scrambled up a waterfall (which was named, not surprisingly, after Palden Lhamo herself), and just about dived off its top in a fit of divine senselessness. When the inner dance came to an end, I found myself standing at the edge of the waterfall cliff, staring peacefully into 'the valley of death', as the shaman later put it. Upon nearly killing my body a second time, I finally convinced myself—perhaps for the sake of my lovely family—that I would not become so hopelessly insane as to undertake a third inner dance exercise, let alone a tryst and union with Palden Lhamo, who could perhaps only be attained at the very moment of my own annihilation.

The shaman was ultimately gracious enough to let me 'be', but he left me with a dramatic and cryptic message. 'Silly boy,' he roared, gnashing his teeth like a fuming beast as he walked away, 'to conquer and consume Death, you must surrender to her and embrace her, allowing your silly *self* to be conquered and consumed by her.'

Through the following night, I reflected on my inner world, wondering what the shaman had meant. If I completely lost my sense of self (read: sanity), I would almost certainly lose my sense of time, space, life and death. But would 'I' still *be* if my sense of self were lost? Who was 'I' in the first place? Oh, and *was* I? Or was it all an illusion? Anyway, I can now see that the same theme has been repeating itself in Thanggu through all the mystical excitement about 'extinguishing the illusion' of the self to extinguish every form of vulnerability in the face of the 'hazards' that inhabit the physical, temporal world.

Before my half-numb mind fully returns to the slightly sticky situation in Pemba's kitchen, I am tempted to attempt before myself a fuller exposition of the cabalistic inner dances that took over my very being during the ostensibly 'psychotic' episodes of 2012. After all, I might draw some occult power from my memory of it, which might prepare me to face Palden Lhamo today; that is, if she really desires me as an offering!

To be able to perform those contemplative inner dances, I needed the infrastructure of yantra, mantra and tantra, which could be regarded, respectively, as the hardware, software and operating system of the 'computer' that executed my contemplative quest. My breathing human body, with its complex neurological and endocrine apparatus as well as the vital force of prana (the 'electrical energy' powering the 'computer hardware'), acted as the primary yantra or material instrument that physically hosted and enabled the contemplative quest. I also used secondary yantras–contemplative instruments that came in such physical forms as two-dimensional spatial configurations (e.g. geometric diagrams) and three-dimensional bodies (e.g. sheep skulls) that were either materially existent in the outer world or imagined in the inner world as symbolic representations of psycho-cultural phenomena such as certain deep psychological impulses (especially 'sordid' ones) embodied by certain deities. The yantra machinery would become useful only when it was filled with mantras or bundles of meaningful sensory information—especially auditory and verbal (e.g. stand-alone sounds or invocatory chants and songs composed within certain melodic and pitch frameworks), but also visual (e.g. invocatory scripts and sketches)—which drove the cognitive and emotional processes that constituted the contemplative quest. Finally, and most crucially, there was the tantra—a philosophically informed, occultly crafted practical framework for contemplation (including, for example, templates for synchronizing the motion of the breath with certain cognitive and emotional processes). It was within that framework that each mantra was operationalized using the yantra machinery. The key task of the chosen tantra was usually to provide the semantic prototypes of psychic-impulse-embodying deities with which each structural unit of each mantra was encoded.

Upon the coming together of yantra, mantra and tantra, my attention would follow the various movements of my breath, drawing, with the breath-driving 'psychic' prana force, certain intangible, phantom spatial patterns through a series of four, five or seven non-physical chakras (vortex-like 'psychic' energy nodes in the 'subtle body' or sukshma-sharira), which are located along incorporeal vertical flow channels that rise from near the tailbone and the perineum all the way to the top of the head via the abdomen, heart, and throat in the 'physical body', apparently corresponding to the spatial alignment of the various nerve plexuses as well as the hormone-secreting glands of the endocrine system.

The supposed passage of the non-physical prana energy (guided by my attention on my moving breath) through those subtle chakra vortices would trigger certain intense emotional experiences, whose nature would depend on the particular tantrically predetermined inner dance that was performed using the breath and the mind's attention thereon. By progressively increasing the tempo of the psychic dance, the associated emotional experience would be transformed into voluntarily induced audiovisual quasi-hallucinations. The visual content of those quasi-hallucinations could then be projected three-dimensionally—using the power of the culturally conditioned imagination—onto a distant snowy peak, a cloud sitting still on a hill, a boulder, a pebble, a patch of snow, a drop of dew resting on a blade of grass, or just a parcel of thin air. In this manner, a certain 'psychic personality' would be made to come alive in the outer world.

On certain occasions—perhaps with some inspiration from my own ancestral Kashmiri Shaiva-Shakta tantric heritage (especially the contemplative bodily practices associated with the tantras of Vijnanabhairava, Manthanabhairava and Kubjikamata as well as the metaphysical doctrine of Pratyabhijna or 're-cognition')—I would use my own bodily self as the 'projection screen', allowing my sense of bodily awareness to be taken over by the neurochemically projected 'psychic personality'. I would then work my mind up into an emotionally climactic, frenzied, supra-orgasmic state that would enable a sort of ontological union with an imaginary feminine consort-deity—a phenomenon underlain, perhaps, by something like a grand eruption of dopamine in the midbrain. I would therefore be 'possessed' by the culturally constructed 'spirit' of a certain legendary tantric 'goddess', such as Ekajati or Ralchigma ('the wielder-ess of the one power-tuft of hair'), Kurukulla or Rikjema ('the magical wisdom woman'), or others from the mighty Vajrayana Buddhist Dharmapala ('keeper of cosmic order') pantheon; or even Tripurasundari ('the beauteous belle of the three realms'), Kalaratri ('the dark, deathly night'), or any of the eight other formidable Mahavidya ('great wisdom') goddesses who manifest Adi Shakti ('the primordial energy') in my own ancestors' spiritual worlds.

Curiously, for some inscrutable reason, the only goddess I could never fully manifest and climactically unite with was Palden Lhamo. Nevertheless, whenever I did arrive at an extraordinary, mind-saturating state of incorporeal quasi-coital fusion with any other goddess, I would temporarily lose my sense of space and time, and would usually go completely, blissfully silent for a very long time, often whilst 'feeling' an emotional intensity that 'felt' impossible to completely 'feel' within the realm of the senses, given the limits of my brain. Afterwards, I would find myself drenched in tears of awe and gratitude. That extraordinary, seemingly miraculous sense of awe and gratitude would persist for weeks or months, sprinkling the magic of its heavenly beauty over my everyday this-worldly experiences. However, there would be an incompleteness or vagueness about the memory that would remain of the prolonged climax, which might best be described as an exposure to a sort of 'singularity', or to a sudden dissolution of all ontological discontinuities and an immersive insight into the unity of all that is and is not, was and was not, and will be and will not be.

Another way—perhaps inspired by Vedantic advaita (Sanskrit for 'non-duality') or Sufic wahdat al-wujud (Arabic for 'unity of being')—to express that ineffable, elusive sense of dissolution and union would be to describe it as the devastatingly blissful coming of a love that is timeless and free from the duality of lover and beloved, subject and object. Yet another characterization of the above climax would be as a transformed, liberated state of consciousness, in which the viewer, the glance, and the view merge into one another, so that all that exists is an all-encompassing dimensionless-ness—a transcendental viewer-less, view-less vision of the ultimate reality (represented, for example, as Brahman by Vedantist mystics, Shiva by Shaivite mystics, Allah by Sufi mystics, and Ik Omkar by Sikh mystics) or the absence thereof (described, for example, as shunyata or voidness by Buddhist mystics). This particular exposition of metaphysical union resonated with three solitary wandering pirs (elderly Indo-Persianate Muslim Sufi ascetics) I encountered later on in 2012, whilst roaming the high, icy ridges of the Pir Panjal Mountains, where Panchaladeva, an enigmatic enlightened being of yore, is believed by some to be in a state of perpetual meditative absorption.

The stick-bearing itinerant pirs came across as unworldly, gentle-hearted, sentimental and quite love-intoxicated, much like the lute-bearing 'Ashiq and Bakhshy' bards of medieval Turkic realms, who would wander from village to village in search of their Beloved, often traversing formidable terrains along the way. Raised within the syncretic Kashmiri Rishi mystical tradition (with many influences from the better-known Kubrawi, Qadiri, Naqshbandi and Chishti Sufi orders), the pirs spoke rather poetically of their philosophies and lived experiences of wujud (existence), haqq (the ultimate truth), ruh (the spirit), qalb (the spiritual heart), the seven stages of nafs (the self) in its journey towards perfection, and the seven stages of 'ishq or hubb' (love) in the lover's inward journey towards fana fi al-mahbub (annihilation and absorption into the Beloved).

One of the three pirs, a white-turbaned tarana-saz or 'song-crafter' had been composing trance-intensifying alliterative verses in Persian, Gojri and Urdu for over sixty years. He sang of 'didar-i dildar dar dil-i dil' (Persian for 'a glimpse of the Beloved in the heart's heart') in the dark and deep double harmonic major scale (the Arabic Maqam Hijaz Kar or the Indic Raga Bhairava), later explaining to me how one's relationship with that inner Sweetheart who reposes in the secret chamber of one's heart—the very core and essence of one's being—is projected onto every relationship one forms in the outer world. As the tarana-saz spoke, he repeatedly uttered aspirated sounds such as 'hu', which, he revealed, acted as stimulants during his breath-borne psychic ascents and descents. When I told him that those sounds were reminiscent of the tantric 'hum' and 'hrih', he turned to his beloved Baba Nanak and remarked, 'Hu, hum, you, I, this, that—isn't everything an echo of the one primordial sound ... "Ik

Omkar" [the core metaphysical principle in Sikhism, denoting the one ultimate reality]!'

Within the context of mystical love, the oldest of the three pirs, Bachcha Mubarak ('the blessed child'), introduced me to jism-i latif and lataif-i sitta—the Perso-Arabic mystical concepts that relate, respectively, to the 'subtle body' (equivalent to the Indic sukshma-sharira) and its psycho-spiritual organs or psychic energy nodes (somewhat analogous to the chakras). Interestingly, he repeatedly cited Sanskrit verses from the ancient Brihadaranyaka ('Great Forest') Upanishad whilst revealing the ontological poetry behind the psychological dynamics associated with khafi (aka latifa khafiya)—the sixth of the seven lataif or subtle psychic organs (presumably comparable to the tantric ajna or 'third eye' chakra)—through which one is said to receive the gift of intuition, extrasensory insight and inspiration required to transcend the barriers imposed on the consciousness by one's senses of temporality, materiality and individuality.

In the self-hypnotic process of untying certain psychic 'safety knots' that would reveal the beauty of khafi (perhaps with some help from the pituitary and pineal glands in his physical body), Pir Bachcha seemed to spontaneously drift out of his individual consciousness into mine. He was briefly able, through some inexplicable mechanism, to access and graphically describe my most recent thoughts and some of the memories that I had acquired during the previous week or so. 'Gosh, the pheromones in my sweat can't possibly be so powerful as to transmit all of that information to the old man's head!' I remember thinking to myself. All he said by way of explanation was that he did not mean to show off or anything; he simply wanted me to see how, only by the grace of the Almighty, anyone with a loving heart and a certain amount of istiqamat ('steadfastness') could experience the intuitive power of khafi and use it to tap into other worlds of zehn-o-zaman ('mind-and-time'), but only for noble purposes. 'Vow, with every breath you take, to shine in nur al-haqq ('the light of Truth')!' he whispered, slowly turning his gaze to the sublime softness of the afternoon sun.

I had to leave Pir Bachcha at dusk, but before that, he walked me up a golden meadow to a shimmering pine nut tree that stood alone on the crest of a rocky ridge, watching over the deep gorge of the thunderous Chenab. 'Meet Shajr Mubarak, my blessed tree!' he exclaimed, before clearing his throat to recite in a sonorous, grandfatherly voice the Ayat an-Nur ('Verse of the Light' in Arabic) from the Quran, which weaves a whole world of wonder around a certain 'blessed tree'. The solitary tree was bursting with birds; it seemed to be a sort of oasis for them.

A chubby large-spotted nutcracker provided some very loud, shrill background music as the Pir began to narrate the story of his life (and that of the tree): 'I left my parents' home and a hundred buffaloes at the age of fifteen, and crossed over into the realm of mahabbat-o-marifat [mystical love and inner knowledge]. One evening, after I had spent a few minutes in quiet muraqabat [meditation] at this very spot, I spontaneously arrived at the threshold of the Beloved's home. After witnessing my hal [spiritual state], my murshid [spiritual teacher, guide, and mentor] received a laudatory dream-visitation from the sixteenth-century Kashmiri saint Hazrat Resh Mir Saeb. In the dream, he commanded that a chilghoza [pine nut] tree be planted at "the blessed spot" so that I—whom he named Bachcha Mubarak, "the blessed child"—would have a rich source of bodily nourishment as well as the uplifting company of very many nut-eating birds as I grew older and more prone to farsudagi [fatigue], due to which I might err spiritually and, as a result, have to bear the sharp pain of hijr [separation from the Beloved]. Subsequently, a handful of pine nut seeds, extracted from a great tree that sheltered a pretty little shrine to Adi Shakti at Ishtiyari in the nearby canyon of Paddar-Pangi, were brought to this ridge and sown at the blessed spot with the wonder word "Bismillah". One of those seeds has grown, by the grace of Allah, into this beautiful, bustling, bountiful tree! Those were the days of Gandhiji's Quit India Movement, so the tree must be about seventy years old now.'

As I bade adieu to the adorable pirs of Pir Panjal, I concluded that they were pursuing essentially identical spiritual quests and undertaking similar neurochemical manoeuvres to those of tantric mystics, except in two respects. Firstly, they never invoked or meditated on any form-possessing, impulse-embodying deity, although one of them maintained the devotional practice of mentally engraving various imagined forms of the Arabic spelling of 'Allah' within his spiritual heart, albeit with a constant awareness, with every breath, of the formlessness of the Almighty. Secondly, they always regarded the grace of their timeless Beloved, the wahid (one and only) Allah—rather than the agency of their own karma—as the sole means by which any mukashafat (revelation, as if by 'the lifting of a veil') or transcendental insight would 'come' to them. They would often burst into tears as they recalled such 'comings', reminding me of the endearing words of a young female Eastern Orthodox Christian tourist I had once found meditating inside a megalithic chamber tomb that had been carved out of a glacially transported boulder in a damp, peaty valley on the cold, stormy island of Hoy in Orkney: 'There are blessed moments when Immanuel comes to me, when true love seeps into me ... Those are my Christmases!'

Love was indeed the central theme of my electrifying and truly 'Himalayan' encounters with both the tantric shaman and the Sufi ascetics. The shaman taught me to travel to the very bedrock of the mind, rescue from the repressive clutches of matter and morality every unwholesome instinct (e.g. fear, hate, angst, insatiety) and every ensuing psychological impulse (e.g. rage, lust, avarice, envy), and bring it to the fore, so that it could then be fully revealed and celebrated in the brilliant light of love's dimensionless-ness, and ultimately torrefied into nothingness by that very light. He showed me how that process would lead to the extirpation of the illusion of the time-bound, death-enslaved self, and along with that, the realization of absolute freedom from all worldly vulnerabilities and sufferings.

The ascetics, through their own pursuits of dissolution and absorption into dimensionless love, uncovered a similar potential for total spiritual liberation from the constraints of time and matter. They made me see that one's love-ward journey through the inner world unveils progressively truer, freer, sweeter, more radiant, more beautiful, more peaceful, more compassionate, more just, more powerful, more fearless, more perceptive, more creative, more useful and more fulfilled versions of oneself in the outer world, until one loses oneself to love.

Back in Pemba's kitchen, my poor little self is still faced with the twirly khabze and the hot milk. The two are sitting in my lap, gazing at me as if they were the very eyes of Palden Lhamo. What am I to do? Am I afraid that I might die as soon as I let them into my body? Or am I prepared to look Death in the eye and let her gaze slay my fear of her, even if that fearlessness were to come at the cost of my mortal life? Is this my second chance to become one with Palden Lhamo, and through her, with dimensionless love? Have I turned into a mystic, a moonstruck geographer of the inner world?

In a moment of transcendence, I let the khabze and the milk in.

The day passes, and nothing unusual happens to my body, except some mild flatulence. In my sleep, she appears as her smoke-clad, donkey-riding self, holding a bone-staff and a triple-edged bayonet in her two left hands, and a blood-filled skull-chalice and a scorpion-handled broadsword in her two right hands. I open my eyes. She is still here, looking into her own eyes through my eyes. I am drenched in her, she in me. Behind the snows, the horizon is blood-red. It is dawn.

Dissolving every horizon
In the slumberous snows of peace,
A silent sigh fills me
With echoes of ecstasy
And blows me out to thee—
A dance of the free
Only closed eyes see.
We are eternity!

It was whilst conducting geographical fieldwork in the Himalaya that I witnessed what I have tried to describe in the essay. Sections of the text have been reproduced or adapted from my doctoral dissertation: Kaul, V. (2019) 'Holistically understanding and enhancing the adaptation of remote high-mountain communities to hydrometeorological extremes and associated geohazards in a changing climate', University of Sheffield (Supervisors: M. Watson, J. Jones, D. Swift).

Acknowledgements

My gratitude to the universe for allowing me to curate this book of wisdom and learnings. I am indebted to all those whose words appear in these pages. A hat tip to Krishan Chopra and Somak Ghoshal who set me on this journey. Thank you, Amrita Mukerji, for your patience and kindness always, and thank you, Udayan Mitra and Ananth Padmanabhan, for your belief and support. Bonita Vaz-Shimray for understanding the essence of the book and the inspired cover design. Sidharth, for bringing the stories to life with your drawings. Sukhman Khera for helping me begin on this anthology and seeing it through to the first draft. Thank you, Anisha Lalvani, for the initial edits and consistent help. Tanima Saha for your perseverance in putting it all together. To so very many others, too many to mention individually, my heartfelt gratitude.

Notes on the Contributors

Holly Gayley is a scholar and translator of contemporary Buddhist literature in Tibet and associate professor in the Department of Religious Studies at the University of Colorado Boulder. She is the author of *Love Letters from Golok: A Tantric Couple in Modern Tibet* (2016) and editor of *Voices from Larung Gar: Shaping Tibetan Buddhism for the Twenty-First Century* (2021).

Andrew Quintman is a scholar of Buddhism in Tibet and the Himalaya, and associate professor in the Department of Religion at Wesleyan University. He writes, teaches and lectures about Buddhist literature and history, sacred geography and pilgrimage, and visual cultures of the Himalayan region. His new English translation of *The Life of Milarepa* was published by Penguin Classics in 2010.

Walter Yeeling Evans-Wentz (1878–1965) was an American anthropologist and writer who devoted his life to the study of Tibetan Buddhism. He is best known for the English translation of *The Tibetan Book of the Dead* (1927). He also translated *Tibet's Great Yogi Milarepa* (1928), *Tibetan Yoga and Secret Doctrines* (1935) and *The Tibetan Book of the Great Liberation* (1954), and wrote the preface to Paramhansa Yogananda's *Autobiography of a Yogi* (1946).

Ranjit Hoskote is a poet, cultural theorist and curator. His collections of poetry include *Vanishing Acts: New & Selected Poems 1985–2005* and *Die*

Ankunft der Vogel. His poems have appeared in *Akzente, Boulevard Magenta, Fulcrum, Green Integer Review, Iowa Review, Nthposition* and *Wespennest.* Hoskote was a Fellow of the International Writing Program, University of Iowa (1995), writer-in-residence at Villa Waldberta, Munich (2003) and research scholar in residence at BAK/ basis voor actuele kunst, Utrecht (2010 and 2013).

Navtej Sarna is most recently the author of the novel, *Crimson Spring.* His earlier books include the novels *The Exile* and *We Weren't Lovers Like That*, the short story collection *Winter Evenings* and several works of non-fiction. A professional diplomat for nearly four decades, Sarna was India's Ambassador to the United States, High Commissioner to the UK, Ambassador to Israel and Secretary at the Foreign Ministry.

Author/editor of over fifty books, hundreds of academic papers, and thousands of newspaper/periodical articles, **Makarand R. Paranjape** is a long-standing professor of English at Jawaharlal Nehru University. He also served as the Director, Indian Institute of Advanced Study, Shimla. Among his recent publications is the book-length study, *Swami Vivekananda: Hinduism and India's Road to Modernity* (HarperCollins India, 2020).

Alexandra David-Néel (1868-1969) was an opera singer, a Buddhist scholar, a prolific author and one of the foremost women explorers of her time, the only European woman to have been honoured with the rank of a Lama. She was the author of several books, among them *My Journey to Lhasa* (which recounts her visit to the Tibetan capital in 1924, at a time when it was closed to outsiders) and *Initiations and Initiates in Tibet.*

Rajiv Mehrotra has been a student of His Holiness the Fourteenth Dalai Lama for forty years. He serves as the secretary and trustee of the Foundation for Universal Responsibility of His Holiness. He has authored nine books. As an independent documentary film-maker, commissioning editor and producer, Mehrotra has won thirty-two National Awards. He serves as the managing trustee of the Public Service Broadcasting Trust.

He has served on numerous committees and boards and was a judge for the Templeton Prize for Religion.

Paramhansa Yogananda (1893–1952) was a spiritual guru and founder of the organization, Self-Realization Fellowship. After starting a school where young boys could receive a well-rounded education, he went to the US in 1920. In 1924, he began a tour of lectures across the country. In 1925, he founded the Self-Realization Fellowship with the first centre in Los Angeles. In later years, he started several other centres. In 1946, he wrote his bestselling *Autobiography of a Yogi* that has sold over five million copies and been translated into many languages.

Sujata Prasad is an author, art columnist, curator and heritage conservationist. A former civil servant, she is currently advisor to the National Gallery of Modern Art, and serves as an expert on the Department of Science and Technology's Scientific Advisory Committee for Heritage Research. She is a member of the governing board of the Institute of Human Development, and part of the Asia-Pacific chapter of the World Crafts Council. She is the author of several books, the most recent being an acclaimed biography of Jayaprakash Narayan. She is the editor of National Gallery of Modern Art's newly launched journal of art and aesthetics and many important museum publications.

As a media person, **Romola Butalia** worked in print, visual and digital media. She is the editor of India Travelogue and co-founder of Save Kumaon. As a practitioner and teacher in the traditions of the Himalayan yogis, her given name is Sriji. She has written two books—*In the Presence of the Masters* and *Sri Babaji Immortal Yogi of the Himalaya*. Her search for wisdom and joy led to a continuing tryst with the Himalaya, where she lives a reclusive life.

Madhu Tandan lived for seven years in Mirtola Ashram, beyond Almora, where every experience was viewed as an opportunity to grow. Her life there, threaded by her dreams, inspired her first book, *Faith & Fire: A Way Within*.

She has since written three more books, *Dreams & Beyond: Finding Your Way in the Dark*, *Hemis: A Novel* and *The Logic of Dreams*, besides contributing short stories to anthologies. She has conducted dream workshops and presented papers on religious dreaming at international conferences. She and her husband live in the hills of Sattal, with the birds and butterflies.

René von Nebesky-Wojkowitz (1923-1959) was a distinguished Austrian anthropologist who went to Tibet and the neighbouring mountain countries to study the legends, customs and religious traditions of the Himalayan people. His book *Oracles and Demons of Tibet* (1956) was the first detailed study of Tibetan deity cults.

Devyani Mungali is the daughter of Swami Rama and has been an educator for more than thirty years. She is the founder of the Sanskriti Group of Schools, Pune. She is passionate about fostering creativity in children and has published three poetry books in Hindi and one in English. She has learnt the Tanjore and Warli styles of painting and is also a trained Bharatnatyam dancer.

Bhushita Vasistha is a writer based in Nepal. She is currently attending an MFA in writing programme in the United States under Fulbright Scholarship.

Sidharth, originally a signboard painter, has a diploma in painting from College of Art, Chandigarh. He has trained in fresco painting, thangka painting techniques, Madhubani paintings and Kashmir papier mâché from masters of the crafts. He has held many solo shows and participated in group shows, nationally and internationally. He is also a recipient of various awards. His works have been acquired and displayed by museums in India and other countries. An author, documentary film-maker, sculptor and painter, Sidharth is a multifaceted artist.

Poet, academic and translator, **Jaspreet Mander** regards poetry to be her calling. She is a full-time writer based in the UK. She has written three volumes of poetry volumes and has a master's degree in creative writing from Leeds Trinity University.

Nirupama Dutt is a poet, columnist and translator writing in English and Punjabi. Her works include the biography of Punjab's Dalit icon, *The Ballad of Bant Singh*, and an English translation of Gulzar's anthology of poetry, *Pluto*. She has published several books of poetry and prose.

Tsering Döndrup was born in 1961 in Qinghai, China. He began writing in the early 1980s and has published numerous collections of short fiction and four full-length novels. His work has been translated into several languages, and he is the recipient of a number of Tibetan, Mongolian and nationwide literary prizes in China.

Christopher Peacock is a PhD candidate at Columbia University.

Dr Jono Lineen is a curator at the National Museum of Australia, where he manages the country's largest social history project, Defining Moments in Australian History. His research focuses on the relationship between storytelling, walking and creativity. As a young man he spent almost twenty years travelling the world working as a forester, ski racer, baker, fisher, mountain guide, humanitarian relief worker and writer. His books include *River Trilogy, Into the Heart of the Himalayas*, *Perfect Motion* and *Searching for Breath*.

Tshering Tashi is a writer based in Bhutan. He has written several books and regularly contributes articles to Bhutan's national newspaper. He is one of the Directors of the Bhutan Echoes, Drukyul's Literature Festival.

Bijoya Sawian is a writer and translator from Meghalaya. Her highly acclaimed translations of indigenous culture from Khasi into English have been published by the Vivekananda Kendra Institute of Culture Guwahati. Sawian's works of fiction are *Shadow Men: A Novel and Two Stories* (nominated for the Tagore Literary Prize 2020) and *A Family Secret and Other Stories*.

Dr Alka Pande is an art historian, curator, arts manager, prolific writer and winner of many prestigious and highly coveted awards in India and abroad. Her major fields of interest are gender, identity, sexuality and traditional arts and heritage. She has been passionately involved with the world of visual arts for more than three decades now. She serves as a consultant art advisor and curator of the Visual Arts Gallery at the India Habitat Centre in New Delhi.

Dr Vaibhav Kaul is a mountain geographer and multidisciplinary artist. He studies changing physical and cultural landscapes in some of the farthest reaches of the Himalaya.

Copyright Acknowledgements

'The Living Presence' by Holly Gayley

First published in *Buddhadharma* (Winter 2007). Reproduced with permission.

'Milarepa' by Andrew Quintman

First published on The Treasury of Lives, https://treasuryoflives.org/biographies/view/Milarepa/3178. Reproduced with permission.

'Lal Děd' by Ranjit Hoskote

Reproduced with permission from *I, Lalla: The Poems of Lal Děd*, tr. by Ranjit Hoskote (Gurugram: PRH India), 2013 (reprint edition).

'The Sage from the Valley of Flowers' by Swami Rama

Reproduced with permission from the book *Living with the Himalayan Masters* by Swami Rama.

'Reincarnation' by Rajiv Mehrotra

Reproduced with permission from *All You Ever Wanted to Know from His Holiness the Dalai Lama on Happiness, Life Living, and Much More* (New Delhi: Hay House), 2009.

'The Handsome Monk' by Tsering Döndrup

Reproduced with permission from *The Handsome Monk* (New York: Columbia University Press), 2019.

'Into the Heart of the Himalayas' by Jono Lineen

Reproduced with permission from *Into the Heart of the Himalayas* by Jono Lineen (New Delhi: Speaking Tiger Books [Indian subcontinent] and Pottersfield Press [Canada]), 2020.

'Magic and Mystery in Tibet' by Alexandra David-Néel

Excerpted from *Magic and Mystery in Tibet* by Alexandra David-Néel (New York: Claude Kendall), 1932.

'My Interrupted Flight toward the Himalayas' by Paramhansa Yogananda

Excerpted from *Autobiography of a Yogi* by Paramhansa Yogananda, 1946.

'Where the Gods Are Mountains' by René von Nebesky-Wojkowitz

Excerpted from *Where the Gods are Mountains: Three Years Among the People of the Himalayas*, tr. Michael Bullock, (New York: Reynal and Company), 1957.

'Tibet's Great Yogi Milarepa' by W.Y. Evan Wentz

Excerpted from *Tibet's Great Yogi Milarepa* by W.Y. Evan Wentz (Kathmandu: Pilgrims Publishing), 1928.

Index

Adi Shakti (the primordial energy), 302

Adi Shankaracharya: Shakti Peetham Stotram by, 281

Aham Brahmasmi, 140

Akhandananda, 67

Alakh Purush, 135–136

Anahata Chakra, 139

Anahat Nada, 139

Anandamayi Ma, 198

ancient souls: Goraknath, 56; Machendranath, 56

Arya Samaj, 124

Asanga, 129; *Yogacharbhumi,* 128

Ashish, Madhav, 6, 148

ashram, 153, 155, 210; aimed at self-sufficiency, 152; Kainchi, 165, 168, 171; Kakrighat, 169; life at, 156; Mirtola, 161; personal identity in, 158–159

Avalokiteshvara, 4, 295

Baba Nanak, 304

Bachcha Mubarak, 304–305

Badrinath, 141, 194

Bareilly, 116

Benares, 114, 118, 157

Bhagavad Gita, 115*n*41

Bhakti Marg (or path of devotion), 139

Bhavani, Rupa, 49

Bhavya, 129

Bodh Gaya, 127, 195

Bodhisattva, 4

Borges, Jorge Luis, 213

Brihadaranyaka, 304

Brilliant, Elaine (Girija): *Sometimes Brilliant: The Impossible Adventure of a Spiritual Seeker and Visionary Physician Who Helped Conquer the Worst Disease in History,* 165–166

Brilliant, Larry, 165

Buddhahood, 105

Buddhism/Buddhist, 93, 109, 124–126; esoteric, 256; material world as maya, 294; rebirths in, types of, 111; Tibetan Vajrayana, 284, 287;

Vajrayana tradition, 295; Yogacara, 49
Bull, Sara Chapman Thorp (Dhira Mata), 74

cartographers, 209
Chakravarty, Sharat Chandra, 80–81, 87–88
Champawat, 141
Chandi Path, 275
Chhota Kailash mountain, 140
Choephel, Gendum, 6, 129
Cho rite, 188
creator, concept of, 108
Cultural Revolution (1966-76), 13

Dalai Lama, 253, 260; Fourteenth, 101–111; Thirteenth, 5, 92–98, 103, 127
Das, Lakshman, 167
Dass, Ram (Richard Alpert), 165, 172, 174
My Journey to Lhasa, 92*n*34
Detsen, Trisong, 288
Devbhoomi (the Land of the Gods), 168
Devi Bhagvatam, 275
Devi Mahatmya, 274, 281–282
Devi Mahatmya of the Markandeya Purana, 279
Dharmakirti, 129
dhuni sadhana, 144
dhuni temples in Uttarakhand Himalaya: Goljyu Deva, 135; Harijyu Deva, 135; Narasimha avatar of Lord Vishnu, 135; Shyamnath, 135; Siddhanath, 135
Dorje, Lama, 291
Dorje, Taksham Nuden, 12
Drakpa, Rechung Dorje, 23
Drong, Alak, 228–229, 234, 236–237, 239
Drukpa Kunley (the Divine Madman), 3
Dungkar Gompa in Chumbi Valley, 183
Dus Mahavidya Temples, 281
Dwarka, 116

ego-principle, 120, 120*n*47

Faqir, Shams, 49
folklore, 3, 278, 281, 287

Gabori Gufa at Paharpani, 144
Ganga-Mai (Mother Ganges) temple, 246–248
Gangotri, 246–248
Garhwal, 168
Gaumukh, 218
Gendün, Akhu, 227–228
ghosts, 111
Goddess Parvati, 2
Golu Devata, 3
Gudari Baba, 190, 192–193
Gurdas, Bhai, 54, 56
Guru Dattatreya, 136–137
Gurudongmar lake, 289
gurudwara (Sikh place of worship), 194; Gurudwara Sahib, Manikaran, 55
Guru Gorakhnath, 169

Guru Rinpoche (Padmasambhava), 3, 12, 14, 20, 97*n*38, 287–290, 297
Gyatso, Gendün, 226, 228–243
Gyatso, Tenzin, 103
Gyeltsen, Mila Sherab, 18
Gyephang (aka Raja or 'King' Ghepan), 297

Hammond, Nell, 84
Hardwar, 114
Hari Parvat, 77
Harrer, Heinrich: *Beyond Seven Years in Tibet,* 252–253
Hazrat Resh Mir Saeb (Kashmiri saint), 305
Hemkund, 194
Hemraj, Mahapandita, 128
Heruka, Tsangnyon, 18, 21; *The Hundred Thousand Songs of Milarepa,* 20
Himalaya, 2–5, 8, 114, 116, 252
Himalayan Institute of Yoga Science and Philosophy, Illinois, 202
Hindu/Hinduism, 51, 248, 277–278; life, goals of, 246; material world as maya, 294; Sanatana Dharma, 276, 281
hypothyroidism, 270

individual ego, hindrance to devotion, 212

jaagar festival, 280
Jal Samadhi, 2
Jarala Pass, 127
Jayaswal, K.P., 130
jealousy, 211
Jnanasri, 129
Jobs, Steve, 165
Jong, J.W. de, 256
Josey, Khyungpo, 18

Kahluria, Bhim Chand, 60
Kailash Manasarovar Parikrama, 7
Kailash peak, Tibet, 7
Kalidasa: *Kumarasambhava,* 65
Kalimpong, 90, 92–93, 95, 128, 176, 178, 187, 189
Kamasutra, 129
Kangchengyao Mountain, 287, 289–291
Kargyen, Nyangtsa, 18
Kashmiri Rishi mystical tradition, 303
Kashmiri Shaiva-Shakta tantric heritage, 301
Kashmiri Sufism, 49
Kashmir Śaivism, 49–51
Kashmir Śaivite, 50
Kawaguchi, Ekai: *Three Years in Tibet,* 126
Kebalananda (Shastri Mahasaya/Ashutosh Chatterji), 117–118, 120–121
Khandro, Sera, 13
Khasi hills/Khasi religion: practice of divination, 265, 269; prayers to U Blei (imageless god), 262, 264–267, 269; Shillong (capital of Meghalaya), 264; U Thlen (snake vampire), 262, 268–269

Kinnaras, 4
knotted thunderbolts, 178
Kriya Yoga, 119
Kshir Bhavani, Kashmir, 77
Kumaon, 2–3, 5–6, 70, 134, 138, 144–146, 150, 164, 167–168, 171–173, 274–275

Laal Baba, 7, 217–223
Lal Děd (also known as Lalleśvarī or Lalla Yogini), 46–51
Lashar Valley, 290
Levi, Sylvan, 125
Lhamo, Khandro Tare, 4, 13–15
Lhamo/Lhamos, 232, 241
Lhatso, 232–236, 238–240, 243
Lingpa, Terdak, 13
Lodro, Marpa Chokyi, 18
Lohaghat, 141
Lord Hanuman, 168
Lord Shiva, 2, 135–136, 141, 247, 272, 277

MacLeod, Josephine, 74
Mahaketongwa (the Great Caller), 258–262
Mahasaya, Lahiri, 117–121
Mahasiddha Saraha, 169
Mahayana Buddhism, 51
Mahayuga, 142
Maneshwar temple, 141
Mansadevi, 198
Marxism, 124, 130
Mathur, Pulkit, 68*n*5
Matsyendranath, 137
Mayavati, 69–73
meditation, 6, 12, 20–22, 26, 28, 37, 42, 57, 67, 70, 119, 135, 145, 152, 188, 194, 198–199, 247, 254, 256, 260, 305; cathartic, 210–211; deep, 222–223; Kriya, 117; stop internal chatter of thoughts, 152
Meister Eckhart, 153
Menmo, Jomo, 13
Milarepa, 4–5, 18–23, 169
Milarepa, Jetsun, 3, 26–33, 36–43; hymn on way to see gods, 33–35
Mishra, Durvek, 129
Mitra, Pramadadas, 67
Mohammedanism, 80
monastery: Mindroling, 13; Nagto Kyiphug, 258; Nyizer, 241; Samye, 261; Shula Gompa, 252
myth, 276

Nagarjuna, 129
Nagarjuna mountain, 209
Nagas, 4
Naljorpa, 96*n*37
Namkha Bardzin deity, 183
Naropa Chos-drug or Shad-dharma ('Six Doctrines'), 298
Neem Karoli Baba, 3, 6, 162, 198; different names of, 167–168; established dhams and ashrams on sanctified spots of Sombari Baba, 169; established Hanuman Garhi Temple on Nainital, 168; Kainchi Dham ashram, 172–173; life of, 164–165, 167; part of

Crazy Wisdom tradition of Himalayan adepts, 169; personality and extraordinary powers, 171; relationship between Swami Chidanandaji, 170–171; scattered footprint of devotees and disciples across world, 165–166, 174; spiritual head of Indian families, 167; trips to Kumaon Himalayas, 168
Neo-Platonists, 152
Noble, Margaret (known as Sister Nivedita), 73–77; *The Master as I Saw Him,* 83
non-dualist Kashmir *Śaivism*, 50–51
Nund Rishi (also known as Sheikh Nur-ud-din Wali), 49–50
Nyima, 179, 181–183, 186–187, 189
Nyingma school of Tibetan Buddhism, 13, 287, 297

Oldenburg, Sergei, 125
Osho sanyasins, 210–211
Otto, Rudolf, 125

Padmasambhava, 4
Page, Larry, 165
Palden Lhamo goddess, 8, 284, 297–300, 302
Paldrön, Mingyur, 13
Panchaladeva, 303
Pande, C.D., 164
Pande, Lilu, 190
Pande, Mukul, 2
Pandrenthan shrine, 77–78
Paramhansa Yogananda, 113–121; *Autobiography of a Yogi,* 5, 138
Paranjape, Makarand R., 5
Parivena, Vidyalankar, 125
Parmanand, 49
Pathak, Siromani, 146
Phipps, Alexander, 6
Phuntsok, Lobsang, 187–188, 258
Pindari Glacier, 143
Pir Buddhu Shah of Sadhaura, 60–61
Pir Panjal Mountains, 303–306
Plotinus, 153
Pragyaparamita, 128
Prakash, Medni, 59
Pramanavarttika, 129
Prasada, Jaya, 175
Puranas: Devi Bhagavat, 281; Kalika, 281; Matsya, 281; Shiva, 281; Skanda, 281; Vishnu, 281

Quintman, Andrew, 4
Quit India Movement of Gandhi, 305

Ramana Maharshi, 153, 198
Ramayana, 120*n*46
Ramsay, Henry, 134
Ranjit Nagara (huge war drum), 58
Razdan, Krishna Joo, 49
Red Lantern Bar, 229, 232, 238, 240
religious identities in Kashmir, 46
religious symbols, 160
Rinchen, Gampopa Sonam, 23
Rishikesh, 62, 66–68, 114, 138, 172

river: Alaknanda, 2; Bhagirath, 218, 247–248; Ganga (Ganges), 7, 157, 172, 203; Indus (Sindhu), 7; Jachu or Lashar Chu, 286–287, 289–290; Kosi, 127; Lachen Chu, 286; Parvati, 55; Tista, 286; Yamuna, 5, 59
Rumi, 153

sacred bodies in Jachu or Lashar Chu river: Shaka Cho, 286–287, 289–291; Sherabu Cho, 286, 292; Yulha Khangsa, 286
sacred sites of southern and western Tibet, 20
sadhaka, 140
sadhu/sadhus, 2, 132, 143, 150, 158, 244; as Hindu ascetics, 246; of noble countenance, 115; -vani, 3
Śaiva Siddhanta system, 50
*Śaiv*ite tradition, 50
Sankaracharya, 69
Sankrityayan, Jaya, 126
Sankrityayan, Rahul, 5–6, 122–123; arrested in crackdown on communists, 130; associated with Congress Socialist Party, 130; *Baisvin Sadi,* 125; conferred title of Tripitakacharya, 125–126; *Darshan-Digdarshan,* 130; *Digha Nikaya,* 125; dropped original name Ram Udar Das, 125; *Ghumakkad Shastra,* 124; imprisoned in 1922 and in 1924, 124; interest in Buddhism, 125; journey of, 124; journey to Kalimpong, 128; Kalimpong journey, 128; *Majjhim Nikaya,* 125; search for *Pramanavarttika of* Dharmakirti, 128; study of Pali Tripitakas, 125; *Tibbat mein Sava Vars* and *Yatra ke Panne* (travel diaries), 126, 128; translated Communist Manifesto, 129–130; visited to Tibet, 126–129; *Volga se Ganga Tak,* 130
Santarakshita, 126–127
Sastri, K.S. Ramaswami: *Reminiscences of Swami Vivekananda,* 64–66
Savarni Manvantar, 142
Sengge, Mila Dorje, 18
Sengge, Mila Doton, 18
Se, Phunkhang, 258
Sevier, Capt. James Henry, 70, 73
Sevier, Charlotte Elizabeth, 70, 73
Shakespeare: *Macbeth,* 154
shakti peethas: Jwalamukhi temple, Himachal Pradesh, 8, 279–280; Kamakhya temple, Assam, 8, 279–281; Naina Devi temple, Nainital, 8, 279–280; Shardapeeth, 8; Vaishno Devi, 8
Shamanist, 99
Shantideva, 105
Sharma, Aneg Singh, 167
Sharma, Dharam Narayan, 167
Sharma, Durga Prasad, 167
Sherab, Lobsang, 127
Shivalik Mountains, 218
Shri Siddhi Ma, 6, 162, 172–175
Siddha Baba Bhairav Giriji, 142
siddha gurus, 135

siddhas, 5, 56–57; chimta as divya astra, 135–136; dhuni trishul or trident, 135–136; merges with universal consciousness, 141
Siddhashram, 145–147
Siddha traditions, 6
Sikh gurus: Guru Gobind Singh, 5; (*Bachittar Natak,* 58, 61; battle of Bhangani, 60–61; camp at Paonta Sahib, 59–60; challenge from Raja Bhim Chand of Bilaspur, 59; influence among people, 59; spent early years at Anandpur Sahib, 58; tenth Guru, 58); Guru Nanak, 5, 54; (also known as Nanak Lama or Rimpoche, 55; on Dark Age, 56; emphasis on meditation and spirituality, 57–58; explain various concepts, 57; meetings with siddhas and yogis, 57; on salvation, 56; visited settlement of Manikaran and Janakpur, 55)
Sil, Narasingha P., 83–84
Sjanti, Ratnakar, 129
Skoll, Jeffrey, 165
Sombari Baba, 168–169
Spiraling Vine of Faith, 14
Sri Aurobindo, 83, 198
Sri Gorakh Babaji, 145–146
Sri Gorakshanath, 136–137
Sri Haidakhandi Babaji, 137–140, 142, 145–146, 169; difference in talking to sanyasin and others, 142–143; encounter with Sir Henry Ramsay, 134; power of dhuni and chimta, 134
Sri Krishna Prem, 161
Sri Madhava Ashish (Ashishda), 150–161
Sri Matsyendranath, 136, 142
Sri Ramakrishna Paramahamsa, 66, 73, 83–84, 88
Sri Sombari Babaji, 134, 140–141
Sri Yashoda Mai, 161
Sri Yogesh Bahuguna, 171
Srutis, 142
Stein, Aurel, 125
Sudarshan Chakra, 8
Sufic wahdat al-wujud, 302
Sumeru Parbat, 56
Swami Chidanandaji Saraswati, 6, 162, 170
Swami Niranjanananda (Nityniranjan Ghosh), 74, 82
Swami Parmananda Puriji, 137–140
Swami Rama (Kishori), 6, 190–195, 197–205; *Living With the Himalayan Masters,* 200; *Love Whispers,* 202, 204
Swami Sadananda (Sharatchandra Gupta), 74
Swami Shivendra Puri (known as Thanapatiji), 141, 143
Swami Swarupananda, 74; founded Advaita Ashrama, 71
Swami Turiyananda (Harinath Chattopadhyay), 74
Swami Vishuddhananda Puriji, 138
Swami Vivekananda, 5, 65–69, 88–89, 169; company of female disciple Margaret Noble (Sister Nivedita),

73–77; founded Ramakrishna Mission on 1897, 69; travelled to Himalaya and Almora, 69–72; visit to Amarnath and Kshir Bhavani, 77–88

Tantra, 49
Tantra Chudamani, 281
tantric goddess: Ekajati or Ralchigma, 302; Kalaratri, 302; Kurukulla or Rikjema, 302; Mahavidya, 302; Tripurasundari, 302
Tantrism, 256
Tashi/Tashis, 232
Thangka paintings, 127
Thapa, Amar Singh, 248
The Britannica Yearbook of Science and the Future, 201
The Lineage of Nyizer Monastery, 232–233
Thumo training, 188
Tibetan calendar, tenth month of, 226
Tibetan Revolutionary Party, 129
Tibetan traditions: as Bhairava, 7; as Mahakala, 7
Tondup, Lhagpa, 178–181
Trotsky, Leon: *Bolshevism and World Peace,* 124–125
Tsakpuwa, Geshé, 23, 26, 28–31
Tsang, Nyizer, 233
Tsangyon Heruka, 169
Tsogyal, Yeshe, 4, 12–15
Tulku, Rimpoche Dando, 258

Upanishads, 152–153, 304
Uttarkashi, 248–249

Vaivaswat Manvantar, 142
Valley of Flowers, 6, 190, 192–194
Vardharajan, Lolitha, 278
Vasubandhu, 129
Vedantic advaita, 302
Vedas, 118, 118*n*44
veda vakya, 140
Vidyasagar, 60
Vishnu Purana: on Ashwatthama, 142

walking long distances skill in short time: Lopen Chuki (master), 254–256; Lung Gompa (mediates on wind or Kang jor or fast legs) in Tibet and Bhutan, 252; Sen-nichi-kaihou in Japan, 252; tshampa, 253–254
World Health Organization (WHO), 165–166

Yamunotri, 246
Yogacara school (also known Vijnanavada), 51
yoga/yogic, 49; Dzog-chen, 298; Nidra, 6; techniques, 139; Tummo, 298
Yugas: Dwapar, 142; Kali, 142; Satya, 142; Treta, 142

About the Editor

Namita Gokhale is the author of twenty-one books, including eleven works of fiction, and editor of numerous anthologies. Her acclaimed debut novel, *Paro: Dreams of Passion*, was published in 1984. Recent works of fiction include *The Blind Matriarch*, *Jaipur Journals* and *Betrayed By Hope*.

She is also co-founder and co-director of the Jaipur Literature Festival.

Namita is recognized both for her writing and her commitment to multilingual Indian literature and cross-cultural literary dialogue. She was the Sahitya Akademi (National Academy of Letters) awardee for 2021, and received the prestigious First Centenary National Award for Literature in 2017.

30 Years *of*

HarperCollins *Publishers* India

At HarperCollins, we believe in telling the best stories and finding the widest possible readership for our books in every format possible. We started publishing 30 years ago; a great deal has changed since then, but what has remained constant is the passion with which our authors write their books, the love with which readers receive them, and the sheer joy and excitement that we as publishers feel in being a part of the publishing process.

Over the years, we've had the pleasure of publishing some of the finest writing from the subcontinent and around the world, and some of the biggest bestsellers in India's publishing history. Our books and authors have won a phenomenal range of awards, and we ourselves have been named Publisher of the Year the greatest number of times. But nothing has meant more to us than the fact that millions of people have read the books we published, and somewhere, a book of ours might have made a difference.

As we step into our fourth decade, we go back to that one word – a word which has been a driving force for us all these years.

Read.